PS3509.L4386845

6.50

D1264333

THE MYSTICAL PHILOSOPHY
OF T. S. ELIOT

The Mystical Philosophy of T. S. Eliot

By
FAYEK M. ISHAK

Associate Professor of English
Lakehead University

COLLEGE & UNIVERSITY PRESS · *Publishers*

NEW HAVEN, CONN.

TO THE MEMORY
OF MY PARENTS

Acknowledgments

I wish to acknowledge with gratitude the helpful advice and valuable criticism of Professor Kenneth Muir and Mr. R. T. Davies of the University of Liverpool.

I am also more than grateful to the late Mr. T. S. Eliot, O. M., who most willingly gave me the chance to have an interview with him on October 19, 1961.

My deep obligation is further due to Dr. W. G. Tamblyn, President of Lakehead University, and Dr. J. G. Rideout, Chairman of the Department of English, for their generous support of the manuscript.

For the competent services of their professional staffs, I am greatly indebted to the following: the British Museum Library, particularly the MSS Department and the North Library, the Westminster City Libraries, the National Central Library and the University Library of London, the Library of Congress, the Bodleian Library, the University, Brown, Picton and Hornby Libraries of Liverpool and the Library of Harvard University.

But the unfailing devotion and help of my wife and the constant encouragement of my brother are more than I can ever hope to put into words.

Finally there remains the pleasure of expressing my appreciation to the following authors, editors and publishers for their courteous permission to reprint extracts from works under their copyright ownership:

Faber and Faber Ltd. for the Works of T. S. Eliot (Canada).

Harcourt, Brace & World, Inc., for the Poetry and Prose of T. S. Eliot (U. S. A.)

A. & C. Black Ltd. for *Indian Thought and its Development*, 1936, *The Mystery of the Kingdom of God*, 1925, *The Mysticism of Paul the Apostle*, 1931 and *The Philosophy of Civilization*, 2 Pts. by Albert Schweitzer (World rights).

Burns & Oates Ltd. for *The Complete Works* of St. John of the Cross, trans. and ed. by E. Allison Peers, 1935 (Reprinted 1957), 3 Vols. and *A History of Philosophy* by Frederick Copleston, 1950, Vol. II.

Cambridge University Press, New York, for *From Ritual to Romance* by Jessie L. Weston, 1920 (Reprinted 1957), *The*

Acknowledgments

Myth of the Magus, 1948 and *Rainer Maria Rilke,* 1941 by E. M. Butler.

Charles Scribner's Sons for *The Degrees of Knowledge,* 1959 and *The Range of Reason,* 1953 by Jacques Maritain; also for *Freedom and the Spirit,* 1935 and *Spirit and Reality,* 1939 by Nicolas Berdyaev (U. S. A.).

Geoffrey Bles Ltd. for *The Degrees of Knowledge,* 1959 and *The Range of Reason,* 1953 by Jacques Maritain; also for *Freedom and the Spirit,* 1935 and *Spirit and Reality,* 1939 by Nicolas Berdyaev (Canada).

The Clarendon Press, Oxford, for the *Metaphysical Lyrics and Poems of the Seventeenth Century,* ed. by Herbert J. C. Grierson, 1921 (Reprinted 1958) and *The Works of Thomas Kyd,* ed. by Frederick S. Boas, 1955 (Non-exclusive world rights).

Constable & Co. Ltd. for *Western Mysticism* by Dom Cuthbert Butler, 1922 (World English language rights, excluding the U. S. A.).

Harper & Row for *Western Mysticism* by Dom Cuthbert Butler, 1922 (U. S. A.).

J. M. Dent & Sons Ltd. for *The Heart of Darkness* by Joseph Conrad, 1956 (U. S. A. and Canada).

Harold Matson Company, Inc., for *The Creative Element,* 1953 (Copyright 1953 by S. Spender) and *The Destructive Element,* 1935, Reprinted 1938 (Copyright 1936, 1963 by S. Spender) by Stephen Spender (U. S. A.).

Jonathan Cape Ltd. for *The Destructive Element* by Stephen Spender, 1938 (World rights excluding the U. S. A.).

A. D. Peters & Co. for *The Creative Element* by Stephen Spender, 1953 (World rights excluding the U. S. A.).

The Harvard Advocate for photostatic copies of Eliot's "On a Portrait," Vol. LXXXVI, Jan. 26, 1909, "Humouresque," Vol. LXXXVIII, Jan. 12, 1910 and "Spleen," Vol. LXXXVIII, Jan. 26, 1910.

Harvard University Press for *The Confessions* of St. Augustine, trans. by William Watts, 1912 (Reprinted 1931), 2 Vols. (World rights).

The Hogarth Press Ltd. and St. John's College, Oxford, for the *Duino Elegies,* trans. by J. B. Leishman and Stephen Spender, 1939 (Reprinted 1948), *Requiem and Other Poems,* 1949 and *Selected Works,* Vol. II, 1960, trans. by J. B. Leishman.

New Directions Pub. Corp. for *Requiem and Other Poems,*

Acknowledgments

1949 (Copyright 1957 by New Directions) and *Selected Works,* Vol. II, 1960 (Copyright 1960 by Hogarth Press Ltd.) by Rainer M. Rilke, trans. by J. B. Leishman.

W. W. Norton & Co., Inc., for the *Duino Elegies* by Rainer M. Rilke, trans. with Notes and Com. by Stephen Spender and J. B. Leishman, 1939 (Reprinted 1948). Copyright 1939 by Norton & Co.; copyright renewed 1969 by S. Spender and J. B. Leishman. With the permission of the publisher.

Hutchinson Publishing Group Ltd. for *The Cloud of Unknowing,* trans. by Ira Progoff, 1959 and *The Physical Phenomena of Mysticism* by Montague Summers, 1950.

Librairie A. Hatier for *T. S. Eliot et la France* by Edward J. H. Greene, 1951.

Macmillan & Co. Ltd., London, for the *Selected Letters of Rainer Maria Rilke* (1902-1926), trans. by R. F. C. Hull, 1946.

Mercure de France for *les Oeuvres Complètes de Jules Laforgue,* 1922.

Methuen & Co. Ltd. for *Mysticism: A Study in the Nature and Development of Man's Spiritual Consciousness* by Evelyn Underhill, 1911 (Reprinted 1930) and *The Wheel of Fire* by G. Wilson Knight, 1930 (English language rights in the U. S. A. and Canada).

Oxford University Press, London, for *The Cloud of Unknowing and the Book of Privy Counselling,* ed. from the MSS. by Phyllis Hodgson, 1944 and Philip Martin's *Mastery and Mercy: A Study of Two Religious Poems, "The Wreck of the Deutschland"* by *G. M. Hopkins & "Ash Wednesday"* by *T. S. Eliot,* 1957 (International rights).

Oxford University Press, New York, for *The Achievement of T. S. Eliot* by F. O. Matthiessen, 1935 (Reprinted 1958).

Routledge & Kegan Paul Ltd. for *The Personal Principle: Studies in Modern Poetry* by D. S. Savage, 1944 (World rights in the English language) and the *Philosophies of India* by Heinrich Zimmer, 1951 (World rights excluding the U. S. A.).

Princeton University Press for the *Philosophies of India* by Heinrich Zimmer, 1951, copyright by Bollingen Foundation (World rights in English excluding the British Commonwealth).

Russell & Russell for *T. S. Eliot: A Selected Critique,* ed. by Leonard Unger, 1948. New York: Russell & Russell, 1966.

Professor Leonard Unger of the University of Minnesota for his essay "Ash Wednesday" in the above selection.

Acknowledgments

The Swallow Press for *Reactionary Essays on Poetry and Ideas* by Allen Tate, 1936; now incorporated into *Essays of Four Decades*, 1968.

Universitetsforlaget, Oslo, Norway for *Poetry and Belief in the Works of T. S. Eliot* by Kristian Smidt, 1949.

The University of Chicago Press for *T. S. Eliot's Poetry and Plays: A Study in Sources and Meaning* by Grover Smith, 1956.

Professor Grover Smith of Duke University for his work *T. S. Eliot's Poetry and Plays: A Study in Sources and Meaning*, 1956.

Contents

Introduction   13

I. The Landmarks of Eastern and Western
Mysticism: Its Relationship to Different
Channels of Thought   17

II. The Philosophy of Eastern and Western Mysticism   30

III. Traces of Mystical "Awareness" and "Nostalgia"
in the Early Poems of T. S. Eliot   45

IV. Versatility of Levels in the Mystical Meaning of
"The Waste Land"   65

V. The Liturgical Mysticism in "Ash Wednesday"   87

VI. The Mystico-Symbolical Connotations of the
"Four Quartets"   107

Conclusion   136

Appendix   156

Notes   162

Selected Bibliography   217

Index   221

Introduction

Since the beginning of the twentieth century, there has been a growing interest in the study of "mysticism." The monumental work of Miss Underhill, *Mysticism: A Study in the Nature and Development of Man's Spiritual Consciousness* (1911), gives a clue to the awakening of this interest which is not limited to academic circles. But, with the broadening of scope, a great deal of irrelevant material has been added and the outcome is the resultant muddle in the field of systematized scholarship. At any rate, "mysticism" was able to absorb nearly everything that was ascribed to it. But the cry for specialization has been reechoed since the early decades of our era more than ever before.

The appearance of Dean Inge's *Christian Mysticism* at the turn of the century (1899) and Sir Sarvepalli Radhakrishnan's *Indian Philosophy* in two volumes (1923-27), has partly filled the gap in the West as well as the East. The work of the German scholar Mr. Rudolf Otto has brought the two channels together and his *Mysticism: East and West* (1932) is valuable in the field of comparative study. He builds his thesis on the assumption of conformity to the spiritual experience and hastens to prove it by selecting two great representatives of Oriental and Occidental philosophy of mysticism, namely the Indian Acharya Sankara (A.D. 788- ?) and the German Meister Eckhart (1250-1327). He elucidates the spirit of kinship that is exemplified in the works of both by referring to the Upanishads and the Bible. But this is only the preliminary step that brings us to the more striking parallelism of their subtle systems of speculation which culminate in the revelation and unity with the eternal Being, the invisible and the inexpressible. These systems are based on what Professor Otto calls the *intuitus mysticus* which is intimately related to the higher modes of perception.

The recent publication of Fumio Masutani's *Comparative Study of Buddhism and Christianity* (1957) deals with the affinity between the lives of Christ and Buddha and cites also certain instances of "faith" in which the two religions are contrasted; the one appeals to the soul, whereas the other rests

13

on the elevation of human nature, although, perhaps, the two methods are inseparable. But Mr. Masutani points in his argument to the fact that Christianity is the religion of love and Buddhism is that of mercy.

Jack C. Winslow's *Christian Approach to the Hindu* (1958) deals with the Hinduist "belief" chronologically to indicate the gradual development from nature-deification to the recognition of the ultimate Reality behind all phases of phenomenal metamorphoses. This concept of Reality, in line with the Advaita metaphysics, is monistic in character and it is, in this sense, synonymous with the notion of Godhead in Western philosophy. On this basis the writer develops his thesis and illustrates his viewpoint by referring to the similarities between Hindu meditation and Christian prayer insofar as they both rely on concentration and aim at communion with God or with what he calls the "paranormal power ('vibhuti')."

Arthur Osborne's *Buddhism and Christianity in the Light of Hinduism* appeared in 1959 but it is a superficial treatment of the subject. The approach is mainly geographical and the writer is concerned, more or less, with the locale from which these religions sprang. Doctrinal convictions are touched upon as the interest widens to cover Taoism and Islam. The work is neither scrupulous nor profound and the investigation does not convey a fresh approach to the previous lines of thought.

Here in this extensive area of "mysticism" not only does the East meet the West but also poetry is associated with the philosophy of the "spirit." The mating of the poetic experience with religious inspiration has now become a commonplace, thanks to the studies of recent theologians (Nicolas Berdyaev 1874-1948 and Albert Schweitzer 1875-1965), abbots with philosophical bents of mind (Dom Cuthbert Butler 1858-1933 and Henri Bremond the abbé 1865-1933), psychologists and essayists (William James 1842-1910 and Aldous Huxley 1894-1963). Their investigations in these related fields have revealed the consistency of the spiritual tradition. The saintly experience in the form of ecstasy or visionary elation is not far removed from the imagist experience of a spiritual poet. Both experiences hold in common an attempt to rise above trivialities and superfluities. There may be certain differences in media but the ultimate end of perception is the same. The inspiration of the poet and the moment of insight with the mystic are interrelated. In philosophical poetry, however, there has always been an aura of suggestibility, a mysterious sensibility and a profound "search" for subtleties in and above human nature that link this type of poetry with the most fundamental problems of the mystical experience which can be termed *trans-animation* and *metapsychosis*. The intuitive communication of these elevated planes of consciousness is, moreover, within the true nature of poetry and the intrinsic area of mysticism.

It is significant that some of the great mystics are poets and this fact is exemplified in the Spanish mysticism of the sixteenth century (for example, in the mysticism of St. John of the Cross 1542-91). On the other hand, poets who have a religious bent of mind may penetrate into the domain of the "spirit" and impart experiences that bear striking affinities with those of the most devout Saints. The Metaphysical School of the seventeenth century in England provides us with a happy example of reciprocity between poetry and liturgy in the poems of George Herbert (1593-1633); poetry and modes of nature transcendentalism in the poems of Henry Vaughan (1621-95); and child intuitionism in the poems of Thomas Traherne (1636-74). Whatever experiences these poets may approach, they turn out in the end to be valuable contributions for the perpetuation of our spiritual heritage. The enrichment of this heritage is largely dependent upon individuals in whom these elements are wedded; its growth relies upon the ethical climate of the age; but its decline is a matter of uprooting beliefs in the general "mess of imprecision."

What is called the "fermentation" of this trend is the degree of restlessness that is relevant to modern society and the insistent demand to remold our ideology and build up some sort of reasonable guidance.

T. S. Eliot has undertaken the task of providing a vivid portrayal of this elaborate problem and his poems reveal the crosscurrents which characterize our complex civilization. There are certainly questions and dilemmas that are still open for further discussion. But the poems supply the clue to the orientation of the poet's thought. And, in spite of the great bulk of material—whether expository or critical—that has dealt with Eliot the poet, very little attention has been paid to the philosophy behind the poems and practically less to their mystical connotations. In fact, none of the inquiries bear the name "Mystical Philosophy" as they deal mostly with syntactical and other literary devices. Even then, relations among the various methods of approach have shown that any relevant investigation is indispensable in formulating a consistent and coherent assessment of the poems as an integral work of art.

F. ISHAK

Lakehead University
Port Arthur

It is safe to write that no [word] in the English Language has been misused in such variations and vagaries, so misunderstood, so distorted in endless, question-begging, [irrelevant], and often meaningless contradictions as the term "Mysticism".[1]

M. SUMMERS

CHAPTER ONE

The Landmarks of Eastern and Western Mysticism: Its Relationship to Different Channels of Thought

I *The Meanings of the 'Mystical Experience'*

The word "mysticism" is one of the most misused words in our day. Mr. Butler refers to the fact that it is applied to many branches of knowledge:

to theosophy and Christian science; to spiritualism and clairvoyance; to demonology and witchcraft; to occultism and magic; . . . to revelations and visions; . . . to poetry and painting and music of which the motif is unobvious and vague.[2]

Though mystical experience might be related to all these branches, it is not pantheistic[3] in its content. It may approach pantheism through the transcendence[4] of the inconceivable absoluteness of God who is, at the same time, immanent[5] in the world of becoming; but, be it observed at the outset that mystic transcendence denotes flight and union of soul with the Divine. Max Nordau in his definition of "mysticism" to which Dean Inge refers, touches upon this interrelationship between mysticism and pantheism:

the word "mysticism" describes a state of mind in which the subject imagines that he perceives or divines unknown and in-

17

explicable relations among phenomena, discerns in things hints
at mysteries, and regards them as symbols by which a dark
power seeks to unveil, or at least to indicate, all sorts of marvels.[6]

This is the phenomenal aspect of "mysticism" which is more
appropriate to define pre-Christian "mysteries," the "marvels"
of occultism, or the Wordsworthian deification of the "unknown
and inexplicable relations among phenomena," and the Law-
rencian "dark power" of Nature. In purely theological terms,
however, "mysticism" has come to mean the "union with God:
in non-theistical contexts it also means union with some principle or other."[7] This is the "unitive experience" in mysticism
which is considered by Mr. Gall as the epitome of the divine
"relationship of the individual human spirit to the Universal
Spirit, God."[8] In his view too, "mysticism" is an experience
and a philosophy: it is the experience of the divine oversoul
and the philosophy of the absolute Reality; the mystical experience that leads to the perfection of self and the philosophy
of "regeneration and unification."[9]

The clue to the perfection of self is the disinterestedness in
"matter" and sensuous indulgence, the quenching of "desire" and
the removal of attachment; it is the "regeneration" of human
nature. This is why Mrs. Fisher considers "mysticism" as "the
being and becoming of all that is best and highest in human
nature."[10] It is the unfolding of "human nature" in its aspiration
for the divine Essence and its yearning for "truth, reality [and]
the Kingdom of Heaven."[11] It is the mystic quest for the
Absolute which necessarily transcends "sensational, phenomenal,
mediumistic, or materialistic Spiritism,"[12] and aims at the redemption of human nature, the attainment of the "lost garden"
and the spiritual erection of the "new Jerusalem."

The "quest for the Absolute" is the mystic's "great adventure
... in the exploration of the unmapped realms of Reality."[13]
It is the "exploration" that is carried out by the soul in the
realms of detachment and self-surrender, in the states of grace
and in the sources of spiritual revelation, for "mysticism" in
Professor Berdyaev's view is "a revelation of revelations, a revelation of the realities behind symbols."[14] Normally mystical symbols stand for the realities of eternity and universality, the realities of emanation[15] and immanence that imply a spiritual
penetration of the soul into the domain of transcendence. The
transcendental experience is usually associated with divine immanence, for the essence of the spiritual quest of the mystic

is the immanence of the Divine in the inner recesses of the
human soul. It is the revelation of universality in finitude,
of eternity in temporality, and transcendence in normality.
Miss Underhill refers to this fact in her elaborate definition of
"the true mystic" as the person

> in whom the transcendental consciousness can dominate the
> normal consciousness, and who has definitely surrendered him-
> self to the embrace of reality.[16]

The idea of domination here necessarily entails the emergence
of self from "normal consciousness" to a state of exaltation. It
begins with an act of self-surrender and develops to a purgatorial
state which signifies the transition from the world of matter
to the visionary world of intuition, partly through the prism
of the mystic soul and partly through a long process of identification and communion with the absolute Being. Hence, the
mystic is able to live at different levels of experience and is
always aware of the different operations that take place in
both mind and soul.

These intellectual and spiritual "operations" have been expounded by St. Bonaventura (1221-74)[17] in his definition of
"mysticism" as

> an act of the intelligence [that] concentrates its gaze upon the
> supernatural vision of things eternal; and having seen intellec-
> tually, and seeing, known and being certain, remains rapt in bliss-
> ful admiration.[18]

This is a happy example of the insight of a great Saint who deftly
welded the intellectual and rapturous powers in mysticism into
a harmonious whole. "Mysticism" for him is a matter of concentration which is an essential concomitant of pure contemplation. It paves the way to the perception of "supernatural visions"
and the transcendence of "things eternal." The aim of this
"act" of concentration is the blissful rapture of the soul in its
union with God.

"Mysticism" is, thus, the realization of spiritual consciousness
which is "necessarily above or beyond the ordinary mundane
consciousness of the physical personality."[19] It marks "a triumph
over creatureliness,"[20] a triumph over the world of atomism and
a realization of "the Divine mystery inherent in the innermost
depths of being."[21] In its aspiration for the ineffable, mystical
experience is capable of transcending "the categories of the

world, all objectified forms, all our conceptions,"[22] for space and time are the preliminary footholds of the transcendental world.

This "mystical experience" is not a matter of Bergsonian "élan vital," a vital force exercising its sway aimlessly or irresistibly through obstacles, but the intuitive perception of eternity and the attainment of Being. It is the fullness of experience or the transition from dilemma and strife to the peace that is beyond human understanding. It is the purification of self through a purgatorial crisis that unshackles all our earthly bound experiences.

*   *   *

Obviously these definitions illustrate certain levels of "mystical experience," but none of them is all-embracing or all-inclusive. Some of them concentrate on the phenomenal aspect of mysticism (as Butler's or Nordau's), others refer to the mystical experience in terms of interrelationship between actuality and transcendence (as Gall's, Berdyaev's, Miss Underhill's and St. Bonaventura's), while a third category typified in the writings of Mrs. Fisher is satisfied with a psychological interpretation of "mysticism." The problem of "activity" and "passivity" in mysticism was hardly touched upon and the few remarks in this respect are left open for further argument.

Mystical experience does not necessarily entail "passivity" for the contemplative life of the great Saints was full of activity. In fact, the fruits of contemplation are the spiritual services that a Saint renders his community in particular and the whole world at large in matters of moral guidance and wise direction to the springs of truth and wisdom. At the dawn of Christianity great ascetics did not hesitate to lead the people to righteousness and keep up the torch of faith amidst the dark waves of persecution. St. Athanasius of Alexandria (A.D. 298-373),[23] and St. Jerome (A.D. 340-420), for example, took an active part in defending the Church against schism and atheism. In both Eastern and Western Churches, moreover, the "monastic founders or legislators ... signalized the vice of idleness as the one most to be dreaded in the monastic life."[24] And with the development of manual work, fine arts were cultivated with great success.

Furthermore, the problem of "inwardness" and "outwardness" in the study of "mysticism," and consequently in defining it, has received very little attention. The experience of the mystic is the development of self or its evolution from "without" toward the "within." It is a process of concentration directed to the realization of the upper constituents of the soul which are the Higher Soul and the Supraconscious Self. It is the revelation of "the apex of the soul [*apix mentis*]"[25] or the summit where all forms of love meet. It is also the realization of the inner consciousness of the mystic that opens the "inward" gates of Transcendence where reality abides.

"Outwardness" connotes the dictates of reason and the imprints that it leaves on our ordinary daily life. It is also the raging thirst of the ego for credulity and sensationalism. It represents all abuses of superfluity and the drawbacks of "desire," the obsession with material profit, and the loss of moral values.

The journey of the mystic has come to signify a transition from the illusion of "outwardness" to the reality of "inwardness," and, in this crucible of self-development, the soul gets rid of the dross of egotism and the remains of earthly desires. Having thus reached spiritual maturity, the mystic is now able to penetrate into the "inward" significance and reality of things, whereas the majority of the human folk are content to dwell on appearance and "outwardness." He discerns their sources and the principles that govern them. His "inwardness" will thus reveal myriads of vistas that are completely unknown to most.

These definitions, too, in addition to several others on the subject, have completely overlooked the "individual" in relation to what may be called the "sociological" values of mysticism. Viewed as a personal relationship with the Divine, mystical experience "unfolds" the personality of the mystic. It brings him in contact with cosmic and divine powers which imbue the self with visionary perception. From this mystical experience, the "re-born" self emerges in a state of blissful *connaissance*. All possibilities of life are rediscovered and all conceptions are reconstructed. These acts of rediscovery and reconstruction mark the "sociological" value of mysticism. It is the mystic view of life in its wholeness, and this is what I may call "active mysticism." It is an experience in the meaning and significance of life, its hidden worthiness and its essence.

The value of "sociological" mysticism is, thus, the adjustment of the moral issues of life and the heightening of its spiritual consciousness. It is this creativeness of ethical responses that has given "sociological" mysticism its elevated rank in redeeming society and in rehabilitating human history at large.

The literature of Eastern and Western mysticism abounds with evidences of divine influence in hoisting the banner of truth, banishing the shadows of doubt and dispersing the clouds of skepticism. The *Confessions* of St. Augustine, St. Teresa's *Way of Perfection,* and Dame Julian's *Revelations of Divine Love* are instances of spiritual experience which denote an invasion into a larger range of "being" beyond the veils of temporality and concreteness. They have guided humanity at crucial moments in its long history and have saved it from the tyranny of schism and the devastation of doubt.

Consequently, "mysticism" is the development of self from the "outwardness" of appearance and attachment to the "inwardness" of truth, wisdom and beatific love, or, from a state of ordinary consciousness to the penetration of soul into the domain of transcendent Reality and union with the Divine; its value is the "unfolding" of the mystic's personality and the spiritual awakening and enlightenment of society. Henceforward, the objective of "mysticism" is the physical, psychical, and spiritual purification through a long process of self-development. It is the release from the fetters of physical cravings and nervous derangements. The results—from the individualistic point of view—are the sublimation of the instinctive life of the mystic, the widening of his scope, the elevation of his aims, and the growth and integration of his personality. From the "sociological" standpoint, mysticism aims at the moral amelioration of society. On the purely philosophical level, it rebels against the domination of "reason." The realization of these views, as a whole, has rendered mysticism more popular nowadays than it has ever been since the seventeenth century.

II *Mysticism in Relation to Various Types of Philosophy:*
the Interpretation of Reality

(a) *Dissatisfaction with Ratiocinative and Empirical Thought*

During the last three centuries there has been a growing interest in rationalism which is associated with technological progress and the gradual loss of the simple vicissitudes of life. This rational trend goes back to the time of the Greek philosophers, and, though the belief in the ratiocinative ability in man was shaken after the decline of Sophism, this trend was propagated again in the Age of Reason. The group of rationalists who appeared on the stage of philosophy, for instance, Descartes (1596-1650), Spinoza (1632-77) and Leibniz (1646-1716), preached the gospel of reason and were successful in building up scales of values based on "abstract ideas." But a great philosopher like Descartes was not satisfied with the truth of the reasoned method as his *Discours de la Méthode* (1637) shows,[26] for he "aimed at constructing a universal science based entirely on rational intuition."[27]

On the other hand, exponents of empiricist[28] philosophy rely upon sense-perception in building their theory of knowledge and in trying to find out relations between sense-data and scientific reasoning, like those typified, for example, in the writings of John Locke (1632-1704), David Hume (1711-76) and Bertrand Russell. The Empiricists, however, in concentrating upon sense-perception, or the relation between sensation and perception,[29] have closed the door against other forms of experience as media for knowledge, that is, moral, artistic and mystical experience. They hold a firm conviction for the ability of senses "to portray" facts, whereas thoughts distract them. Modern Empiricists, however, like Bertrand Russell, have relied upon this notion in supplying us with a basis for gaining knowledge. Commenting on Russell's theory, Albert Einstein says that

> the concepts which arise in our thought and in our linguistic expressions are all—when viewed logically—the free creations of thought which cannot inductively be gained from sense-experiences.[30]

In Einstein's sense, it is rarely denied that "sense-experiences" are of little help in gaining our "concepts." For the acquisition of fresh data, however, we may rely on inference which is a matter of "intuition," whereas analysis is usually an act of rational thought. In this view, intuition "gives us access to concrete reality and enables us to expose the erroneous character of accepted scientific concepts."[31] These concepts are usually refuted by coming generations, but the accessibility to mystical reality depends not so much on our discursive reasoning as on our intuitive perception.

(b) *The Philosophical Basis of Intuition: Its Supremacy over the Intellect*

In fact, the great ascetics in the East and the West relied wholly on the intuitive perception of visions in conveying any meaning behind their revelations. This does not mean that faith works against reason, but as Mr. Hocking puts it, "faith is ... an intuition; and while its discoveries could never be contrary to reason, they might well be 'beyond reason'."[32] "Intuition" is then essential to faith and to what Santayana calls "spiritual wakefulness"[33] which is concerned with the awareness of "pure essence" rather than "material existence."

It might be interesting to note that Spinoza in dealing with this relationship was wavering between repudiation of "reason" and conviction that it

regard[s] things not as contingent, but as necessary. It perceives this necessity of things truly . . . But this necessity of things is the necessity itself of the eternal nature of God.[34]

And thus Spinoza adroitly relates the "necessity" of the reasoning process to the eternity of God. But his theory does not hold ground in the sense that Schopenhauer's (1788-1860) differentiation, for instance, between the scientific and intuitive methods as the observations of phenomena and the perception of the correspondence among them, is clear-cut.[35] The latter has gone further in recognizing the reality behind these processes as "one vast will, appearing in the whole course of nature, animate and inanimate alike."[36] It is identical with the "will of the universe which is one and timeless."[37]

Following this line, Henri Bergson (1859-1941) associates intellect with "space" and intuition with "time"[38] for

space, the characteristic of matter, arises from a dissection of the flux which is really illusory ... Time, on the contrary, is the essential characteristic of life or mind.[39]

This concept of "time" as a major feature of life that is intuitively perceived has exercised some influence on Eliot's *Four Quartets*. It is what Bergson calls "duration." Bertrand Russell explains it as "the very stuff of reality, which is perpetual becoming, never something made."[40]

In this way, intellection is knowledge in fragmentation which is normally limited to resemblances among objects; whereas intuitionism is knowledge in its entirety which is based on true speculation. The intuitive vision of a poet or an artist who "enters into things"[41] steps the threshold of inspiration and results in the creation of great works of art in moments of insight. This insight which is not far removed from mystical perception is characterized by "a unity, a simultaneity, a wholeness"[42] which is quite different from "the laboured processes of the intellect."[43]

In dealing with this problem, Dean Inge has chosen a midway between "reason" and "feeling" but he seems to favor the outlook of rationalizing "intuition." At any rate, his enthusiasm for "reason" appears to have cooled down when he refers to it as "dry formalism" and "cold rationalism." In a later work, however, *Mysticism in Religion,* he asserts that reason has failed to be "the basis of a religion or the substitute for it"[44] because "it practically denies the validity of spiritual intuition,"[45] and concludes that "this intuition must be a factor in what we believe about reality; it means that reality is spiritual."[46]

(c) *Rationalism, Naturalism, and Mysticism in Relation to Reality*

Though rationalist, empiricist, and naturalist philosophies have, in this way, explained the domination of intellect, they have also obliterated any meaningful apprehension of true knowledge. In keeping an eye on reality, however, both rationalism and empiricism are "not denied but rather illuminated by spirit."[47] Naturalistic realism eventually deduces the existence of the Divine from the rudimentary facts of life. Evidently it does not satisfy the ultimate end of absolutism in the mystic quest for the revelation of reality for it is involved either in partial relationships or in myriad types of autosuggestibility.

In the domain of the "spirit," reality is neither extrinsic nor ratiocinative; it is the reality of the "inward" life. Spiritual reality is not determined by time and space alone; it is the eternity of Being. Rationalistic reality in the way expounded by Einstein is dependent upon time-space as it exists in pure relativity to the observer. Naturalistic reality is based upon the psychic life of man; whereas spiritual reality manifests itself in the mystical experience of the wholeness of life and cosmic positivism. The latter steps the threshold of transcendentalism and discloses the hidden links that bind the microcosm of self to the macrocosm of the Universal Whole.

(d) *Christian Symbolism[48] and Mystic Revelation*

To give expression to this synthetic experience of reality, the Christian mystic may use certain symbolic images which are the media of bridging the chasm between spiritual realities and ordinary daily experience. But in our modern clash of ideologies, we are more inclined to lose hold of the representations behind symbols. And in rationalizing religious symbolism, the purposiveness of divine revelation will remain unknown.

Mystic "revelation," on the whole, penetrates existence and raises actuality to the state of participation in Being. It presupposes conviction and leads to illumination with which transcendent reality becomes immanent. This is the backbone of the mystical experience which is the highest degree of spirituality. It speaks of the elevation of consciousness and the abolition of the artificial barriers that exist between knower and unveiled knowledge as they both merge into each other in front of the absoluteness of the mystic reality.

III The Components of the Mystic Way[49]

(a) The Awakening of Self

The elevation of consciousness is known in mysticism as the awakening of self which is the state of conversion from the worldly life of sensuousness to mystic liberation. Baron Frederich von Hügel speaks of this crucial moment in the life of St. Catherine of Genoa (1447-1510) saying that in one of her confessions "her heart was pierced by so sudden and immense love of God ... [that] she was drawn away from the miseries of the world."[50] Though conversion is a preliminary stage, it may be coupled with the perception of visions. At the age of four William Blake saw the face of God peeping through the window, and when he was eleven, he told his mother that he had seen a tree full of angels.[51] But in most cases seeing visions comes after cleansing "the doors of perception" and loosening the fetters of self-assertion by undergoing a purgatorial process.

(b) The Purgatorio of Suffering

The mystic pilgrimage begins with the trial of purgatory for the self. The element of suffering is essential in the process of purification. Plato considers it important for the removal of sins. Clement of Alexandria (150-215)[52] taught that "fire sanctifies, not flesh or sacrifice, but sinful souls."[53] Origen (185-254), the prolific Alexandrian theologian, considers "the tortures and examinations [of purgatory] as gold in the crucible"[54] where the refining flames cleanse the soul and melt the dross of impurity. Dante also recounts,

> I saw spirits going through the flames;
> wherefore I looked at them and at my steps,
> with divided gaze from time to time.[55]

In this "refinery" venial sins are gradually removed.

The whole of this process is a detachment from antipathies which will set the "real" self free. It "is brought about by contrition, by confession, by hearty amendments"[56] and it "necessarily includes self-discipline"[57] which should aim at the renunciation of selfhood.

These acts of depossessiveness give us a clue to mystic suffering and to the awakening of self to the "calls" of the inward voice and to the orientation of soul toward the world of divine illumination.

(c) *The Illumination of Divine Love*

After the catharsis that took place in the previous stage, the self is emancipated from all earthly entanglements and achieves enlightenment. Miss Descola tells us that

> l'illumination par Dieu lui-même du globe terrestre, c'est la contemplation divine illuminant les facultés de l'âme.[58]

On this illumination of the constituents of self (that is, thoughts and volitions), the whole of the intuitional life is built. True artists, in this state, were able to contemplate the very heart of things, to perceive in them unusual radiance and mystery, and to behold divine love instilled in the humblest as well as the sublimest of objects.

(d) *Visionary Perception*

The illuminative process is incomplete unless it is coupled with the perception of visions. They are usually clothed in images which help the mystic in attributing concreteness to the various planes of Reality particularly at moments of deep absorption. These images are the media by which he is able to crystallize his intuitive perception, his knowledge of the ineffable, his aspirations and revelations, as his soul[59] passes the threshold of "experience" (that is, in the Blakean sense) to the higher realms of transcendence. The revelations of St. Catherine of Siena (1347-80),[60] Rabia (717-801),[61] or nearly the whole host of mystics, are translated into verbal form as they emerge to the surface of consciousness.

(e) The Dark Night of the Soul[62]

Within this period of revelations, the mystic may undergo an experience of imperceptibility and spiritual dryness which St. John of the Cross calls "the dark night." Miss Underhill speaks of it as the "Divine Dark" or "the Uncreated Light in which the Universe is bathed."[63]

The Spanish Saint tells us that the reason why it is necessary for the soul to pass through this "dark night" is that

> all the affections which it has for creatures are pure darkness in the eyes of God, and, when the soul is clothed in these affections, it has no capacity for being enlightened and possessed by the pure and simple light of God . . . ; for light cannot agree with darkness.[64]

These affections and pleasurable desires shroud it in mists of distraction. That is why, in its aspiration for enlightenment

> l'âme a renoncé aux plaisirs de la terre et à l'enchantement des êtres.
> Il lui faut, maintenant, noyer dans les eaux sombres de la nuit active ses "puissances" spirituelles. Et d'abord, libérons l'entendement des sensations, images, concepts et révélations qui ne sont pas de Dieu.[65]

It has thus renounced all sensory images and all concepts that used to link it with the sensuous world.

Mystical "darkness" also entails austere suffering during "la nuit active" which is normally accompanied with a growing sense of unworthiness[66] on the part of the mystic. His selfhood which is now fully devastated after this series of mortifications gives way to the ascent of the soul to the spiritual domain. It is her last emergence from the world of "becoming," the delusive world of "desire," the mirage of the earthly bound aspiration, and the meaningless monotone of matter clashing against matter.

The "dark night" is, thus, "the Entombment which precedes the Resurrection,"[67] the purging of the soul and the liberation of its transcendental Eros[68] from the prison of the flesh and its flight toward the Absolute. It now verges on the Divine whose sanctifying love enhances it in exaltation.

(f)   *Unification and Its Aftermath*

The ecstatic union between the soul and the Logos marks the culmination of the strenuous Way of the Mystic, as

> l'âme, enfin parvenue au terme de son voyage mystique, se détache, dans un grand arrachement, du corps crucifié. Dieu l'absorbe et se confond avec elle.[69]

It would be futile to try to approach this state of utter detachment comprehensively for our reasoning is of little help here. A verbal interpretation would be a vain attempt to reduce the loftiness of the "moment" to the flatness of tangibility. Yet, paradoxically enough, words and images are the only media whereby the mystic is able to give expression to these realities.

At any rate, this state of mystical union tightens the spiritual bonds of intimacy and divine love. These bonds have kept the early believers true to their creed in the tragic moments of unrest and religious persecution.

IV

Considering these stages of mystical experience, one may conclude that they mark a whole systematization of the conscious and spiritual life of the mystic. The development of his soul culminates in a state of unification which is a fruition of a long struggle against the egoistic self. It is an act of conquering selfishness for the sake of character-building, quenching the thirst of "desire" to assure the integrity of personality, piercing the transcendental sphere for moral well-being, and embracing "divine love" for the sublimation of earthly sentiments. These steps are meant, in fact, to bring out what is sublime in human nature so as to lead, in the end, to the perception of truth.

CHAPTER TWO

The Philosophy of Eastern and Western Mysticism

The study of comparative mysticism has revealed to us the
fact that mystical speculation has its roots in the millennium
before the Christian era. In India the clue to its mysticism,
which has remarkably influenced the poetry of T. S. Eliot, is
the quest after reality in the spiritual world that is crowned
by Brahman or Buddha. In the case of Brahmanic mysticism,
it took the form of a mystical realization of the true Self called
"Atman." With the Buddhists, it is the manifestation of "the
unconditioned Being" through an ascetic system of self-discipline
based on ethical righteousness.

I Indian Mysticism

Brahmanic and Hindu Mysticism[3]

The aim of Brahmanic mysticism is the "discovery of the Self
['Atman'] as an independent, imperishable entity, underlying
the conscious personality and bodily frame."[4] According to
Brahmanism, the world of attachment is the delusive world of
flux and changeable forms. Behind them are the first causes,
only to be discovered through the knowledge of the transcendental Self which remains unknown because of people's
ignorance ("avidya")—the root of all earth-born delusions. It is

30

mainly through an act of "interior awareness ('anubhava')" that we can conquer this self-begotten nightmare of "ignorance." To the realization of this aim in a "spirit" of humility, Indian mysticism consecrates its full efforts. But before coming to this cherished end, it is necessary to trace the stages of progression in this type of mysticism that throw light on the poetry of T. S. Eliot.

II *Traces of Mystification in the Rig-Veda*

The doctrine of sacrificial ceremony is the backbone of the whole range of mystification in which the ancient religions were shrouded. In China Taoist initiates believed in their identification with the mysteries of nature. In India the hymns of the Rig-Veda which were brought by the Aryans when they migrated to India from Central Asia in the sixteenth century B.C., extol the idea of mortifying the flesh for the sake of the revival of the soul. Though many deities of atmospheric origin like Indra[5] and Varuna[6] are scattered in the whole bulk of the Veda, they all melt into the concept of the one Supreme Being called Prajapati.[7] He is the lord of life and death and the recognized symbol of immortality.

In this sense, the underlying theme behind these hymns is that of unity in diversity, and the philosophical framework upon which they are built is the belief in monotheism. The gods "were looked upon as the different embodiments of the universal spirit."[8] The unfolding of this "spirit" will normally lead to the revelation of the innermost Self. But Vedic mysticism stopped at this point. Investigations into the act of revelation together with the permanent reality behind the seeming plenitude of terrestrial formulas were developed in the Upanishads.

III *The Mysticism of the Upanishads*

> In the whole world there is no study so beneficial and so elevating as that of the Upanishads. It has been the solace of my life, it will be the solace of my death.[9]
>
> SCHOPENHAUER

The thesis of elaboration in these philosophical tracts is the communion with the Supreme Being. There is a shifting here from the "outwardness" of nature-deification in the Rig-Veda to the "inwardness" of Self. The *Katha Upanishad* which is considered by the majority of Indian scholars to be the most illuminating of the whole Upanishads, states

> the wise who knows the Self as bodiless within the bodies, as unchanging among changing things, as great and omnipresent, does not grieve.[10]

This Self (or the absolute Reality) is mystically transcendental as it exists beyond all created objects, yet, paradoxically enough, they are all revealed through its immanence in them all. It is, in this sense, universal in revealing the cosmic reality behind them. In its oneness and absoluteness, it is identical with Brahman, the supreme Self or the absolute Atman "that is the timeless reality of all things in time."[11]

The aim behind these speculations is that of mystical union which is not so much a matter of "liberation from the world as the experience of being exalted above the world in union with the Brahman"[12] by way of release ("moksa") from the bondage of sensuality. It comes through a process of self-realization which is in itself a distinctive mark in unfolding reality. This is the way to true knowledge which is the main Upanishadic thesis expounded by T. S. Eliot in *The Waste Land*.

It is acquired through an act of elevation above "sense" and karmic rebirth.[13] The result is that the enlightened mystic achieves wisdom after the gradual conquest of his "ignorance" ("avidya") and the subjugation of the karmic substance to the luminosity of Self. It needs, in fact, a great deal of self-discipline to loosen the fetters of the karma (that is, the manifestations of one's aptitudes in his own deeds) so as to gain perception of the absoluteness of the Supreme Reality.

IV *The Mysticism of the Bhagavad-Gita*[14]

> The Geeta is to Hindus what the Bible is to Christians, the Koran to Muslims.[15]
>
> SAYAJI RAO GAEKWAR

The philosophical themes of the Upanishads have received a practical treatment in the Bhagavad-Gita (the Song of the Exalted One) which forms a prominent part of the great epic poem "Mahabharata." As there is no reference to Buddhism in it, we shall not be very far from truth if we presume that it goes back to the fifth century B.C.

The text of the Song speaks of the crucial moments when two great armies of the Bharatas (that is, the Royal Family) were about to fall into combat. One of the leaders, namely Arjuna who is a prince, asked his charioteer to drive him to the field between the two armies where he witnessed his friends and tutors. The words of Arjuna, in this respect, who says

> I do not wish for victory, O Krishna! nor sovereignty, nor pleasures. . . . Even those, for whose sake we desire sovereignty, enjoyments, and pleasures, are standing here for battle, abandoning life and wealth. . . . These I do not wish to kill, though they kill [me],[16]

compose the major theme of the Bhagavad-Gita. The charioteer "was none other than the god Krsna [Krishna],[17] an Incarnation of the Creator, Preserver, and Destroyer of the world."[18] He confesses to Prince Arjuna whose throne was usurped that

> learned men grieve not for the living nor the dead. . . . As in this body, infancy and youth and old age [come] to the embodied [self], so does the acquisition of another body; a sensible man is not deceived about that.[19]

Krishna mixes this doctrine of transmigration with his idea of release from sins. Salvation for him is the result of true perception, which means deliverance from "appearance" and concentration upon the imperishable and eternal One. The right way to perception is the disinterestedness in benefits of actions. In this act of mystic detachment, the active ways of life are identified with cosmic goodness inasmuch as the individual "will" should be involved in the action itself irrespective of its results ("phala"), for "Krishna requires the outward performance of actions in combination with inward renunciation of the world."[20] Mere participation in action is a mark of wisdom for ignorance is attachment to momentary satisfaction. In this way, the Gita does not encourage abstention from action but it claims that the cultivation of mystic detachment is the right approach to our activities.

V *The Mystical Philosophy of the Advaita Vedanta*

With the philosophy of the Vedanta[21] one shifts again to the sphere of metaphysics. It was laid down by Sankara[22] who was in favor of considering substance in a state of fineness to contain the immanent essence of the objectified world, as

> la substance est rigoureusement immanente à tous les accidents, c'est elle qui surrélève en eux son propre être; mais elle ne s'épuise en aucun d'eux.[23]

In this sense, substance is both inside "tous les accidents" and outside them all as "elle ne s'épuise en aucun d'eux." Incorporated in the world of experience, it is limited to the range of human activity and erroneously conceived in terms of transformation. It is only the obscurantism of the ever-revolving and transitory world that bedims it and screens Reality. Paradoxically,

> the appearance of a Universe and its disappearance, the succession in space and time, is that by which alone the eternal simultaneity of the Be-Ness of the One can be expressed.[24]

The "Be-ness" of the absolute One can only find expression in the world of "space and time" which is mystically revealed through the "eternal simultaneity" of Being. It speaks of the mystic relationship between the world of "becoming" and that of Being[25]—and this is the basic inquiry of Vedantic mysticism. It reveals the indwelling identity of the human and the divine which is normally lost in the mists of our world of flux ("maya"). Here lies the fundamental cause for the presence of the pairs of opposites and the apparently irreconcilable elements in the processes of life. Here originates too the denial of Reality in the mundane routine of everyday existence, so long as it is involved in the phantasmagoria of sense-perception, hidden behind the cramming veils of "outwardness" and deluded by our belief in "reason" and "matter."

This is why the goal of the Advaita Vedanta is the ultimate release ("moksa") from everything that used to screen the real Self. It is attained through meditation and complete absorption[26] in the eternity of Being which signifies the meeting of the contradictory elements in existence; hence, in agreement with the Heraclitean aphorism, "the way up is the way down, the way forward is the way back,"[27] and, in Eliot's sense,

> What we call the beginning is often the end
> And to make an end is to make a beginning.
> The end is where we start from.[28]

In this mystical state of reconciliation, the fallaciousness of the material causality of the world recedes gradually. "The way up" and "the way down," "the way forward" and "the way back," "the beginning" and "the end" are completely indistinct in front of the unifying efficacy of the Absolute.

VI *The Ethical Mysticism of the Buddhist Philosophy*

With Buddhism we move to a different level of consciousness, that is, the deliverance from suffering and the series of reincarnations that await the soul. This is why Buddhism concentrates upon freedom from terrestrial attachment and from "the meaningless will-to-live [which] the Buddha calls ... the desire for existence and pleasure."[29] In his view human life entails suffering and sorrow:

> birth is attended with pain, decay is painful, disease is painful, death is painful. Union with the unpleasant is painful, painful is separation from the pleasant; and any craving that is unsatisfied, that too is painful.[30]

The attachment to "desire" gives a transient satisfaction to our greedy appetites and explains, at the same time, the restlessness of humanity.

Only with the abolition of worldly cravings can suffering be mitigated. Happiness is ascertained with benevolent deeds of mercy, as long as one

> endure[s] enmity and forgive[s] evil, not only for the sake of the perfection that is to be attained, but also because in this way something is accomplished in the world.[31]

In this view lies the singular merit of Buddhism which is "simply that of inward purification and moral goodness."[32] Buddha relied mainly upon ethical righteousness insofar as it is based on self-scrutiny and on what he calls the Noble Eightfold Path which ends in "Supreme Enlightenment; the consummation of which is emancipation from the thraldom of Self"[33] through mystical meditation ("dhyana") and the attainment of Nirvana. It is a state of consciousness that denotes the annihilation of wrath and self-deceit, the re-awakening to ethical righteousness and nirvanic peace—which are all the remarkable contributions of Buddhism to Indian mysticism.

In this way the primary concern of Indian mysticism is to acquaint devotees with the absolute Reality which is termed the true Self ("Atman") or the primal Being ("Purusa") through which all the processes of life are mystically revealed. This Reality is both immanent and transcendent for it is fundamentally synthetic in character. The former gives us the clue to phenomenal causation which is the outer manifestation of real existence. Hindu mystics do not countenance this externalization of consciousness. The ultimate aim of their mysticism is the revelation of transcendence in the sphere of "inwardness." For this purpose they stress the theme of renunciation and take it to be the sole way leading to mystical enlightenment.

VII *European Mysticism*

Liberation of the human soul from the delusion of tangibility was also sought in Greek philosophy. Hindu mystics aimed at deliverance by renouncing carnal desires, but Platonic disciples tackled the problem in terms of metaphysical speculation. Though the approach may appear different, the ultimate aim is the revelation of reality in its purity that is untrammelled by sense-perception. Platonism goes even further in professing that the soul before coming to this world used to enjoy the World of Ideas, the abode of the eternal Reality. True knowledge is, thus, a matter of reminiscence that comes to the soul by tearing the veils of seemingness.

VIII *Neo-Platonic Mysticism*

> Plotinus is in the fullest sense the "Father" of western mysticism. He put the vision of God and union with Him as the goal of life for man.[34]
>
> R. Jones

(a) *The School of Philo* (30 B.C.-A.D. 50)

Philo who was nourished in Jewish-Alexandrian philosophy departed from Plato whose bias was toward "reason" in spite of the mystical traits that his philosophy reveals at times. He relied upon the potency of "faith" for mystical union with God. The School of Philo is, thus, termed neo-Platonism and it marks a most fundamental shift in the history of thought from intellectualism to intuitionism. The revelation of reality is not so much a Platonic intellectualization of Ideas as the intuitive perception of the totality of Being.

(b) *The Neo-Platonism of Plotinus*

With Plotinus mysticism moved completely to this domain of neo-Platonism. He worked out the Platonic-Aristotelian antithesis between matter and form into a triple system in which the absoluteness of the One "transcends the Platonic or Aristotelian Nous[35] and is beyond the reach of the ordinary processes of the human intellect."[36] He states that the Absolute

> is none of the things of which it is the source—its nature is that nothing can be affirmed of it—not existence, not essence, not life—since it is that which transcends all these.[37]

From the Nous emanated the World-Soul which is related to the material as well as the spiritual world. The human soul too is associated with both, but it is capable of "passing upward from the sensible world, first to the world-soul, then to the sphere of the intelligence, and finally to the Absolute One."[38] It takes a negative way of contemplation which Plotinus considers necessary for the purification of the soul from attachment to sin.

(c) *Dionysian Mysticism*

In line with this neo-Platonic trend is the mysticism of Dionysius the Areopagite[39] who views this progression in terms of hierarchies. The soul, in its homeward ascent, is united in the end with the divine principle which is its source. By an act of purification, it is capable of passing upward to the celestial hierarchies whence it is absorbed in the Supreme Essence and attains perfection. It becomes, then, a partaker of the beatific vision. With absorption it comes to the final refuge of mystics.

IX *The Mystical Philosophy of St. Augustine*

> Theologian, philosopher, moralist, and tireless champion; it is really through his exquisite sensibility that St. Augustine has remained the contemporary of successive generations.[40]
>
> P. DE LABRIOLLE

Through St. Augustine the neo-Platonic tradition in mysticism came to be known to the West. In fact, he incorporated Plotinian themes in his philosophy because they were subservient to Christian dogma. In his famous *Confessions,* for instance, he manipulates a thesis of the ecstatic ascent of the soul to God and takes the visionary world of "inwardness" to be the basis of illumination[41] and divine love. In the Tenth Book he says:

> Too late came I to love thee, O thou Beauty both so ancient and so fresh, yea too late came I to love thee. And behold, thou wert within me, and I out of myself, where I made search for thee.[42]

For St. Augustine this inward world of revelation surpasses all discursive reasoning. This is why he laments the deviation of people from the wisdom that this revelation entails and stresses the necessity of regeneration in *The City of God* ("De Civitate Dei"). In his convincing way, he defends Christianity against the slogan that Rome has perished in the Christian days and argues that the corruption which is inborn in the hearts of the Romans led to the downfall of Rome: *The Earthly City*—"Civitas Terrena." His aim, in this respect, is the awakening of the aspirations of the earthly city dwellers toward the Heavenly Kingdom which should be the concern of every citizen.

X   *Aristotelianism Versus Augustinianism*

Aristotelianism came into vogue in the Middle Ages because the neo-Platonic trend failed to satisfy the mystical quest for an integrated interpretation of reality. Neo-Platonism is based on an essential dichotomy between matter and spirit, existence and essence. Aristotelianism is based on a synthesis between matter and form. The former

> is passive, the principle receiving being and action; while form [act] is active; the principle giving being and action. These two opposites are harmonized in the substance of the physical thing. Neither matter nor form alone constitute the essence of the physical object, but both together.[43]

This Aristotelian synthesis appealed to the Medievalists. At the same time neo-Platonism that found its Christian interpretation in the hands of St. Augustine continued to influence the history of mysticism in the domain of mystical theology. Aristotelianism that came to the West through the Arabs, most particularly through the works of Avicenna (A.D. 980-1037) and Averroes (A.D. 1126-98), left its imprints on the mystical philosophy of St. Thomas Aquinas (1225-74)[44] whose bent of thought is what I call "speculative intelligibility." With the flourishing of reasoning after the thirteenth century, Thomism continued to flow side by side with Augustinianism representing respectively metaphysical intellection and mystical intuitionism.

XI *The Synthetic Mysticism of St. Thomas Aquinas*

St. Thomas gave a further development to the Aristotelian theory of form and matter by relating them to their primal sources. The "being" of an object, in his view, constitutes its substance (that is, its fundamental reality) which is characterized by certain determining factors, namely "accidents." They may affect the inward being of the object, but mostly re-act upon its outer constituents. At the same time, the existence of "becoming"

> denotes a kind of actuality: since a thing is said to exist, not through being in potentiality, but through being in act. Now everything to which an act is becoming, and which is distinct from that act, is related thereto as potentiality to act; since act and potentiality are reciprocal terms.[45]

The fundamental trait of "becoming" is activity. It is the "act" that gives a thing its actuality and its existence too. The driving force of the "act" is the "potentiality" of the object. Hence, the reciprocity of act and potentiality gives validity and meaning to the existence and "becoming" of such an object.

The relation between "substance" and "accident" is identical with that between "being" and "becoming," "essence" and "existence." The fixation in the "types of perfection" gives us the ultimate differentiation between the finite and the infinite and the Eliotesque point of intersection between time and the timeless. The crystallization of this point of fixation which Eliot calls "the still point" illuminates the mystical conception of the interrelatedness between these "spheres" which should be —according to Thomist metaphysics—hierarchically graded. These levels give us the perfectibility of the elemental essence of all types of existence.

XII   *Dante Alighieri and the Mysticism of Divine Love*

> ...while Scholasticism is the body of Dante's re-
> ligion, Mysticism is the soul, and Love the animat-
> ing spirit of both.[46]
>
> E. G. GARDNER

By the time of Dante, theology was a mixture of Aristotelianism, neo-Platonism, and Christology that came to Dante through
Augustinianism and Thomism. Religious thinking, on the whole,
in the thirteenth century "is not humanitarian: not human, but
divine scientia, fides, et amor,' make Medieval Christianity."[47]
This gives a clue to Dante's preoccupation with the idea of
divine love. With the early death of Beatrice, the poet has
developed an aura of mysticism and a saint-like perception of
a mystic. She is to him "the ideal that has come to life...in
order to impart to the world a ray of the splendour of Paradise";[48] and about whom Dante tells us in the *Vita Nuova:*

> I behold her of so noble and laudable bearing that assuredly of
> her might be said those words of the poet Homer: "She seemed
> not the daughter of a mortal man but of God."[49]

But she is disguised in the poem as another "gentle lady"—rather
a screen behind which the poet could disclose the sacredness
of his love.

In the *Convivio* which is only a development of the *Vita
Nuova,* the major theme is still love and virtue, but it is treated
from a philosophical point of view. The mystical philosophy
of the poem rests on the medieval tradition of *Fin Amor* which is
not so much the demonstration of the poet's learning as giving expression to certain noble sentiments in heightened pursuits.

In the *Divina Commedia*[50] this theme of Platonic love is
mixed with the concept of suffering and the necessity of purification not in the consuming fire of an "Inferno" but in the
refining flames of a "Purgatorio" where the souls are divested of
all sensuality. The suffering of these souls becomes meaningful
through the poet's masterful exposition of deadly sins and carnal
desires. It is coupled with the aim of salvation insofar as it paves
the way gradually to the beatific vision of the "Paradiso"
which is revealed through the mystic image of divine light:

> Meseemed a cloud enveloped us, shining, dense, firm and pol-
> ished, like diamond smitten by the sun.

Within itself the eternal pearl received us, as water doth receive a ray of light, though still itself uncleft.[51]

The "ray of light" that pierces the density of the cloud has
led the poet and his paramour to the diamond-like transparence
of the moon. Its divine illumination has enhanced the whole
atmosphere and created a pearl-like luminosity. With it the
consummation of the poet's vision of the Absolute is brought
home through the all-encompassing power of his mystical love
for Beatrice.

XIII   *The Active Mysticism in the Cloud of Unknowing*[52]

> ... a little book that is one of the finest flowers
> of medieval mystical literature.[53]
>
> A. HUXLEY

Concerning the purpose of *The Cloud of Unknowing*, Dr.
Progoff tells us that it is meant "to provide practical advice for
all individuals interested in achieving a direct knowledge of
God that they might verify by their own experience."[54] It is
primarily addressed to "a young man twenty-four years of age
who was seriously considering taking a step that would com-
mit him to a life of religious dedication as a 'Contemplative'."[55]
In this work there is no severance between contemplation
and activity for the anonymous author says that the "contemplative life and active life are coupled together in spiritual
kinship."[56] He, thus, artfully brings mysticism into closer contact with the workaday life.

The contemplative life here means concentration with such
intensity that the mystic becomes unaware of the outer world
as if he is lost in a "cloud" of darkness. It is not the negation
of light but the lack of knowing that is meant here by darkness.
This state of unknowing "includes everything you do not know
or else that you have forgotten, whatever is altogether dark for
you because you do not see it with your spiritual eye."[57] It is
a state of separateness that usually exists between the soul and
God at the beginning of the Mystic Way. The purgatorial process ensues in the complete submergence of the mystic into a
state of unawareness, a "cloud of Unknowing" through which
he overcomes his personal prejudices and prepares his heart for
"the draught of this love and the voice of this calling!"[58] The

soul is cleansed by "a meek stirring of love"[59] through devotion to Christ. By adoration of "His Godhead and His manhood together,"[60] the work of humility and love is accomplished "in full purity of spirit."[61] With the effective help of grace and charity, God "sometimes send[s] out a beam of spiritual light piercing 'the cloud of unknowing' that is between you and Him."[62] He will then reveal "His secret ways of which man neither can nor may speak."[63] This process of revelation culminates in the unification "with God in spirit, and in love, and in harmony of will."[64]

On the whole, *The Cloud of Unknowing* avows practical mysticism and considers contemplation without action incomplete. It deals with a way of life based on dismissing evil cravings in a "cloud of forgetting" and the approach to a "cloud of unknowing" through the "stirrings of love." The author advocates the passage of the soul from the distractions of egotism to intent concentration. This process assures the mystic that he is advancing along the road of perfection. Here mystical illumination pierces the dark cloud of unknowability and opens in front of the mystic vistas of charitable and virtuous acts.

XIV *Spanish Mysticism*

(a) *St. Teresa and the Mysticism of the "Interior Castle" of Perfection*

In the hands of Teresa of Avila (1515-82), one of the greatest saints the whole of Christendom has ever produced, the themes of renunciation and inward concentratedness in mysticism reached their summit. With this saint the burning desire for "love divine" is coupled with the thirst of her soul for the service of God in a spirit of humility. In the *Way of Perfection* (1565) she asserts that "there is always greater safety in humility, mortification, detachment and other virtues."[65] These are all practiced by her in an atmosphere of inaccessible solitude which, in the case of St. Teresa, ends in the *unio mystica* with Jesus Christ.

In the *Interior Castle* (1577) she develops this theme of perfection and uses the image of the seven mansions to mark mystical development. The soul is viewed here "as if it were a castle made of a single diamond or of very clear crystal, in which there are many rooms."[66] Admission to the Castle is not an easy task for "without complete self-renunciation, the state is very arduous and oppressive."[67] The Carmelite saint reminds that worldly preoccupations usually turn one away from the entrance.[68] At the same time, she did not dismiss this world altogether; on the contrary, she was always keen to translate her prayers into benevolent deeds.

(b) St. John of the Cross and the Mysticism of the Dark Night[69]

St. John (1542-91) has taken the way of the "dark night" to mark the full consciousness of the soul of "her 'strange knowledge' of God's secrets."[70] He tells us that "this dark and loving knowledge, which is faith, serves as a means to divine union in this life."[71] In this state, the Beloved "is truly in the soul and the soul in Him, and each lives in the other, and the one is the other, and both are one through the transformation of love."[72] Necessarily this union is attained by the "way of unknowing" and the *Via Negativa* which link "the Dark Night of the Soul" with fourteenth-century English mysticism as well as Dantesque negativity.

St. John has associated mystical progression with the ascent of the soul to the summit of Mount Carmel: the state of Perfection. Along its way, the soul undergoes a nocturnal experience of perilous torment which is mainly based on the idea of purification. It harbors a belief in asceticism and in the spiritual efficacy of the inward process that is accomplished through liberation from all the fetters of egoism.

XV The Growing Vogue of Secularism and the Orientation of Thought toward Ratiocination

After the collapse of the whole edifice of Spanish mysticism, the needle of thought was oriented toward ratiocination. Eclecticism ceased to be the clue to philosophical learning and speculation. Mysticism was gradually losing ground; its scope was narrowed to passive contemplation and private meditation.

This trend is typical of the Norwich circle of contemplatives among whom Dame Julian[73] (1343-1443) is the most influential figure. She is famous for her *Revelations* which cluster around the main theme of the loss of all righteousness. In her view, lack of steadfastness is the cause of sinfulness; thus, she stresses the fact that "our way and our heaven is true love and sure trust,"[74] whence she finds the remedy and points to the possibility of mystical redemption which "implies the restoration of something lost, the cure of an evil."[75]

This vogue culminated in the mystical speculations of the Cambridge Platonists who flourished in England in the seventeenth century. The leading figures of this group like John Smith (1618-52) and Henry More (1614-87) practiced a sort of cloistered piety, but they relied on "reason" in building up their concepts of truth and ethics. Though they began as Thomists, they verged on the neo-Platonic tradition after their dissatisfaction with "reason" in interpreting revealed truth.

This marked rationalization of revelation which is the basic feature of the Cambridge School, originates in the Cartesian duality (1596-1650) of the extension of matter and the non-extension of spirit. The Kantian theory (1724-1804) of sensationalism and categorization (that is, knowledge of phenomena and pure concepts), the egoistic approach of Fichte (1762-1814), the absolute rationalism of Schelling (1775-1854) and the will-to-live of Schopenhauer (1788-1860) have, moreover, fallen short in giving us any evidence of the absoluteness of the mystic reality. They could only give vent to the human state of consciousness in relation to the world of external objects. Reality, for these philosophers, is a logical systematization of relations that exist between the mind and the outer surroundings.

This rational concept of reality is coupled in the nineteenth century with the growth of scientific materialism. It is followed, in its turn, by a sweeping view of agnosticism that has interpreted the cosmos on purely mechanical bases. It is a natural manifestation of a trend of thought that is mainly devoted to the recognition of reality in terms of conceptualism and sensationalism.

In opposition to this materialistic approach, T. S. Eliot has endeavored to draw our attention to the fountain-source of mystical reality, not by way of ratiocination, but through the threads of mystical experiences that are woven together in the very texture of his poetry.

... it is only a personal prejudice of mine, that I
prefer poetry with a clear philosophical pattern ...
to poetry like Shakespeare's. But this preference
means merely a satisfaction of more of my own
needs, not a judgment of superiority or even a statement that I "enjoy" it more as poetry. I like a
definite and dogmatic philosophy, preferably a
Christian and Catholic one, but alternatively that
of Epicurus or of the Forest philosophers of India;
and it does not seem to me to obstruct or diminish
either the "poetry" or the . . . pattern.[1]

T. S. ELIOT

CHAPTER THREE

Traces of Mystical "Awareness" and "Nostalgia" in the Early Poems of T. S. Eliot

In order to come to a fuller and a more comprehensive assessment of Eliot's poems, one has to trace both the philosophical
and literary influences that were, so to speak, the motivating
forces which gave them shape and color, and, in this sense,
review the whole poetic works through a fresh and an integrated perspective. These forces clustered around the metaphysical quest after reality which eventually gave eminence to
mystical philosophy in art (Benedetto Croce), ethics (Sören
Kierkegaard) and pure abstract thought (Martin Heidegger
and Wyndham Lewis). The inquiry into a synthetic theory of
knowledge gave birth to a neo-Thomist movement led by Jacques
Maritain.[2]

I *The Trend of Thought That Gave Prominence to Mystical
Philosophy as Eliot's Immediate Inheritance*

Since the earlier decades of the nineteenth century, a host of
nomenclatures has evolved out of the term "mysticism" which

has, in fact, suffered many misconceptions. Writers have applied it to any mode of thought that is irrational and they have found great treasure in the psychology of the unconscious. Even the phantasmal appearances of dreams portrayed by William H. R. Rivers[3] drew the attention of the reading public as a phase of mysticism.

In the vagaries of suprarationalism and supernaturalism, many thinkers got mixed up in applying "mysticism" to any sphere of existence that is invisible. It was confused with the occult tradition which took another form at the dawn of Christianity and underwent a complete metamorphosis in the seventeenth century as it came to mean a full mastery of man over the powers of nature. The pre-Christian concept of occultism rests on a belief in the supernatural and the possibility of the human "spirit" to identify itself with certain aspects of phenomena. After the seventeenth century, this vogue has become associated, more or less, with sorcery and with all that is queer, ghostly and fantastic which have obviously nothing to do with mysticism.

The result is that this term has deplorably been associated, particularly nowadays, with this medley of confused and sometimes contradictory views. It is not surprising that mystical experience which is fundamentally based on the "awareness" of self and its direction toward union with the divine Absolute is considered by the majority of modern philosophers as both esoteric and too complicated to be disentangled.

With the development of scientific research, this view has become an integral part of modern thought. Attention has, thus, been deviated from concentration on the *raison d'être* of existence to the workaday life which necessarily entails the shift from the unitive wholeness of outlook to the limitations of mechanistic rationalism. It follows that

> the aim of literature was no longer to confront the totality of life and hand on an imperishable impression; instead, it became concerned with "slices of life." Exaggerated importance being given to segments, the universal note became lacking. This was all in the direction of confusion and lost vision. Certainly those who made it their business to keep us informed of their reactions and repulsions, succeeded only too well in providing a distorted picture of reality.[4]

This line of thought is obviously linked with agnosticism, phenomenalism and pragmatism. They all profess the denial of the

spiritual domain beyond the tangible objects and their interpretation of life and existence is instrumental and sensational.
For the holders of these creeds, any reality beyond phenomena
"was unknowable, because the mind could see things only
through the windows of the senses."[5] The agnosticism of Thomas
H. Huxley (1825-95) and the pragmatism of Dr. John Dewey
(1859-1952) have broken the link between existence and essence,
idea and reality, by relying on sensations and opposing the
motivating power of the "spirit" behind the activities of life.
Inside this limited boundary of human understanding, creativeness was diluted and initiative was paralyzed by checking man's
spontaneity and tying his aspirations to the deadly routine of
the Blakean "dark Satanic mills." This trend which is seeking
un accord avec la science has created a sense of aimlessness in
human perspective and has kept the world closed in a blind
alley. It is no wonder that social upheavals and economic crises
have dislocated the framework of society, and these menacing
eruptions will continue to appear in the world as long as materialism has the preponderance over spiritual consciousness and
outer appearance over essence and meaning.

With this mechanization of life the death knell of the ethical
significance of man's existence was tolled. His repeated immer-
sion into the limited boundaries of his thought has not saved
the world from a pervasive mood of depression and cynicism.
Leading figures in literature and metaphysics sought refuge in
mysticism after their dissatisfaction with pragmatic modes of
thought. Some enthusiasts have gone to the other extreme of
contemplative abstraction; others whose mystical philosophy is
characterized by moderation have concentrated upon a meaningful interpretation of reality. With F. H. Bradley (1846-1924),[6]
one had to plunge into the sphere of unknowability if reality
is to be accessible to him. In his *Appearance and Reality* (1893)
he argues that "appearance" exists only in a state of relatedness
to objects and qualities which have all deluded us from the true
"reality" as they are founded on the inaccuracy of sense-perception. He was even dissatisfied with the mystical transcendental
Self as it is related to the egoistic self, and relies in his perception
of the absoluteness of Being on the "unknowable" that knows
no contradiction. This is perhaps an extreme abstraction of
"reality" which renders it highly inapplicable. But he modifies
his theory when he comes to realize, in Eliot's assessment, that
"no one 'fact' of experience in isolation is real or is evidence

of anything."[7] Bradley too professes toward the end of his work that the "Absolute 'is' its appearances, it really is all and every one of them"[8] and that there

> is truth in every idea however false, there is reality in every existence however slight; and, where we can point to reality or truth, there is the one individual life of the Absolute.[9]

With this all-inclusiveness of the Absolute, the chasm between "appearance" and "reality" is no more broadened.

It is this modified approach to idealism that attracted the attention of Eliot and its influence has never lost hold on him. In point of criticism, it supplied him with the idea of depersonalization;[10] and, in mystical philosophy, it supported his notions of transcendence and absoluteness that have grown to maturity in his poems that appeared after the collection known as *Ara Vos Prec* (1920).[11]

In Europe more than England the metaphysical climate has been dominated by the mystical philosophy of St. Thomas Aquinas since the later decades of the last century. The prevailing trend of neo-scholasticism ever since has been given vent in France by Jacques Maritain (1882-   ) whose mysticism of knowledge rests on a neo-Thomist synthesis of experience and reality, as

> il est exact que la structure du réel est synthétique, et par conséquent ... davantage encore ... que le devenir lui-même du réel est synthétique.[12]

This synthesis is reached by way of abstracting essences from objects "as in the case of God and pure spirits."[13] The importance of this process lies in the mystical perception of the Divine Essence, the ultimate reality that is the end of all knowledge which transcends all vagaries of categorical experience. It follows that the wholeness of Being is determined by "an intuitive vision"[14] of the absolute reality

> [qui] est le privilège de ceux qui agissent dans la lumière de la vision béatifique.[15]

On this basis the vision of Eliot's *Ash Wednesday* is rendered possible as an insight into the reality of *la vision béatifique*[16] that transcends all imperfections and contradictions.

This trend of mystical philosophy that was directed toward the revelation of visionary insight flourished also in Germany in the earlier decades of the twentieth century. It took the form of a metaphysical investigation into the essence of Being. Martin Heidegger (1889-), for instance, in his *Question of Being* relates it to the philosophical notion of nothingness which is the negative aspect of "being." For him both should not only be correlative but synonymous.

Heidegger also relates Being to "time" and takes

monumental history [to be] directed to the future; antiquarian history to the past; critical history to the present. The structure of the whole complex lies in the character of human being as time.[17]

"Time," in this sense, constitutes the structural backbone of human existence as long as "it forms the horizon of all human questioning about Being, that is, of all philosophical thought."[18]

This problem received also proper attention in the voluminous study of W. Lewis in his *Time and Western Man*, but he dealt with it from a different angle. He begins by associating time with the Bergsonian theory of duration[19] and assures us—in agreement with Mr. Russell—that Bergson's[20] "responsibility for most contemporary philosophic thought having the concept 'Time' at the heart of it,"[21] is tremendous in this respect.

He associates it, then, with Spengler's (1880-1936) concept of time-space which is based on his recognition of the "world-as-history,"[22] and takes it to be more adequate than the Bergsonian theory of the time-philosophy in giving full vent to the "image" world of poetry as "the time-world is a world of images; . . . [whereas] the world of Space . . . is a world of 'pure Present'."[23]

This theme is developed in an illuminating article on *The "Chronological" Philosophy of Spengler*. Here Mr. Lewis refers to the German philosopher's differentiation between spatialization and time-sensationalism saying

What is thought takes the "spatial" form; what is felt takes the "time" form. . . . The "time" of Spengler is sensation. . . . And "sensation" is what is "us" (for "We ourselves are Time"); whereas what we "think" is not us, or is not-Self.[24]

Tracing this dichotomy between space and time, Mr. Lewis detects a sort of "subjective disunity" in what he calls the "tactile-observer" and concludes that the "separate treatment of the senses"[25] is the main cause of this division in the "spatio-temporal reality."[26]

This subtle question of "time" is one of the major themes in Eliot's *Four Quartets*. Heidegger considers time in relation to environmental conditions, whereas Eliot manipulates his thesis partly as a cyclic recurrence in the world of phenomena and partly as an integral element in the transcendence of timelessness. Lewis' concept of time as "nothing but space and simultaneity"[27] comes nearer to the Eliotesque view of relating time to eternity. By building up this relationship, Eliot's theme, moreover, has interpreted the totality of existence and gained universality.

With this multiplicity of metaphysical trends that are prominent in modern Western thought, it has become evident that the fundamental aim of mystical philosophy is "to penetrate behind the veil of appearance to some ultimate and abiding reality."[28] The star of this outlook has been in the ascendancy since the earlier decades of our century as a reaction against the nineteenth-century preoccupation with rationality that has beset the world of thought into indistinct and irreconcilable modes. The outcry for a meaningful philosophy behind both literature and metaphysical thought is more than a reaction; it has become a persistent demand for coherence and consistency. Here lies our sole satisfaction in a troubled world in which chaotic distractions have reacted disastrously upon our minds.

II *The Impact of Mysticism on Contemporary English Poetry and the Eliotesque "Via Mystica"*

The modern poet is particularly sensitive to the realization of this view, and he perceives the impact of science over art and literature as an act of monstrosity. The outbreak of world and civil wars has, moreover, swept the remnant belief in social amelioration. Particularly in post-war periods with the breaking down of aspirations, the loss of ethical values, with plunder, exploitation and homelessness, poets have sought refuge in their inner selves not as escapists but as experimentalists who look for the release of the agonized "spirit" in the world of inwardness after losing all faith in the ratiocinative ability of man. This revolution against the dehumanizing effect of scientific machinery was preceded by an awareness of the perpetual menace of tension and alarm:

Over is the tension, over the alarms,
The falling wage, and the flight from the pound,
The privates are returning now to the farms;[29]

of destruction, torture and rumor:

> We hear of towers long broken off from sight
> And tortures and wars, smoky and dark with rumour,
> But on Mind's buried thought there falls no light;[30]

of awe and stricken souls:

> New fears, old tunes cannot induce
> Nostalgia of the sickly soul;[31]

and the passionate appeal (of the unborn infant)

> Against those who would freeze my
> humanity, would dragoon me into a lethal automaton,
> would make me a cog in a machine.[32]

Henceforward, many modern British and American poets would embrace Freudianism which was preliminary to their final refuge in sociological and ethical mysticism; but, present intellectual climate is undeniably alien to the area of mysticism which "is still very much suspect by people who do not feel the desire to grow beyond the habitual and self-indulgent drowsings of their egos,"[33] and recognize the potentiality of the spirit behind all aspects of their lives.

Thus it has become pressing that in this "age of uncertainty ... an age in which so little can be taken for granted as common beliefs [and] assumptions, ... no explorable area can be forbidden ground."[34] Eliot's "explorable area" covers religion, philosophy, and mysticism.[35] His orientation toward the mystical source of spirituality in "an age of uncertainty" speaks of the religious bent of his mind and of the colossal effort he has devoted for the rehabilitation of "spirit," "time," and "history." In his view, it is within the domain of poetry to render possible certain types of experience that are mystical in character. In *The Use of Poetry and the Use of Criticism* runs his pronouncement on the relationship between both:

> that there is a relation [not necessarily noetic, perhaps merely psychological] between mysticism and some kinds of poetry, or some of the kinds of state in which poetry is produced, I make no doubt.[36]

His poems express the poet's experience along the Mystic Way; his quest for the absoluteness of Being culminates in the mysticism of the "invisible" in *Burnt Norton*. The development of his mystical "yearning" is almost Dantesque in its stages of progression from the Inferno of the early poems to the Purgatorio of *Ash Wednesday* and the glimpses of the Paradiso in the *Four Quartets*.[37]

With the help of this mystical progress, Eliot intends to give meaning and depth to our existence and to evoke the very experience that humanity is lacking at present in this clash of ideologies. His media are the vast realms of Eastern and Western mysticism on which he draws heavily together with his vast storage of literary reminiscence. Though the accumulation of all these trends may create a sense of estrangement, the resultant effect is in conformity with our multiple sensibility. It is the outcome of a complexity in "feeling" and "experience" that has become prominent in poetry since Eliot remarked that

> poets in our civilization, as it exists at present, must be "difficult." Our civilization comprehends great variety and complexity, and this variety and complexity, playing upon a refined sensibility, must produce various and complex results. The poet must become more and more comprehensive, more allusive, more indirect, in order to force, to dislocate if necessary, language into his meaning.[38]

Allusiveness is essential in giving expression to a complex meaning. It necessarily creates a sense of esotericism which is not the outcome of present modes of thought, nor is it a re-echo of Eliot's theory that in "the seventeenth century a dissociation of sensibility set in, from which we have never recovered";[39] but, it is, in my view, a "dissociation" that originates in the thought of St. Thomas Aquinas. The flight of Thomist metaphysics from Augustinianism marks an essential fissure in the main European trend of neo-Platonism.[40] Here lies the dichotomy between the *intellectus* and the *perceptio* or between knowledge gained through intellectualization and perceptual recognition.

This view is the result of my dissatisfaction with Eliot's theory of the seventeenth-century "dissociation of sensibility" (1921). The poet himself changed his attitude a little in his Oxford lecture on "Milton" in 1947 and confessed that "we must seek the causes [of the dissociation] in Europe, not in England alone."[41] In 1952 the French critic M. Vallette, after an elaborate analysis of *la décomposition de la sensibilité,* came to the conclusion:

Le résidu de la controverse, sur lequel tout le monde paraît s'entendre, c'est un fait mal nommé, insuffisamment analysé, souvent compris à faux, et même alors non sans donner lieu, "felix error," à d'utiles recherches.[42]

This wave of dissatisfaction was broken in 1957 against Professor Kermode's wise dictum that

the rediscovery of Aristotle, which was the cause of what we understand as medieval philosophy, necessarily involved a dissociation in Christian thought.[43]

I take the "dissociation" to be the result of the irreconcilable elements between Thomism and Augustinianism, or more specifically, between Aristotelian ratiocination and Plotinian revelation.

The fusion of these elements—which were not versatile in pre-Thomist thought—into a unified sensibility, constitutes the structural backbone of Eliot's poetry. His choice of mysticism as an area of operation is deliberately meant to bring these diverse themes into a harmonious whole; and, by relating them to the existing domination of "sense" and "matter," he aims at intensifying the spiritual anarchy of the modern world. His essential purpose is the apprehension of life in its totality and existence in the multiplicity of its levels.

III *The Crystallization of Psychic Experience into States of Profaneness in Eliot's Early Poems*

In the early poems Eliot operates on the level of psychic experience and relates it to different situations. In "The Love Song" the hesitant multiple personality of Prufrock who has measured out his life "with coffee spoons"[44] is unable to reach a decision and "force the moment to its crisis"[45] by making a visit to the room where "women come and go/Talking of Michelangelo."[46] The case in the "Portrait of a Lady" is the reverse, as we have tentative approaches "Of one about to reach her journey's end"[47] to a youth younger than her, to whom she could offer "Only the friendship and the sympathy."[48] He too is suffering from emotional frustration and is unable to face the situation which becomes with Sweeney a state of bewilderment as he identifies himself with "the silent vertebrate"[49] that "contracts and concentrates."[50]

Yet the main interest behind these poems is not so much the psychological neuroses of those characters (that is, the impact of modernity on the unconscious) as the frailty of their "belief" that robs them of a consistent and an integral element that is necessary for the poise and integration of their personalities. This theme crystallizes into an awareness of the loss of moral and spiritual beliefs. It speaks of certain states of profanation committed by those who "can sleep and feed at once"[51] and are practically unable to "refresh the Church"[52] by working for the spiritual revival of its members. Even a hippopotamus, "though perhaps quite cold in faith, has ultimately more favour with God than apathetic Christians"[53] who conceive that "Flesh and blood is weak and frail,/Susceptible to nervous shock."[54] Through the poet's quasi-prophetic vision, he could perceive at an early stage of his poetic development that the "True Church remains below/Wrapt in the old miasmal mist."[55] The edifice of the "True Church" which was once "based upon a rock"[56] is erected nowadays on the "sands" of secularism. Even its "sapient sutlers"[57] are as barren as the worker-bees which "pass between/The staminate and pistillate,"[58] with their "hairy bellies."[59] They are launched adrift the sweeping hurricane of the "material ends."[60] Instead of working for the spiritual salvation of humanity, clergymen have busied themselves with the "masters of the subtle schools"[61] who "are controversial"[62] like Origen and have, moreover, given vent to sectarianism. It is no wonder, then, that "the sable presbyters"[63] of the Church "never stir/To gather in its dividends."[64] On the other hand, the theologians who have tackled many problems are no better than a Sweeney "Stirring the water in his bath"[65] on Sunday. Their controversies are as futile as Sweeney's shifting "from ham to ham."[66] It is a deliberate contrast to the image of "the Baptized God"[67] that is depicted by "A painter of the Umbrian school."[68] This picture the poet has seen in front of him during the morning service on Sunday.[69] The scene of baptism in the wilderness which it illustrates is now "cracked and browned."[70] Instead of the angelic voice announcing: "Thou art my beloved Son; in thee I am well pleased,"[71] the whole atmosphere is cracked with the noises of diabolical inventions; and the "clear" gospel of love "is browned" with futile sophistications.

In a sweeping touch of ironic contrast to these phases of modern sordidness, Eliot manipulates a theme of the doctrinal permanence of "The word within a word, unable to speak a word."[72] Obviously Eliot is drawing here on "The Twelfth Sermon" of Bishop Andrewes on the "Nativitie"[73] in which we read

> The worke of the day is *invenietis,* to find Christ. We shall not be the better for *natus est,* if we finde Him not. Finde Him we cannot, if [first] we finde not a "Signe" to finde Him by . . .
>
> What is our "Signe" now? Why, was this "Signe" a signe of? There needs no streining at all; of "humilitie" (cleere) . . .
>
> "Signes" are taken for wonders: (Master we would faine see a "Signe," that is, a "miracle"). And, in this sense, it is a "Signe," to wonder at. Indeed, every word [here] is a wonder: Τὸ Gp ξφos "an infant"; *Verbum infans,* the "Word" without a "word"; the "eternall Word" not hable to speake a "word"; A wonder sure. And the στωαρνανίοπos, "Swadled"; and that a "wonder" too. He, that (as in the 38 of "Iob" he saith) "taketh the vast bodie of the maine Sea, turnes it to and fro, as a little child," and rolls it about with the swadling bands of "darknesse"; . . . There lieth He; the "Lord of florie," without all "glorie."[74]

The mysticism of the Incarnation, of the "Verbum infans," is "swaddled"[75] with the "darknesse" of doubt and overshadowed nowadays with the corruption of a sickening civilization in which the Jewish owner of Gerontion's house "Spawned in some estaminet of Antwerp,/Blistered in Brussels, patched and peeled in London."[76] He "spawned" more greedy youngsters, "blistered" with money-seeking transactions, as he "patched and peeled" the rottenness of his articles. After his restlessness, he comes to settle in an area of "Rocks, moss, stonecrop, iron, merds."[77] It is one of barrenness, decay and industrialization. In this urban milieu, even the goat that symbolizes instinctive lust, is emaciated and sick. The area is peopled with the housekeeper who "keeps the kitchen, makes tea,"[78] pokes "the peevish gutter";[79] and with all those who follow the deadly routine of life either by enslavement to a machine or running after material profits.

For the spiritual revival of this society, came the "eternall Word" of God, the Divine Logos, to send peace to the whole world "In the juvescence of the year."[80] But "In depraved May"[81] the innocent Lamb of God was crucified in spite of the "signe" that was given to the Pharisees after their demand: "Master we would faine see a Signe, that is, a miracle." At any rate, the "flowering judas"[82] of man's betrayal and the imprisonment of his ego in a "chestnut" of hesitation give sufficient evidence that "the tiger springs in the new year."[83] The divine wrath[84] will undoubtedly devour us all as "unnatural vices"[85] since "the wrath-bearing tree"[86] of original sin has become unspeakably obtrusive.

Also the sacrament of the Holy Mass which is meant for the spiritual development of people by becoming sharers of the divine substance, had "To be eaten, to be divided, to be drunk/ Among whispers."[87] Obviously these whispers are the result of uncertainty. They emanate from the "Vacant shuttles"[88] of hollow mentalities that "Weave the wind"[89] in restlessness and confusion.

Throughout the history of the race, human beings have been distracted and deceived by their "whispering ambitions."[90] They have been guided along its "cunning passages"[91] by fleeting vanities, and could only find their way out of its labyrinthine mazes by following "the craving" for "desire" which "famishes"[92] as soon as it is realized. Man's restless motivation is to run after what I may call "a belief in disbelief" or a hesitant recognition of "What's not believed in, or if still believed,/ In memory only, reconsidered passion."[93] It is a belief only insofar as it exists in memory and gives birth to a momentary passion. This abstention from belief naturally "propagates a fear."[94] It may create certain virtues which "Are forced upon us by our impudent crimes."[95] Virtues like righteousness and sympathy are of no ethical import if they are practiced out of fear or for the mere avoidance of evil. They do not flow spontaneously from deeply felt emotions as was the case with our former ancestry when the Divine Logos was near their hearts. Immediately the symbol by which the divine and the human meet, "was removed therefrom/To lose beauty in terror, terror in inquisition."[96] It has lost its glamor through the terror of make-believe and the futility of the associated inquiry. They have "adulterated" human passion and hampered people's senses against any sort of spiritual revivification. Only the profit and the loss "of their chilled delirium,/Excite the membrane,"[97] and set their hearts aquiver for material anticipation. The wheel of Fortune will ever go on turning and "multiply" its ups and downs; the spider will then weave its cobwebs of financial "operations" and the "weevil" will never delay in accomplishing its destructive ends.

IV

Considering these early poems collectively, it is easy to notice that there is a theme of love running through them all and acting as a binding force. But this love is very far indeed from its divine concept that was distinguished and recognized by medieval theologians to embrace the whole of humanity. It is the secular love of created beings, conventional in outlook, possessive in aim, perverted and abortive in media. It is physical in its glorification of "sense" and its orientation toward the immediate realization of "desire," not the universal or spiritual love of Eastern and Western mystics which aims at union with the Divine and is usually presented in terms of a lover wooing his mistress.

The love theme in these poems too is more personal than objective in its manipulation of certain emotional states. Though it stands for types of perversions and neurotic abnormalities, its psychological content is one of limitation. The inability of Prufrock to get rid of fear and "spit out all the butt-ends of [his] days and ways";[98] the youth's failure to break the "Capricious monotone"[99] inside his brain in the "Portrait of a Lady"; the griefs and pangs of agonized parting which should be accomplished "As the soul leaves the body torn and bruised,"[100] instead of the girl's autumnal resentment in "La Figlia Che Piange," are instances of particularized rather than generalized aspects of love.

This theme of particularization is removed from the subtleties of an all-inclusive outlook that binds its diverse elements to the wholeness of a fully integrated experience; it has only given vent to specific reactions as those of Rachel with her "murderous" attacks and the lady "in the Spanish cape"[101] who "Tries to sit on Sweeney's knees"[102] in "Sweeney Among the Nightingales."[103] It operates on an area of pettiness and insignificance: "But where is the penny world I bought/To eat with Pipit behind the screen?"[104] The image is effective for its ironic touch in contrasting the "penny world" with the privacy of what is eaten. Here the pomp and glory of the materialistic world is reduced to the worthlessness of a penny that speaks of the limited aspirations of Pipit and her friend. The fact that their world is very cheaply bought is indicative of its rapid transience. The values they hold and extol should be fleeting too insofar as they derive their content from the nature of this world. Moreover, the idea of secrecy ("behind the screen") which brings the question to a climax, denotes not only the whimsical waywardness by which simple and instinctive acts are accomplished but the psychological introversion of the operators.

Viewed in retrospect, this theme of perverted love in the early poems is mixed with certain macabre utterances that betray a death-longing. For Prufrock "There will be time to murder and create"[105] and time to think of "death as the eternal Footman"[106] and hear "the mermaids singing, each to each"[107] "Till human voices wake us, and we drown."[108] The desire for submergence into "the chambers of the sea"[109] and identity with "a pair of ragged claws/Scuttling across the floors of silent seas"[110] are all symptoms of a psychologically devastated personality waiting for death. Prufrock aims too at drowning his ego in the fathomless depths of fantasy by shutting himself up from reality. He is fettered by his repeated failures that haunt his actual life and curse his love.

This erotic theme in the "Portrait of a Lady" terminates in the youth's wishful thinking of his lady's death:

and what if she should die some afternoon,
Afternoon grey and smoky, evening yellow and rose;
Should die and leave me sitting pen in hand
With the smoke coming down above the housetops.[111]

The same sepulchral atmosphere envelops the love story of the waiter in "Dans le Restaurant" who thinks his fate to be similar to the drowned Phlebas: "c'était un sort pénible/Cependant, ce fut jadis un bel homme, de haute taille."[112] Burbank too, the American tourist, ends his unrequited love with Princess Volupine by "meditating on/Time's ruins,"[113] and the collapse of civilization.

This blending of the love theme with the *memento mori* is reducible, in the end, to the eternal relationship between Eros and Agape, the motivating power of love and its freedom from possessiveness.[114] Viewed against a background of psychic wholesomeness, the conflict between the Hellenistic Eros and the Christian Agape could be synthesized as in Caritas on a basis of sacrifice which may verge in sublimated cases on self-abnegation. But Eliot's erotic theme in the early poems is far from this happy issue and it does not portray any remarkable trait of development toward it. It operates on a setting that is agonizingly deficient and chaotic. It is clothed in an unhealthy and sickening atmosphere: "When the evening is spread out against the sky/Like a patient etherised upon a table."[115] Here the metaphysically startling image stresses the wavering of Prufrock between a nostalgia for life and a hope for paralyzing the ego under the anaesthesis of forgetfulness.

The prevalent imagery, at any rate, that frames this setting is one of boredom, of the "Streets that follow like a tedious argument/Of insidious intent";[116] of the pitchy darkness of "the soot that falls from chimneys";[117] and of "the smoke and fog of a December afternoon."[118] It is "An atmosphere of Juliet's tomb,"[119] of loss and fate, of grudgery and hasty decisions. It is the atmosphere too of the "darkened room"[120] in which the soul is moved

> by fancies that are curled
> Around these images, and cling:
> The notion of some infinitely gentle
> Infinitely suffering thing.[121]

Here is the premeditation of the soul on no other suffering save its own and presumably those which are similar in being launched adrift the stream of affliction. Hence, it "stretched tight across the skies/That fade behind a city block."[122] Its life is governed by shadowy "appearances" which are set against "The burnt-out ends of smoky days."[123] This extinction of a collapsing civilization has aggravated many wise mortals who are helplessly left in a state of agony after the visualization of "the thousand sordid images"[124] that speak of the destitution and emptiness of the "vacant lots."[125]

These images, on the whole, are not only metaphysical but symbolist too and most of them show a blending of both. It is worth noting, however, that Eliot came across the French Symbolists through his reading of Arthur Symons' book *The Symbolist Movement in Literature* in its second publication in 1908.[126] He expressed his indebtedness to it saying that "the Symons' book is one of those which have affected the course of my life."[127]

Miss Starkie stresses the fact that Eliot

> found particular stimulus in Laforgue because he expressed,
> even more than Corbière or Baudelaire, the problems of his own
> age, and he renewed poetry since he had understood modern
> man.[128]

As early as *Spleen* (1910) the influence of Laforgue (1860-87) is evident in such lines:

> And life, a little bald and gray,
> Languid, fastidious, and bland,
> Waits, ... [129]

which recall Laforgue's

> Alors, le grand bouquet tragique de la Vie!
> Les mornes violets des desillusions,
> Les horizons tout gris de l'ornière suivie,[130]

and "Mais il est temps encore!"[131] that gives birth to an un-expected tone of cynicism which is characteristic of both poets.

In *Humouresque* (1910) which is modeled "After J. Laforgue" too, traces of the French poet's preoccupations with "La Lune" are marked in Eliot's "His who-the-devil-are-you stare;/Trans-lated, maybe, to the moon,"[132] and "Your damned thin moon-light, worse than gas—"[133] which are reminiscent of Laforgue's *dilettante Lune*[134] and *vagabonde Lune*[135] as the moon is like the "silent spy"[136] who trespasses upon the affairs of people.

The influence of Laforgue continued after the very early poems and is evidenced in the interior monologue[137] of "The Love Song of J. Alfred Prufrock" (1910-11), the provocative image[138] in the "Portrait of a Lady" (1910), the conversational tone[139] of "Conversation Galante" (1909), and "Dans le Res-taurant" (1916-17).

Before the voice of Laforgue dies out in Eliot's poetry, we hear echoes of Gautier (1811-72) recalling "L'Hippopotame":

> Je suis comme l'hippopotame:
> De ma conviction couvert,
> Forte armure que rien n'entame,
> Je vais sans peur par le désert.[140]

With Eliot this personal conviction reinforced with a *forte armure*, is extended to embrace the majority of believers.

Above all, Eliot has learnt from these French Symbolists the use of deliberate contrasts, abrupt transitions, dramatic situations, as-sociational themes, irregular *vers libre*[141] and economy of words.

Parallel to this trend, but not completely bereft of it, is the influence of the Imagist Movement which was given birth when T. E. Hulme (1883-1917)[142] who is *l'initiateur du mouve-ment*[143] established the Poet's Club in 1908. With the supremacy of Ezra Pound (1885-   ) who is *l'animateur*,[144] it crystallized into a belief

> in technique, . . . in the mastery of all known forms and systems
> of metres, the insistence on precision, the avoidance of convention
> and cliché, of rhetoric and inversions.[145]

T. S. Eliot was attracted to the Imagists at the beginning of his poetic career, but soon developed into far-reaching horizons. Their insistence on the concreteness of detail falls short in giving full expression to his poetic visions. Before coming to this later stage in Eliot's poetic development, it is interesting to observe the reaction of the reading public. A book review of the early poems and lyrics that appeared before 1919 contains the following:

> Mr. Eliot is certainly damned by his newness and strangeness;
> but these two qualities, which in most art are completely un-
> important, because ephemeral, in him claim the attention of even
> the serious critic. For they are part of the fabric of his poetry.[146]

The reviewer takes the example of "The Hippopotamus" and considers it "perilously near the pit of the *jeu d'esprit*."[147] This seeming levity may be the by-product of "newness," but it conceals underneath an intense seriousness in the usage of imagery. The apparent "strangeness" arises from the poet's conviction that poetry "may help to break up the conventional modes of perception and valuation which are perpetually forming, and make people see the world afresh, or some new part of it."[148] Henceforward, the Eliotesque image, in addition to its nonconventional trait, is both panoramic and kaleidoscopic as it projects the spectra of a whole life-cycle:

> when I am formulated, sprawling on a pin,
> When I am pinned and wriggling on the wall,
> Then how should I begin
> To spit out all the butt-ends of my days and ways?[149]

It is also characterized by ambivalence and paradox which are the result of fusing dissimilars—the commonplace and the otherworldly, the secular and the mystical:

> At mating time the hippo's voice
> Betrays inflexions hoarse and odd,
> But every week we hear rejoice
> The Church, at being one with God.[150]

It may elaborate a theme of condensation through the device of the metaphysical "conceit" in a single line like "I have measured out my life with coffee spoons,"[151] in which the trite generality (of Prufrock's life) is ironically particularized by a relatively insignificant article.

This symbolico-metaphysical image in the very early poems gives way to the mystico-symbolical image in such poems as "Gerontion," "The Hippopotamus," and "Mr. Eliot's Sunday Morning Service." In "Burbank with a Baedeker: Bleistein with a Cigar" it shifts to what may be called the "aesthetic image." Obviously these images are functional rather than ornamental, organic architectonics and not loose pendants. They are interrelated and most of them show a blending of various elements. The theme of aestheticism in the last poem, for instance, has given vent to

> le sens esthétique qui apparaît comme un grand maître en mysticisme. Il crée en nous une croyance expressément inverse de celle qui nous persuade en l'état normal de la réalité du monde extérieur.[152]

It is entwined in Eliot's poem with the modern psychological conception of sublimation through art which is unknown to Princess Volupine and her associates of modern Italy toward which

> The horses,[153] under the axletree
>   Beat up the dawn from Istria[154]
> With even feet.[155]

The absence of any aesthetic sense is mostly deplorable in the Venice of today where

> A lustreless protrusive eye
>   Stares from the protozoic slime
> At a perspective of Canaletto.
>   The smoky candle end of time
> Declines.[156]

The contemporary "protrusive eye" is incapable of having a full "perspective of Canaletto" as it is dipped in "the protozoic slime" that has deprived it of its usual luster. The exuberance of Canaletto is set against a background of "defunctive music"[157] and the "smoky candle" of modern industrialization that marks the end of civilization.[158]

This thematic-imagistic relationship may appear in the poems to be loosely connected, but it is richly connotative in its associations. Eliot's adroitness is evidenced here in his accumulation of discordant elements and his telescopic method which may result at times in such syntactical ambiguities as "flowering judas,"[159] "the wrath-bearing tree,"[160] "the mensual turn of time"[161] and "the anguish of the marrow."[162] At any rate, "s'il [Eliot] favorise une ambiance ambigüe, c'est pour y faire/éclater plus vivement de fulgurantes éclaircies."[163] The pervading impression, however, in addition to this element of liveliness, is one of sinuosity by which metrical fibres function in heterogeneity. Apparently the whole process is synthetic insofar as it blends disparate elements into a harmonious whole.

Yet this heterogeneous outlook is not final, but it is essential for the poet who aims at building up an envisaged homogeneity based on the refinement of sensibility or the elevation of instincts above the material and sensuous distractions of life. Eliot looks forward to drawing attention to the existence of various other layers of experience which are vital for creating any taste and criterion of beauty. The cultivation of this taste rests in many ways on its nurture with what is permanent in values and what is integral in concept. Necessarily it would function in a social milieu through communion with the sensibilities of others. Aesthetic taste, in this sense, should be genuinely objective insofar as it aims at creating an "awareness of the true nature of reality underlying the superficial appearances of things."[164]

These aspirations are difficult to realize as far as Eliot's early poems are concerned owing to the presence of psychic frustration and total loss of a spiritual belief. Though this problem runs through most of the poems and its portrayal has been worked out on many a level of experience, perhaps no real solution has been attempted.[165] In the main, the attitude of the "True Church"[166] in facing sin and evil, is one of utter passivity, but the gathering of antagonistic sects is in some respects the first step toward a pervasive issue of real unity[167] and true understanding. Instead of "compassing material ends"[168] the "sapient sutlers"[169] should draw upon the essence of mystical theology and bring together the "passionless" folks that are divided against themselves. In essence as well as in purely objective values, mystical religions are not far from each other,[170] and the nature of the solution should bear relevance to the multiplicity of these divisions. Its motivating power should necessarily be a wholesome and constructivist unity that will bring the "friction" of sectarianism to an end and relieve humanity from the "pricks" of narrow-mindedness and futile controversy.

V

As a whole, these early poems are essential for the mystical development of the soul. At this early stage, they are mainly concerned with the exploration of the setting in which they will operate. Streaks of bafflement coupled with corrosive irony are quite natural in facing a world wholly given to strife and egocentric ends. In this milieu, both emotional perversion and ethical starvation help to portray the scene of degeneration. The nonchalance of those who are mainly concerned with "mystical religion" has become more and more bewildering. Rescuing the numberless folks from imminent destruction is not a far cry in the wilderness that goes unheard, but a necessity of snatching humanity from a devouring doom which is the responsibility of all sincere and conscientious thinkers.

...it would be difficult to imagine a completer transcendence of the individual self, a completer projection of awareness [other than those expressed in *The Waste Land*].[2]

F. R. LEAVIS

CHAPTER FOUR

Versatility of Levels in the Mystical Meaning of "The Waste Land"

The foregoing themes of frustration and loss in the previous poems take a firm foothold in Eliot's longer poem *The Waste Land*.[3] Futility and despair play havoc on the minds of its inhabitants; lust casts them asunder and renders their land unproductive; abortive love has deadened the soul; and complete separation from the elemental symbolism of existence has dried up the springs of rebirth. It is no wonder that hope in this "barren" land of modern civilization is only a mirage. Flight to past recollection or "mixing/Memory and desire"[4] is the only shelter for a devastated ego that seeks refuge in phantasmal "appearances." There is no escape from the abiding reality which we try to evade as a natural result of the decline of "belief" in mystical symbolism which used to be universally acknowledged by our former ancestors.

I

Eliot in this poem follows the life-cycle of torment that was suggested by the Grail legend.[5] The main theme of Miss Weston's *From Ritual to Romance*, of a soil that is blighted with a curse, is associated in *The Waste Land* with the "Unreal City,"[6] the post-War suffocating atmosphere of London,[7] the Baudelairian

Fourmillante cité, cité pleine de rêves,
Où le spectre en plein jour raccroche le passant![8]

and the Dantean *Inferno* in which sighs are exhaled and possibilities of repentance are too narrow.

For the dwellers of this land, the coming of April with the earlier showers of spring is mostly cruel because "the disengagement of the self from death into life which April symbolizes, is painful."[9] The rebirth of nature meant for the ancient generations in the East (for example, India, China and Egypt) as well as the West (for example, Greece), the spiritual rebirth of humanity and was associated with the sacrificial ordeals out of which the soul of man was transformed into a state of purity and mystical bliss. For them the "sprouting" of nature is a prototype of the spiritual transformation of man, to which modern civilization remains insensitive. We stick to the darkness of "the dead land"[10] and the wintry evenings that "kept us warm, covering/Earth in forgetful snow."[11] The inhabitants of the modern world have completely lost the significance of the age-old aphorism that "life comes out of death"—the way to spiritual life is one of Purgatorio in which the egoistic self is totally diminished marking the "inevitable dissolution which must precede new life."[12]

Life comes out of the death of Osiris or Orpheus with the burial[13] of his effigies. It symbolizes the mystical deliverance of people through the death of the corn-god, and his resurrection is indicative of a prosperous life of fertility.[14] But this life-giving symbol is utterly unknown to the Stetson[15] of the modern world whose ritual is disturbed by "the sudden frost."[16] He is also haunted by the seemingly friendly intervention of the Dog[17] which will dig up its hidden reality. Mr. Williamson rightly considers the Dog

> more important than Eliot's transformation of Webster;[18] rather it is the transformation, for it develops the ambiguity of the planted corpse.[19]

Even then, it is doubtful whether the effigy will "bloom this year"[20] or will be lost "in forgetful snow."[21] This loss of fertility[22] is associated in *The Waste Land* with "the idea of infidelity and betrayal"[23] hinted at by Lil's friend:

> think of poor Albert,
> He's been in the army four years, he wants a good time,
> And if you don't give it him, there's others will, I said.[24]

It is all symptomatic of the boredom of love which is degraded
in contemporary society to a mechanical relationship:[25]

> When lovely woman stoops to folly and
> Paces about her room again, alone,
> She smoothes her hair with automatic hand,
> And puts a record on the gramophone.[26]

This automatism of love, which is conceived in the poem in the
"sterile" abstraction of a chess-game, is reminiscent of the biting
satire behind the series of seductions in Middleton's plays. In
A Game at Chesse the White Queen's Pawn is raped by the
Black Bishop's Pawn "in the heat of Game";[27] and in *Women
Beware Women* the Duke of Florence was able to seduce Bianca
by engaging her mother-in-law in a chess-game "that will
beguile time."[28] Undoubtedly it has all struck the death-knell
of the mystical glamor of love as it used to be associated with
the sublime and the sanctifying efficacy of truly Christian mat-
rimony. Nowadays, it is "The sound of horns and motors, which
shall bring/Sweeney to Mrs. Porter in the spring,"[29] instead of
the lullings of "sweet Thames"[30] that used to attract the nymphs
to their paramours.[31]

So too the Grail procession that was basically meant for initiation, is now ironically turned into "A crowd" of people flowing
"over London Bridge."[32] This image of the crowds has enlivened
the mystical significance of the poem as it is reminiscent of
Dante's *Inferno* where "the dreary souls of those ... who lived
without blame,/and without praise,"[33] are tortured. In his stu-
pefaction the poet Dante tells us "I should never have believed
death had/undone so many."[34] Though the image speaks of
a Sibylline wish to die[35] and of utter loss of hope, it is through
the death of the carnal self that the real Self enjoys internal
and mystical fortitude. It is thus what may be called a death-in-
life image that is symbolically significant on both levels. It
gains universality through association with the symbolico-mys-
ticism of death and the horrors of the "Limbo" and the desperate
atmosphere of the "endless wailings"[36] of those who linger in
suspense. Its symbolism is not that of a private arbitrary creation
but of an "objective correlative"[37] that exists in the mind of the
hermaphrodite Tiresias who is "the most important personage in
the poem,"[38] as what he "sees, in fact, is the substance of the
whole poem."[39] As he is blind, he perceives through his mind's
eye that each person, in his unimaginative way, is fixing "his

eyes before his feet."[40] After all, he is the "Hypocrite lecteur!—
mon semblable,—mon frère!"[41] The point of resemblance here is
the state of "spiritual lassitude"[42] that pervades all.

Commenting on this last part of "The Burial of the Dead,"
Edith Sitwell grows unusually enthusiastic in describing it as a

> miracle of poetry, so magical in its power of evoking the deepest
> movements of the soul, so intensely poignant . . . [that] sense
> and language are one living, suffering being, and cannot be
> separated without destroying their life.[43]

It is not only the simple welding of "sense and language" but
the deliberate mating of intellect and emotion that accounts for
Eliot's preoccupation with the "association of sensibility" which
he endeavors to restore.

At any rate, the culmination of the previous state of unwill-
ingness to undergo initiatory rebirth into a Baudelarian ennui
renders the sacrificial death of the Phoenician sailor in "Death
by Water" a justifiable process. His drowning is predicted by
Madame Sesostris, the "famous clairvoyante,"[44] who warned him:
"Fear death by water."[45] The modern fortuneteller uses "a
wicked pack of cards"[46] and "is known to be the wisest woman
in Europe!"[47] But her ancient Egyptian ancestress used to derive
her inspiration from the wisdom of the *Corpus Hermeticum*
which is based on the mystical symbolism of "initiation."

The loss of this wisdom throughout the ages supplies us with
the architectonic clue to the basic concept behind the mystical
significance of the whole poem. This concept is stressed through
the poet's reference to the emptiness and sterility of the modern
waste land where the inhabitants have lost all contact with the
connotative meaning of mystical symbolism.

The drowning of "Phlebas the Phoenician,"[48] who is "the
Smyrna merchant,"[49] has become, thus, a necessity; and, it symbolizes the death of the fertility god whose effigy used to be
thrown into the waters of the Nile, Tigris, and Euphrates. It is
also the symbol of the fruitful death of Alonso, Ferdinand's
father, in *The Tempest,* at which the Ariel hinted in his Song
saying: "Those are pearls that were his eyes."[50] These deaths
which are sacrificial in character are not everlasting; Alonso
had to "suffer a sea-change/Into something rich and strange"[51]
before his rescue from the shipwreck and his association with
Prospero who announces: "I'll deliver all."[52] The effigies too in

due course begin to sprout through the slaying of the corn-god[53] which may be the symbol of the crucifixion./Nature is, however, relieved with the resurrection, and its budding with April showers is thus symbolically significant for the mystical revival of the soul. But the showers are lacking in the contemporary waste land where the inhabitants have blindly shut themselves away from the "gleams" of reality and spiritual revelation. They are gradually suffering the suffocating atmosphere in a "decayed hole among the mountains"[54] above which the "black clouds"[55] are not loaded with the reanimating drops of rain, but clothe the whole scene in the sepulchral darkness of death. It is the paralyzing atmosphere of the one who "was neither/Living nor dead"[56] and of those who "are in rats' alley/Where the dead men lost their bones"[57] and are thus deprived of a peaceful death.

Against this scene of phantasmagoria and sickening decay is the possibility of regenerating the "Unreal City"[58] through mystical deliverance by way of sacrificial death which is charged with all the possibilities of rebirth. The passage of the drowned Phoenician sailor along "a current under sea"[59] speaks of this inevitability of suffering. It is a reiteration and a prolongation of the same theme developed at the end of "Dans le Restaurant" where the poet ironically shifts from a waiter's need of a bath "Tiens, voilà dix sous, pour la salle-de-bains"[60] to a reference to "Phlébas, le Phénicien"[61] whom

> Un courant de sous-mer l'emporta très loin,
> Le repassant aux étapes de sa vie antérieure.[62]

He has passed through the stages of *sa vie antérieure* recapitulating in a flash of insight all his previous phases of development before "entering the whirlpool"[63] that symbolizes the decisive moment of mystical surrender and the Buddhist freedom from attachment to possessiveness.[64] But Phlebas' death "shows the failure of false efforts at redemption"[65] as he is still held to "the wheel"[66] of desire ("tanha") and suffering ("dukkha").[67] In the words of Buddha which are cited by Mr. Humphreys, the Founding President of the Buddhist Lodge, London, 1924 (now the Buddhist Society):

> Verily it is this thirst or craving [for desire], causing the renewal of existence, accompanied by sensual delight, seeking satisfaction now here, now there—the craving for the gratification of the passions, for continued existence in the worlds of sense,[68]

that breeds suffering. This message is addressed in Eliot's "Death by Water" to the "Gentile or Jew,"[69] to those who are still governed by passion and frustrated by the cravings of the flesh.

These symptoms of attachment lead naturally to the possibility of cleansing through infernal asceticism. The very title of this part of *The Waste Land* is taken from "The Fire Sermon" of Buddha in which the Blessed One addressed the congregation of friars saying:

> Everything, O Bhikkhus [friars], is burning. And how, O Bhikkhus, is everything burning?
> The eye, O Bhikkhus, is burning; visible things are burning; the mental impressions based on the eye are burning; the contact of the eye [with visible things] is burning; the sensation produced by the contact of the eye [with visible things], be it pleasant, be it painful, be it neither pleasant nor painful, that also is burning. With what fire is it burning? I declare unto you that it is burning with the fire of lust, with the fire of anger, with the fire of ignorance; it is burning with [the anxieties of] birth, decay, death, grief, lamentation, suffering, dejection, and despair.[70]

The main thesis of this Sermon is the burning fire of lust. In the words of M. Greene

> l'amour qui ne se propose d'autre but que la satisfaction immédiate du désir charnel est un feu qui consume; il ne régénère pas, il tue.[71]

This consuming fire could be quenched, however, by way of detachment[72] from "eye-consciousness" and sensual indulgence. Passage through the purgatorial flames will cleanse the soul and assure the devotee that he is following the Mystic Path to righteousness.[73]

St. Augustine also, after stating

> To Carthage then I came, where a cauldron of unholy loves sang all about mine ears,[74]

earnestly expounded the "burning"[75] nostalgia for flight to Him and exclaimed:

> How did I burn then, my God, how did I burn to fly from earthly delights towards thee, and yet I knew not what thou meanedst to do with me![76]

For St. Augustine too

> everything was offensive, yea, the very light itself; and what-
> soever were not he, was alike painful and hateful to me, ex-
> cept groaning and weeping.[77]

He then prays God to protect his soul against

> these seducements of the eyes..., lest my feet wherewith
> I am to enter upon my way, should be ensnared; yea, and I
> lift up mine invisible eyes unto thee, and thou wouldst be
> pleased to pluck my feet out of that snare.[78]

And, pleading for the mercy of God, St. Augustine concludes on a
note of mystical certainty that is characteristic of great saints
and says:

> Thou wilt pluck me [out], O Lord, thou wilt pluck me [out]
> because thy mercy is before mine eyes.[79]

St. Augustine appears to use the phrase "plucking out" with
reference to a snare, but Eliot in saying

> Burning burning burning burning
> O Lord Thou pluckest me out
> O Lord Thou pluckest[80]

has apparently had in mind the phrase: "a brand plucked from
the burning" which is based on the Old Testament verse:

> And the Lord said unto Satan, the Lord rebuke thee, O Satan;
> yea, the Lord that hath chosen Jerusalem rebuke thee: is not
> this a brand plucked out of the fire?[81]

Detachment from the Augustinian "seducements of the eyes"
and the Buddhist "impressions based on the eye," however, comes
by loosening the snares of "desire" and the transition of the
soul across the burning flames of an Inferno. These predicaments,
in fact, give the clue to the ethical mysticism of the poem, for
it is through these media that the Heavenly Kingdom on earth[82]
and the nirvanic exaltation[83] are attained.

These "two representatives of Eastern and Western asceticism"[84] are associated here by Eliot for they reach this state of
exaltation in much the same Mystic Path of detachment from
sense-indulgence.[85] Their mystical philosophy of asceticism is

relevant to the contemporary waste land in which there is no
sign of life save the bones "Rattled by the rat's foot"[86] and where

> the nightingale
> Filled all the desert with inviolable voice
> And still she cried, and still the world pursues,
> "Jug Jug" to dirty ears.[87]

This twittering of seduction has deadened the "voice" of con-
science; and, against the wisdom of the past, "still the world pur-
sues" the "thoughts of a dry brain in a dry season."[88] Even Tiresias who has "foresuffered all"[89] types of lust, simply sat down "by
the waters of Leman[90] . . . and wept."[91] In his Babylonian captivity, he is unable to loosen the chains of "desire" and release
himself from the bondage of attachment.

With this abstention of the protagonist (Tiresias or the
quester of the Grail) from infernal "burning," the poet reiterates
the mystical symbolism of suffering and develops in "What
the Thunder said" a theme that is mainly concerned with the
world of "inwardness." He links this Inferno to which the soul
is exposed partly with the Christian mysticism of the crucifixion[92] and partly with the Brahmanic mysticism of the "three
cardinal virtues." In the *Brihadâranyaka-Upanishad* one reads
that

1. The threefold descendants of Pragâpati,[93] gods, men, and
   Asuras [evil spirits], dwelt as Brahmakârins [students] with
   their father Pragâpati. Having finished their studentship
   the gods said: "Tell us [something], Sir." He told them the
   syllable *Da*. Then he said: "Did you understand?" They
   said: "We did understand. You told us *Dâmyata*, Be subdued." "Yes," he said, "you have understood."

2. Then the men said to him: . . . "You told us, *Datta*, Give."
   "Yes," he said, "You have understood."

3. Then the Asuras said to him: . . . "You told us, *Dayadham*,
   Be merciful." "Yes," he said, "you have understood."
   The divine voice of thunder repeats the same, *Da Da Da*,
   that is, Be subdued, Give, Be merciful. Therefore let that
   triad be taught, Subduing, Giving, and Mercy.[94]

Professor Max Müller stresses the fact that the Upanishad philosophers "were concerned with [these] three important stages
which they preached as with a voice of thunder."[95] But before
these dicta are brought into realization by benevolent enact-

ments, the protagonist of *The Waste Land* had to suffer a most direful journey across the desert where "Sweat is dry and feet are in the sand,"[96] and

> the dead tree gives no shelter, the cricket no relief,
> And the dry stone no sound of water. Only
> There is shadow under this red rock.[97]

It is a continuation of the theme of suffering in "Death by Water" where Phlebas' life is brought to a tragic end:

> He who was living is now dead
> We who were living are now dying
> With a little patience.[98]

Though the first line is interpreted by a considerable number of commentators in terms of the fertility-god, it may also mean the death of Christ (before the resurrection), and the loss of self in the phantasmagoria of a worn-out make-believe. The idea of death is hinted at in the opening lines of "What the Thunder said":

> After the torchlight red on sweaty faces
> After the frosty silence in the gardens[99]

of Gethsemane and those adjoining the Golgotha where Christ used to have his moments of divine speculation, the people were exasperated before His trial by Pontius Pilatus was over. The deadly silence which was coupled at times with the Disciples' regression was broken by "the shouting and the crying"[100] of hard-hearted unbelievers: "Crucify 'him', crucify 'him'."[101] The scene then shifts to "the agony" of the crucifixion "in stony places";[102] and, with the death of Christ, thunder and lightning broke "over distant mountains,"[103] piercing the darkness of the place.

The notion of the resurrection is reinforced in the poem with the protagonist's bewilderment that "There is always another one walking beside you/Gliding wrapt in a brown mantle."[104] Failing to realize the mystical significance of the redemption and having his share in the "frosty silence" that is removed from the warmth of true belief, the protagonist suffers another initiatory process hoping to reach the chapel in the end.

The parching drought which he experiences on his way across the desert is that of the "carious teeth that cannot spit."[105] "Even silence"[106] is denied on the "dead mountain,"[107] "But dry sterile thunder without rain"[108] breaks its desolation. The "red sullen faces"[109] of monks who "sneer and snarl/From doors of mudcracked houses"[110] which he encounters on his way, bring to mind the ascetic mysticism of monastic solitude.

On coming to the Chapel Perilous among "the tumbled graves,"[111] he perceives that it is empty, but in the Grail legend, the quester "finds on the altar the body of a dead knight, covered with a rich samite, a candle burning at his feet."[112] He is identified here with the dead knight who failed in his message which is also the case in *The Waste Land.* A "cock stood on the rooftree"[113] to remind him of the austerity of his mission. Though its main function in the poem is to herald the peeping of dawn, it is not daylight with the protagonist nor is it the "damp gust"[114] bringing the rain of spiritual revival. The quester[115] has failed in grasping any meaning behind the Upanishadic utterance: *Datta, Dayadhvam, Damyata,*[116] that is, give, sympathize, control.[117] He is still preoccupied with the "empty rooms"[118] of the desolate self where "the beneficent spider"[119] weaves its webs of past recollection. He has given himself up to the reverie of "aethereal rumours"[120] that will keep him "in his prison"[121] away from the reality of mystical release.

In this state, he "turns his eyes inwards upon his own soul... only to find there a gallery of horrors which repentance and faith alone can dispel,"[122] as Mr. Peter finely puts it. He is here linked with those who long for deliverance from the imprisonment of the carnal self and the aridity of a meaningless ideology. This view helps the poet to recapitulate the former themes which are not only intensified but driven home through the mysticism of suffering. This is, perhaps, the cornerstone in the structural symbolism of *The Waste Land.* The morbidity of enslavement to selfish desires has led to "the present decay of eastern Europe,"[123] the destruction of "London Bridge"[124] with the breaking down of all aspirations for salvation and mystical revelation,[125] to the madness of Hieronymo in seeking revenge,[126] and to the necessity of refinement in the cleansing flames of Dante's *Purgatorio.* It is no wonder that the protagonist identifies himself with the speaker in G. de Nerval's sonnet *El Desdichado* in his inconsolable melancholy[127] and longs for the freedom of the sparrow like Procne in *Pervigilium Veneris* who expressed it in her questioning: "Quando ver venit meum?/ Quando fiam uti chelidon, ut tacere desinam?"[128]

But the protagonist of *The Waste Land* is unable to realize that he is far removed from the true meaning of his journey as he is still unaware of the Upanishadic wisdom of silencing sensual cravings. Only by treading this path, he may come to "Shantih shantih shantih"[129] or "the Peace which passeth understanding."[130] This is the reverse of Mr. Williamson's interpretation that "the Sanskrit commands, supported by the Upanishad ending, sound like the mad talk of Hieronymo, and hallucinative vision appears to end in madness."[131] Both the commands and the ending play an essential role in drawing attention to the dangers of self-imprisonment and the possibility of attaining "peace" through sacrifice and the realization of the Upanishad benediction.

II *The Spiritual Flaccidity of the Hollow Men*

The prevailing theme of "the emptiness of life without belief" finally "resounds with sickening fear and desperation in 'The Hollow Men'."[132] This poem speaks of the dryness of the contemporary life of "cactus land"[133] where "stone images"[134] of death "Are raised."[135] Its major theme is not that of the death-in-life of *The Waste Land* but "death's other Kingdom"[136] where the "violent souls"[137] rest. We "Are quiet and meaningless/As wind in dry grass,"[138] whereas they were "violent" in facing death with the courage and certitude of true believers. Our quietness and inability to take any action have transformed our life into the death of a "hollow valley"[139] where "the stuffed men"[140] are no more than "Shape without form, shade without colour,/Paralysed force, gesture without motion."[141] In their crippled gestures and formless shapes, they are unable to undergo the mystical suffering of an Inferno.

Their shrinkage to "such deliberate disguises"[142] and their dwelling on "death's dream kingdom,"[143] introduce the theme of nightmare and the flight of the Hollow Men from reality. The protagonist who is an example of their emptiness,[144] abstains from "that final meeting/In the twilight kingdom"[145] of mystical religion. He prefers "the dead land"[146] of his inner self to the "final meeting"[147] of Truth through "the supplication"[148] to faith and acceptance of mystical revelation. His spiritual flaccidity is that of "a fading star"[149] which presides over the valley of death where the "broken jaw"[150] of suffering will "stuff" the men in their resting place. Here by "the tumid river"[151] of death where they gather[152] before their utter damnation, their eyes[153] are "sightless"[154] and completely blind to the earlier dawnings of mystical illumination.

With the appearance of "the perpetual star"[155] only to those souls that have plunged deeply into the Purgatorio of suffering, the Dantean vision of the "Multifoliate rose"[156] becomes meaningful. It is reminiscent of Dante's visionary absorption in contemplating the Rose of Heaven (the Virgin Mary) and the Apostles after Beatrice's gentle reproof that they should be the object of his praise and not her:

> Wherefore doth my face so enamour thee that thou turnest thee not to the fair garden which flowereth beneath the rays of Christ?
> There is the Rose wherein the Word Divine made itself flesh; there are the Lilies [the Apostles] at whose odour the good path was taken.[157]

But to those who are still turning round "the prickly pear"[158] of sinfulness, the vision is unknown. The root of their negative way of life is their inability to differentiate

> Between the idea
> And the reality
> Between the motion
> And the act[159]

where "the Shadow"[160] of a meaningless existence falls. Mr. Fussell rightly takes this Shadow to be "the inescapable presence of the dead emptiness and the insignificant disorderliness which Eliot sees as the essence of an age without religious faith."[161] It handicaps the way to prayer:

> For Thine is
> Life is
> For Thine is the[162]

and reduces it to broken quibbling. Its interposition "between essence and descent symbolizes the inability to reconcile spirit and flesh, word and deed."[163]

This inability to reach a reconciliation speaks of the hopelessness of the "empty men" who take shadows for realities and are thus deprived of the true meaning of existence. For them "Life is very long" and the way to redemption ("For Thine is the Kingdom") is faintly perceived.

The poem, in this sense, speaks of the various symptoms of depravity and the despair[164] of those who are attached to a meaningless life. Round "the prickly pear" they go completely unaware of any destination or conclusion. Their aimlessness has created the barrier of the Shadow that separates them from the genuineness of existence and offers no possibility of spiritual revivification. Their emptiness is a natural concomitant of a land laid waste; and, it is obvious that "The Hollow Men" has added another dim stroke to the already dark picture of *The Waste Land*.

III

In fact the dilemma depicted in this picture of the devastated land has aroused a good deal of critical controversy to the extent that it is no exaggeration to consider *The Waste Land* as epoch-making. Critics who have dealt with it, though their analyses are more or less irreconcilable, mostly fall into three major groups: those whose views are known for their moderation; those who are enthusiastic enough to condemn the whole thing on a basis of obscurity or complexity; and those who are unable to face any commitment by either developing or refuting a certain view and are content to remain indifferent. The writings of the third category hardly deserve the name "literary criticism," and, it is mainly with the first two groups that any assessment is relevant.

A preliminary analysis of the poem will show that it operates on many levels of experience ranging from Buddhist asceticism, Augustinian mystical philosophy, Dantean infernal death, anthropological cults, to modern settings of treachery and lust. It "sounds chaotic[165] enough, yet all these things are definitely fused; the result is symphonic, not episodic,"[166] as Professor Dobrée wisely remarks. Each theme leads to a final dilemma of "facing life and death without the spiritual and intellectual certainties which sustained an earlier generation."[167] The loss of all significance behind these aspects of human experience and the mystical meaning that used to be attached to them sounds the keynote of *The Waste Land*. The theme of despair that is associated with this loss is emphasized through the poet's apparent preoccupation with the ironic juxtaposition of the exuberance of ancient mysticism and the numbness of contemporary industrialization. Professor Greene has rightly noted that

par les nombreux parallélismes et contrastes qu'il [Eliot] établit
avec diverses époques du passé, par l'évocation des mythes
les plus anciens de l'humanité, enfin par le ton prophétique
qui se fait entendre par moments, il est certain qu'il a
voulu présenter une vision de la vie contemporaine qui s'élargit
jusqu'a embrasser tous les temps.[168]

The clashes of all these themes are sifted in the crucible of *le ton
prophétique* which is heard from the Thunder in the Upanishadic
aphorism. The result is not only the crystallization of a single
vision but a series of kaleidoscopic visions that mark the multiple stages in the mystical advancement of the soul.

Failing to appreciate this point that is fundamentally based
on a thesis of associationism has led some critics to consider
the poem lacking in matter of development. But it may portray
an integral phase in the *Via Mystica* of the soul. This does not
mean that the poem "exhibits no progression"[169] or "ends where
it began"[170] in exactly the same state, as Dr. Leavis interprets
it. At the end of the poem the soul has passed through the Inferno of the Waste Land and has explored mystical experiences
of which it knew nothing. In the beginning it was enveloped
in the darkness of "the brown fog";[171] in the end, the "flash of
lightning"[172] has pierced these thick layers of a collapsing
materialism which is the reverse of Miss Gardner's interpretation
that "the close is darker than the beginning."[173] The last part of
the poem speaks of "the faint moonlight"[174] of a waning civilization, "the violet light"[175] of a restlessly wandering soul
seeking salvation, and the sudden "lightning"[176] that has led it
finally to the refining fire in Dante's *Purgatorio* where Arnaut
Daniel pleads:

> "*Ara vos prec,* per aquella valor
>   que vos guida al som de l'escalina,
>   sovegna vos a temps de ma dolor."
> *Poi s'ascose nel foco che gli affina.*

["Now I pray you, by that Goodness which guideth you to the
summit of the stairway, be mindful in due time of my pain."
Then he hid him in the fire which refines them.][177]

Moreover, the sea that proved to be treacherous when Isolde's
ship was not in sight

> Oed' und leer das Meer

[The sea is waste and void][178]

and Tristan bewailed his misfortune, became calm at the end of the poem. Hence, "The boat responded/Gaily, to the hand expert with sail and oar."[179] After the sacrificial "passage" of the soul, its steerage should be left to the expert hand of a sublime power to direct its sails to the harbor of Peace ("Shantih"). Even "the wind's home"[180] after the turmoil and cyclonic devastation of the modern Waste Land. The parching drought of "the dry stone"[181] and the desperate sound of wind become the "damp gust/Bringing rain."[182] Though rain did not actually fall at the end of the poem, the situation is not one of a "hopeless sojourn"[183] as Dr. Leavis puts it. The "damp gust" is not to be completely bereft of hope for it is a symptom of the coming of rain.

In this sense, the mystical state expressed in the poem is synonymous with Dante's *Inferno* in its portrayal of the aridity of the "dry sterile thunder without rain"[184] and the restlessness of those who "can neither stand nor lie nor sit."[185] This means that the poem is not merely a cry for the past; it gives us above all "a panoramic view of spiritual exhaustion,"[186] of the falsity and artificiality of the "hooded hordes"[187] who are "swarming/Over endless plains"[188] and "stumbling in cracked earth."[189]

Obviously the poet is concerned here with the external elements that disturb the soul and check it against any progression toward a state of mystical beatitude whether Buddhist or Augustinian. Thus, the predominant image is one of orderliness as depicted in the following question: "Shall I at least set my lands in order?"[190] From the mystical point of view, it is essential to set one's "lands" in order (that is, achieve internal poise) before he aspires to reach any level of spirituality. But the "lands"[191] are blighted with curses and their Fisher King[192] is suffering from impotence and "the loss of virility in the one [that is, in him] brings about a suspension of the reproductive processes of Nature on the other."[193] Naturally the parching drought of this unproductive land "needs refreshment and a new life. Its sterility is, of course, not physical but spiritual, and its sense of impotence is a dire malady of the soul."[194] These versatile themes are driven home through certain images of violation: "The change of Philomel,[195] by the barbarous king/So rudely forced";[196] of decay and chaos:

In this decayed hole among the mountains
In the faint moonlight, the grass is singing
Over the tumbled graves;[197]

and of destruction: "London Bridge is falling down falling down falling down."[198] Even then, this "heap of broken images"[199] will not set the lands in order; a "dead tree"[200] will only grow "out of this stony rubbish"[201] and a "red rock"[202] will cast a fleeting shadow.

Liberation from the aridity of the "dead mountain,"[203] the delusions of the "empty cisterns,"[204] the dried-up resources of the "exhausted wells"[205] and the enslavement of "each in his prison"[206] of egotism—which are all aspects of the same "panorama of futility"—sounds plausible to the inhabitants of the Waste Land. For Eliot, as M. Häusermann has rightly remarked,

tous les hommes jouent le même jeu monotone, brûlent des mêmes désirs stériles, et ainsi des situations identiques vont en se répétant.[207]

Nevertheless, it is only

by self-restraint through the triple law of the thunder [that we] must prepare for "a deeper communion," attainable not through fleshy love or through the ruined Chapel but through abnegation of [the] will.[208]

This renunciation of the "will" entails the acceptance of suffering which might lead to the deliverance of the modern world from the desolation of its waste land. That the poet has not explicitly pointed this way led a well-known critic like M. Cattaui to state that

Eliot ne nous montre pas la résurrection qu'apporte le Libérateur, rajeunissant la Terre Dévastée, et se substituant au chef déchu, dont la peine est commuée.[209]

It is, in fact, the hope for release that sets the soul in motion across the "burning" flames of the Inferno where sacrifice is the only way toward resurrection and spiritual revival.

This fundamental theme of suffering and release has led Professor Bullough—in agreement with the whole host of commentators[210]—to consider the poet's attitude in The Waste Land "more negative than positive, analytic rather than synthetic."[211] Though this view is sound, the whole poem is not completely bereft of positive and synthetic elements. The Upanishadic aphorism: Datta, Dayadhvam, Damyata[212] (give, sympathize and control), conveys an important message to society today, and it should function on a socially positivistic level, otherwise it would remain a mere abstraction. "What have we given?"[213] the poet asks; and his question is applicable to all in the matter of charity. "Sympathy" with others is incomplete; it is purely negative unless it is coupled with benevolent deeds to remove people's distress in time of anguish. It needs the ability "to control" desires. Sacrificing selfish ambitions is thus essential for the relief and betterment of the larger community.

On the side of the analytic attitude, Signor Gamberini states that

> Il poeta aveva sentito la necessità di esprimere un mondo assai complesso, ne aveva visti i lati che non sono contingenti, ma eterni.[214]

> [the poet has strongly felt the need of investigating a complex world, considering things not as they are incidental, but in view of eternity].

Eliot is here justified in dealing with various levels of human experience ranging from the mundane to the highly mystical. His analysis of this "complex world" is not limited to a single method and his treatment of the subject is extended to embrace not only contemporary civilization but human modes of thought since the dawn of history.[215] The result is not one of mere accumulation but as Professor Greene has happily put it:

> l'effet général qui se dégage de cette puissante composition, c'est le sentiment de l'unité essentielle d'une expérience humaine très variée et très complexe.[216]

It is a synthetic unity[217] that allows room for the variety and complexity of human experience.

The centripetal force behind this synthesis is a theme of "belief," whether mystical or non-mystical, that focuses all these levels of experience. This theme in relation to *The Waste Land* is tackled by Mr. Spender and Professor Richards. The former states that "the whole structure of Eliot's poem is based on certain primitive rituals and myths"[218] rather than on "accepted belief."[219] Though it is not an accepted belief in the modern religious sense of the term, these rituals used to dominate the spiritual life of the ancient civilizations which Mr. Spender acknowledges in his treatment of the subject. Obviously this does not mean that *The Waste Land* effects "a complete severance between his [Eliot's] poetry and 'all' beliefs,"[220] as Professor

Richards puts it. As early as 1927 Eliot firmly states: "I cannot for the life of me see the 'complete separation' from all belief"[221] and confesses in his essay on "Dante" (1929) which is reprinted in his *Selected Essays* (1917-32) that "Mr. Richards' statement ... is to me incomprehensible."[222] But in *The Use of Poetry and the Use of Criticism* (1933), he analyzes the statement saying that it "might mean that it was the first poetry to do what all poetry in the past would have been the better for doing"[223] and humbly dismisses this suggestion. He adds that it

> might also mean that the present situation is radically different from any in which poetry has been produced in the past: namely, that now there is nothing in which to believe, that Belief itself is dead; and that therefore my poem is the first to respond properly to the modern situation and not call upon Make-Believe.[224]

Saying that "Belief itself is dead" is another way of referring to the complete absence of all values. "Belief" has now degenerated, but the idea of its annihilation will result either in utter negation or in a chaotic state that is impossible to redeem. A society without "belief," whether secular or mystical, material or spiritual, is not worth its salt. The statement, in this sense, separates poetic sensibility from all "belief."

Obviously the poem is based on an intimate relationship to "belief"[225] both ancient and modern, anthropological and purely religious, Buddhist and Christian. It is dominated not only by a belief in the sacrificial efficacy of pre-Christian ritualism, but also by the Augustinian faith in the possibility of redemption through the purgatorial "snares" of suffering.

Running through the whole of the five Sections that compose *The Waste Land* is the comprehensive belief in the necessity of deliverance from the bewildering chaos of the contemporary civilization. Even shortly after the first publication of the poem on December 15, 1922, Mr. Lucas shrewdly remarks that

> the gist of the poem is apparently a wild revolt from the abomination of desolation which is human life, combined with a belief in salvation by the usual catchwords of renunciation—this salvation being also the esoteric significance of the savage fertility-rituals found in *the Golden Bough*, a watering, as it were, of the desert of suffering soul.[226]

This belief in its operation on the multiple levels of the poem has gained richness and profundity. On the emotional level, the sterility of love is viewed in terms of a chess-game. The restoration of love to its former state of glamor and wholesomeness means the regeneration of an intrinsic plane of human life. On the mystical level, it takes the form of liberating the self from the momentary ambitions of life by regaining the original meaning of existence that is deeply rooted in ancient rituals; and, on the social level, it is relieving humanity from its haunting miseries in the way predicted by the Upanishadic wisdom. On the purely literary level, Mr. Smidt speaks of "an awareness of connectedness of wholeness co-existing with the prevalent awareness of dissolution,"[227] and points to the fact that "Eliot's objects and fragments are so often broken"[228] as to direct our attention to the presence of "an ideal, complete existence in which they are whole."[229] In this sense, the poet believes that his fragmentary reminiscences will build a harmonious integration out of the present crisis. It is, in other words, the ability of form to reshape content, or more specifically, the literary form to reorganize the content of our civilization which is not easily realizable.

All these experiences express the need for a coherent "belief" which has become mostly pressing in a society that is "incapable of self-sacrificing devotion and no longer held together by the bonds of love and faith."[230] This does not mean the negation of "belief" but merely its decline[231] owing to the obsession of mankind with other transitory values. Even the Hollow Men of the contemporary "cactus land,"[232] though their state speaks of vacuity in either matter of reality or tradition, are also the guys that are "stuffed" with "meaningless" ideologies.

Sharing these beliefs of the poet, however, is not essential for the appreciation of his poetry for that wouldn't give us "a groat's worth more of understanding."[233] A non-Catholic, for instance, is capable of enjoying the *Divina Commedia* and apprehending the development of its themes. At the same time, Eliot has not disregarded the fact that

> it may be in practice easier for a Catholic to grasp the meaning, in many places, than for the ordinary agnostic; but that is not because the Catholic believes, but because he has been instructed.[234]

Instruction is then essential for apprehension, which does not mean "merely knowledge of books or words, any more than . . . belief."[235] This intellectual belief is subservient in the case of the

Commedia to the poetic belief of Dante the poet, and his religious belief as a man. Thus the human in Dante does not necessarily hold the same beliefs and convictions as the poet in him. But both branches, in Eliot's view, are nurtured by the intellectual belief which is their life-vein. The emotional belief, moreover, plays a fundamental role in the crystallization of both types of belief with a traditional bias in the case of a religious belief toward "faith" which is its backbone. With poetic belief the intellectual and emotional elements are blended together, and, in the case of good or genuine poetry particularly in metaphysical poetry, they can hardly exist in separateness. The degree of effectiveness rests on the poet's ability to weld these elements happily together without betraying any sense of violence or inconsistency. This view conforms so well to one's notion of *The Waste Land;* even though the intellectual side may be dominant, it is deftly interwoven with the various other elements that constitute the intricate network of the whole poem.

Eliot, however, is too adverse to the projection of personal beliefs in poetry and here he is consistent with his critical theory of objectivity in art. The "beliefs" in *The Waste Land* are neither personal nor do they belong to a certain specific limitation of existence. They are concerned with humanity at large, with aspects of life and death, and with Eastern and Western modes of thought. Even to this extent, one feels, at times, that the voice of Eliot is still there[236] and is heard in such personal pronouncements as "I read, much of the night, and go south in the winter"[237] and "These fragments I have shored against my ruins"[238] and formerly in "After such knowledge, what forgiveness?"[239]

At any rate, the major concept of "experience" in *The Waste Land* is the transition from doubt to "belief" (conviction) which is followed by a sacrificial process that brings the quester nearer to the realities behind the wisdom of initiation and surrender. Here the poet is justified in weaving "these fragments" of mystical knowledge, that pervaded the eras of the past, in the very texture of his poetry. The result—as Mr. Spender remarks—is that the poet "has made an artistic whole"[240] out of them.

Concerning this problem of allusions, whether literary, mystical or a mixture of both, Mr. Maxwell stresses the view of "Eliot's acceptance of traditional literature as his poetic world,"[241] and builds up the Eliotesque theory of symbolism on a blend of references to several traditions, the purpose of which is to reaffirm and illuminate what has gone before, by its relation of the poem's setting to these traditions.[242]

In fact, this process of shifting and blending is more than a reaffirmation of previously experienced activities; even more than what Professor Bullough terms "the density of colour resulting from the recognition of the original source and its relation to the new context";[243] it is what Professor Brooks takes to be a "transference of items from an 'innocent' context into a context in which they become charged and transformed in meaning."[244] This transformation of meaning accounts for the ambiguities and paradoxical subtleties of the poem. It underlies what Sir Maurice Bowra happily considers "a contrast between the ideal and the actual [by fusing] into a single phrase a complex emotion,"[245] or what Miss Drew calls "the fusion of disparate materials into a re-creation."[246] The outcome is not merely one of accumulative condensation but of ironically multiple reference. The elaborately developed "fragments" of European and Asiatic thought, moreover, conform to Eliot's theory of the continuity and simultaneity of tradition.[247] Mr. Melchiori calls them "the outcrops of the deep strata of past culture"[248] which the poet has shored against the ruins of a collapsing civilization. Obviously they have gained profundity and fresh significance through the universality of their mystical symbolism in much the same way as old stones acquire new radiance by relating them to an exuberant setting.

In "The Burial of the Dead," for instance, the burial of effigy is charged with universality through its symbolic reference to the mysticism of death; the "sprouting" of vegetation is the resurrection of the spirit from the suffocating atmosphere of modern industrialization; and, the "hyacinth garden,"[249] that symbolizes fertility, is for Eliot a mystical moment of "looking into the heart of light."[250]

On the whole, *The Waste Land* portrays the state of "a society without values, an exhausted civilization, gesturing impotently in accordance with the barren formulas of a worn-out humanism."[251] Its alienation from the true meaning of life is due to a serious ethical malady. Modern people are content to remain inept in all matters of righteousness, and here Eliot is speaking to them: "not in terms of their victimization by society or by ontological disability, but in terms of their having perpetuated their own condition."[252] The root of our stagnation lies in procrastination. It is the attitude of indifference that has deprived the modern man from all the wisdom of the past and has created a sense of estrangement between him and his Creator, at which Madame Sosostris hinted when she said, "I do not find/The Hanged Man."[253] He was a stranger and now He has become an illusion[254] in the waste land of contemporary urbanism. The mystical significance of the crucifixion is to the inhabitants of the "unreal city"[255] only a "Murmur of maternal lamentation—"[256] of the Virgin Mary over the crucified God. The birth of a Christian era that marks an important stage in the spiritual revival of humanity, is completely lost among "the loitering heirs of city directors."[257]

IV

Consequently Eliot's main thesis in *The Waste Land* is that people are afraid to face the reality of death and undergo any sort of suffering either by way of the life-giving water or the infernal flames. They are so much attached to their selfish ambitions that parting with them would mean their utter collapse. There is no possibility of rebirth as our minds are preoccupied with "the profit and the loss." We are, in this sense, more and more driven away from the true significance of existence and the meaning of mystical symbolism will remain a closed book for us—as it used to be for the quester of *The Waste Land* when he was faced with the benediction of the Upanishads —so long as we remain indifferent either through sheer ignorance or through abstention from the tragedy of life. In our narrow-mindedness we evade the real problems that should have the foremost concern and, in most cases, prefer to stick to the "sweet" reverie of our own private illusion.

CHAPTER FIVE

The Liturgical Mysticism in "Ash Wednesday"

With the poet's apparent dissatisfaction at the conclusion reached in *The Waste Land,* that of a composite wholeness of experience against which he hopes to shore his ruins, he completely relies in *Ash Wednesday* on religious mysticism. Owing to his preoccupation with the purgatorial efficacy of the soul, he mainly develops a theme of "inwardness" and draws heavily upon Christian liturgy,[2] the mysticism of the Dark Night expounded by St. John of the Cross, and the spiral ascent in Dante's Mount of Purgation. The poem thus abounds with images of strife, sensual torment, and spiritual affliction.

I

It opens with a musing on the mysticism of patient endurance:

Because I do not hope to turn again
Because I do not hope
Because I do not hope to turn[3]

In the austerity of his spiritual exile,[4] the protagonist has completely lost "The infirm glory of the positive hour."[5] He thus "rejoice[s] that things are as they are"[6] and gives himself up to the purgatory of the Dark Night.[7] His inability "to turn again" represents a state of despair and loss that precedes the entrance of the soul into the "divine darkness."[8] By way of consolation, he questions himself "Why should I mourn/The vanished power of the usual reign?"[9] Affliction for the "transitory power"[10] of earthly pomp and "the usual reign" of egocentricity is reminiscent of his past agony.

Still he is aware of his desperate state and of his human limitations so long as

time is always time
And place is always and only place
And what is actual is actual only for one time
And only for one place.[11]

87

The oneness of time and place has gained recognition for the moment after his hopelessness in turning again to the source of mystical revelation.

In this state of utter deprivation, he rejoices that he has renounced "the blessèd face"[12] owing to his inability to loosen the fetters of attachment, and goes in a touching regression to his former condition of bitter cynicism. The irony of his rejoicing is that of "having to construct something/Upon which to rejoice."[13] For St. John of the Cross this illusory construction of "something" will lead the soul astray. His way to the summit of Mount Carmel is that of the *Via Negativa* and the renunciation of all carnality and voluptuousness in the Dark Night of the Soul, which link it with the neo-Platonic tradition in Christian mysticism. Hence the protagonist's prayer "Teach us to care and not to care"[14] is relevant to the theme of renunciation, that is, caring for mystical detachment and not caring for the "desires" of this world. For the realization of the objective of the prayer, he appeals to an earthly Lady[15] who "honours the Virgin in meditation"[16] to plead for intercession and snatch him from "the hollow round"[17] of death. Because of this Lady's goodness "And because of her loveliness,"[18] even the dry bones[19] of death will shine with brightness in purgation.

In the Purgatorio of suffering the senses are cleansed through a process of deep concentration that is coupled with moments of utter oblivion:

> As I am forgotten
> And would be forgotten, so I would forget
> Thus devoted, concentrated in purpose.[20]

This state of forgetfulness is necessary in the *Via Contemplativa* and is stressed in *The Cloud of Unknowing* as an issue of intense concentratedness.[21] It is associated with the state of unknowability which is essential for the purification of the soul.

After reaching this stage on the Way to Perfection, the scattered bones celebrate it with a song to the

> Rose of memory
> Rose of forgetfulness
> Exhausted and life-giving.[22]

The rose of the Lady is commemorated as a token of celestial love,[23] but the "Rose of forgetfulness" is that of earthly love which is easily and quickly forgotten. The latter is attained by way of exhaustion; its "inscape" in the Hopkinsian sense, is exhausted in the process, whereas the former is the "life-giving" symbol that revivifies the drooping love of people. It is "The single Rose"[24] in "the Garden"[25] "Where all loves end";[26] the termination "Of love unsatisfied"[27] and the "End of the endless"[28] where torment ceases and Grace is dedicated to the Mother.

With this commemoration of love, the protagonist proceeds toward Purgatory which is reminiscent of Dante's entrance with Virgil to the purificatory Mount through "a gate, and three steps beneath to go to it,/ of divers colours."[29] It recalls also the hierarchy of the Pseudo-Dionysius[30] which gave St. John of the Cross the idea of the mystical ladder.[31] The concept of the "ladder" which is re-echoed in *Ash Wednesday* and the symbolism that it invokes are masterfully expounded in the following unpublished MS:

> In as much as the spare and hard life is a Ladder St[e]ppe ωeri acceptable in the Light of God, as it may appeare by [the] gracious reward/it is therefore ωeri meet . . . to learne to live. . . . [We] thereby may climbe more highle up the Ladder to heaven/Therefore by the holy and unfallible holines of the Scriptures we ought to saye our prayers . . . not many climbe now the hyt in the Light of God.[32]

The purgatorial development of the soul is portrayed here as a way of living or learning how to lead a spiritual life. It is conceived in terms of steps which are normally ten in number; each represents a stage in this mystical progression that culminates in the "gracious reward" of the divine Light.

> Having reached only a preliminary step, our protagonist turned and saw below
> The same shape twisted on the banister
> Under the vapour in the fetid air.[33]

Professor Matthiessen after stating that "the sinister horror of what he saw below him at the first turning is heightened by the very ambiguousness of the expression, 'the same shape',"[34] puts forward two suggestive questions:

> Does it mean a spectre that he has been fleeing from and has felt to be pursuing him up the stair? Or, more terrifying still,

does it mean his own very likeness, thus stressing the obsession with self, the inability of the individual to escape from the bonds of his own identity?[35]

Keeping the purgatorial hill of Dante in mind, to which the poem bears a striking resemblance, I am more inclined to take "the same shape" not only of another similar person but of all the fellowmen who are still struggling with the devil at the bottom of the staircase. The point is driven home in the next sestet with the protagonist's declaration: "At the second turning of the second stair/I left them twisting, burning below,"[36] that removes the doubt of singularity, that is, either the spectre or the individual identity. He, moreover, came to a place where "no more faces"[37] were visible.

On reaching a further step, however, he perceived that "the stair was dark"[38] and plunged deeply into this mystical darkness that effaces all traces of sinfulness.[39] He is guided here by the faint gleam of hope that comes from the "slotted window"[40] though it is "bellied"[41] with the sins of the past "like the fig's fruit."[42] This image of the window brings to his mind "the hawthorn blossom"[43] that symbolically reminds him of "the maytime"[44] of his past sensual life. It is reminiscent too of the "antique flute"[45] that is played on a "pasture scene"[46] and the "Blown hair"[47] of his Prufrockian days when he was deeply affected by the romantic scene of "the mermaids singing, each to each,"[48] and "Combing the white hair of the waves blown back."[49] These are all the representations of worldly "distraction" that mitigate the soul from its objective. The protagonist, then, realized that it is necessary for him to have spiritual "strength beyond hope and despair"[50] and confesses his unworthiness to proceed on the mystical way of ascension:

Lord, I am not worthy
Lord, I am not worthy
    but speak the word only.[51]

Here he is re-echoing the words of the priest in a Catholic Mass[52] just before holding communion.

After confessing his unworthiness, the protagonist appeals to the Lady who walks "between the violet and the violet"[53] that associate her with the liturgical color of the Church. She is dressed "in white and blue, in Mary's colour."[54] She is thus linked also with the Virgin in the whiteness of her purity and the

blueness of her heavenly attire. Paradoxically enough, she went
on "Talking of trivial things/In ignorance and in knowledge of
eternal dolour."[55] These "trivial things" are the unlicensed sen-
sualities before the Purgatorio and the "eternal dolour" is that
of lamentation which ensues. Inevitably the Lady's talk reminds
him of "the years that walk between, bearing/Away the fiddles
and the flutes."[56] The passage of the years has obliterated the
early sensuousness of "the fiddles and the flutes" before ap-
proaching the mystical "ladder" of the soul. In his ascension,
the Lady has brought him to "the new years"[57] of spiritual
revival which he attained "Through a bright cloud of tears."[58]
The dark cloud is here brightened through the mystical illumination of the "veiled sister" to whom he appealed to "re-
deem/The time"[59] through spiritual restoration by which "the
years" acquire new significance. "The unread vision,"[60] in this
way, will be read with fresh meaning and thorough understanding.

The vision then shifts to

The silent sister veiled in white and blue
Between the yews, behind the garden god.[61]

She is walking "between the yews" of symbolic death and immortality but "behind the garden god" of sacrificial rebirth. She
"spoke no word";[62] only

the fountain sprang up and the bird sang down
Redeem the time, redeem the dream
The token of the word unheard, unspoken.[63]

With the eternal fountain of spirituality and the angelic songs of
the bird, time and the dream might be redeemed; till then "the
word" will remain "unheard." The religious awareness and supplication of the protagonist to divine power for the redemption
of the world are re-echoed in his petition to the Virgin that takes
the liturgical form of the *Salve Regina*:

Eia, ergo, advocata nostra, illos tuos misericordes oculos ad
nos converte; et Iesum, benedictum fructum ventris tui, nobis
post hoc exilium ostende.

[Turn then, O Thou our Advocate, thy dear eyes of mercy
towards us, *and after this our exile,* show unto us the blessed
fruit of thy womb, Jesus].[64]

The prayer is a passionate appeal to mercy and its advocation to those who are exiled in the wilderness of the world and who are "weeping and wailing in this valley of tears."[65]

In this earthly desolation, the Word of God, the Logos, is still "unspoken, unheard";[66] hence, "the Word within/The world and for the world,"[67] passes unnoticed by the unbelievers in the mysticism of the Incarnation. With the Nativity "the light shone in darkness,"[68] and "Against the World the unstilled world still whirled/About the centre of the silent Word."[69] The "unstilled world" is still fighting against "the silent Word" that symbolically occupies the center of the Wheel. The whirling world of "sense" and "matter" is unable to grasp the mystery of "the still point." This is why the protagonist echoes the words of the Saviour, "O my people, what have I done unto thee."[70] He then appeals to "the veiled sister"[71] to pray for those who in their naiveté are deceived by the bustle of this world, and for "Those who are torn on the horn between season and season,/time and time,"[72] and waver between denial and faint recognition of the spiritual life. They are torn "on the horn" of agony and restlessness. In the words of Mr. Unger, "they are attracted by two opposing directions, and so are torn between the seasons, times, hours, words and powers of the worldly and the divine."[73] In their hypocrisy, they "affirm before the world and deny between the rocks,"[74] whereas a limited minority have experienced "The desert in the garden the garden in the desert."[75] "The desert in the garden" signifies the mortification of carnality as a necessary purgatorial stage that brings the soul to the mystical revivification of "the garden in the desert."

Still the protagonist is replenished with the desires of the world, "Wavering between the profit and the loss"[76] and with his meditations upon material transactions, "In this brief transit where the dreams cross/The dreamcrossed twilight between birth and dying."[77] In this brief transition to the spiritual world which is only the "twilight" of a lifetime, the dreams of the past cross his mind and engender in him the struggle between body and soul. The "slotted window"[78] of the Third Part of the poem is wide open here as the conflict is broadened to cover the whole of humanity. The "lost heart stiffens and rejoices"[79] "And the weak spirit quickens to rebel"[80] against the tyrannical domination of the flesh. He is thus wrestling with

> the time of tension between dying and birth
> The place of solitude where three dreams cross
> Between blue rocks.[81]

After realizing that life is but "empty forms"[82] or meaningless abstractions that "the blind eye creates,"[83] he resumes his struggle against the "blue rocks" that symbolize the silencing of bodily cravings in "solitude." The "three dreams" of birth, dying, and rebirth that cross his mind assure him that he is still in the Purgatorio of suffering where "The voices shaken from the yew-tree drift away."[84] Here he has learned that people after death had to undergo a necessary process of purification. And coming back to reconsider his fate, he can now hopefully look forward to "the other yew"[85] to be shaken for his deliverance and the attainment of mystical rebirth. His last prayer recapitulates the themes of the poem which are focused here in his petition "not to be separated"[86] from the "spirit of the river, spirit of the sea,"[87] and the spirit of the "garden." His appeal to the Holy Mother is well summarized in the following unpublished MS:

> Blessid Mary mother of god and flouer of virgins vochesafe
> to praye contynually for vs/and as thou mayste and canst So
> obteyne for vs/and chefely faoure vs *at the houer of ouer
> deathe*.[88]

The petition is coupled with the reiteration of "Teach us to care and not to care/Teach us to sit still."[89] The protagonist has come to the full realization of "Our peace in His will"[90] that recalls the words of the saintly Piccarda Donati answering Dante's question: "do ye desire a more lofty place?"

> Brother, the quality of love stilleth our will, and maketh us long
> only for what we have, and giveth us no other thirst.
> Did we desire to be more aloft, our longings were discordant
> from his will and here assorteth us.... *his will is our peace;*
> it is that sea to which all moves that it createth and that
> nature maketh.[91]

With this sense of satisfaction that came after the disturbing conflict between corporeality and spirituality, the protagonist has understood that "peace" is attained by way of detachment and submission to divine Will. Both are essential for the mystical contact with the Divine expressed in the ritual words: "Suffer me not to be separated"[92] which appear in the *Anima Christi:* "Ne permittas me separari a te," [Do not permit me to be separated from thee],[93] and "Let my cry come unto Thee,"[94] which is taken from the *Devotions of the Forty Hours:*

Domine, exaudi orationem meam
Et clamor meus ad te veniat.

[O Lord, hear my prayer,
And let my cry come unto Thee].[95]

It is, after all, a cry of anguish and self-torture that recalls the bitter Passion of Christ on the Cross.

II

The poem in general is underestimated by the majority of critics because of its religious content. Mr. Hicks, for instance, states that

the poetry Eliot has written since his conversion suggests that he has gained little—and may have lost much. In his critical pronouncements he can dogmatically affirm his new faith, but the poems in "Ash Wednesday" are as weak and elegiac as any he wrote in his unregenerate state.[96]

In the view of this critic as well as others,[97] *Ash Wednesday* points the way to the poet's decline only because its theme is mainly based on liturgy and the Catholic Mass. This trend is briefly summarized by Mr. Allen Tate in what appears to be a logical sequence:

the reasoning that is being brought to bear upon Mr. Eliot's recent verse is as follows: Anglo-Catholicism would not at all satisfy me; therefore, his poetry declines under its influence;[98]

and he adds

to accept the poetry seems to amount to accepting an invitation to join the Anglican Church. For the assumption is that the poetry and the religious position are identical.[99]

He then points out the syllogistic fallacy of the argument by stressing the fact that "there is an aesthetic Catholicism, and there is a communist-economic rejection of art because it is involved with the tabooed mode of salvation."[100] Though *Ash*

Wednesday deals in many of its parts with religious dogmas, an "aesthetic" assessment of the whole poem seems to be a wise approach. The poem abounds also with doctrines that are not wanting in matter of ethical value. A "belief" in these Anglo-Catholic doctrines is not essential for the appreciation of the poem. The poet himself has expressed his view in what seems to me a fair conclusion:

> Actually, one probably has more pleasure in the poetry when one shares the beliefs of the poet. On the other hand, there is a distinct pleasure in enjoying poetry as poetry when one does "not" share the beliefs, analogous to the pleasure of "mastering" other men's philosophical systems.[101]

Obviously this viewpoint refutes any identity between the poem and the "religious position" it evokes.

Mr. Tate, at any rate, has put his finger on the crux of the matter when he states that "these six poems are a brief moment of religious experience in an age that believes religion to be a kind of defeatism and puts all its hope for man in finding the right secular order."[102] Here lies the main issue which has led to the previous critical pronouncements; here originates too the censure voiced against Eliot. In an age given up to secularism, it is not surprising to take religion as "a kind of defeatism" and consider a "mode of salvation" a taboo. Literary criticism, too, in this sense, will be narrowly limited to the hard and fast rules of material utility that handicap any aesthetic appreciation in works of art. This attitude that extols the extrinsic rather than the inherent value of art is the outcome of the impact of Pragmatism and Marxism on the various branches of knowledge.

Professor Bullough in what appears to be a more wholesome approach asserts that "the superiority of *Ash Wednesday* over *The Waste Land* is due to the intimacy of the whole conception, and above all to the universality of its intellectual background."[103] He wisely detects this "intimacy" in the restraint of allusions and the simplicity of imagery due to the remarkable influence of Dante in this period. The universality of the poem is derived "from its participation in . . . a coherent religious tradition"[104] based on Biblical and liturgical dogmas.

In the light of these reflections, it is necessary as well to call to mind that the previous phase in Eliot's poetic development culminated in the "fragments" of literary and philosophical reminiscences with which he intends to set his "lands in order"[105] and to unify an already devastated sensibility. Naturally he had to revert to religious mysticism after the devastations of the Waste Land. There is undoubtedly, moreover, the underlying implication that he looks forward to achieve a satisfactory solution of the dilemmas that have so much disturbed his Hollow Men.

But the poet has gone to the other extreme and one feels that the pendulum which began with the anarchy of *The Waste Land* swung too far in *Ash Wednesday* to the extent that it verges at times on complete isolation from the religious concern of society. The poet might be justified in seeking a Purgatorio to the evils of *The Waste Land* and one is convinced that at the end of *Ash Wednesday* the soul is tempered with the sublimities of Christian mysticism, but the shift is almost baffling. It would have been more consistent to bridge the gulf not through a further projection of scenes already familiar but through the "erection" of a poem that is transitional in the true sense insofar as it serves in introducing us to the spiritual climate of *Ash Wednesday* instead of being launched abruptly to it to find ourselves in a completely different milieu.

Though the "Journey of the Magi" (1927), "A Song for Simeon" (1928) and "Animula" (1929) were written in this transitional period, the experience they illustrate is limited more or less to the Word which is "unable to speak a word"[106] in "Gerontion" and apparently these poems add very little to the themes worked out in the early period. They simply compose certain moments of retrospection that allow the poet to move backward and forward in his meditations over past experience. This method has given vent to the themes of oscillation which are the manifested features of this period. In the "Journey of the Magi" the element of hesitation becomes more evident at the end of the pilgrimage with the question of the protagonist who is here the narrator of the incidents they faced on their way: "were we led all that way for/Birth or Death?"[107] Is it for the Nativity or Death that he hazarded his long journey with his compeers (that is, the Magi)[108] among "the cities hostile and the towns unfriendly/And the villages dirty and charging high prices?"[109] He thought that "this Birth was/Hard and bitter agony for us, like Death, our death."[110] His association of His Death with theirs denotes his failure to appreciate the sacrificial death of Christ. For him the Nativity is coupled with "hard and bitter agony" partly because it speaks of the sinfulness of humanity and partly because it has left him with a sense of misunderstanding and bewilderment.

In "A Song for Simeon"[111] this theme is evidenced in Simeon's wavering between the past and the future, the past which he has partly renounced by keeping "faith and fast"[112] and the future which he is unable to face heroically. He is not spiritually prepared to undergo any form of mystical suffering, the ascent on "the saints' stair,"[113] the crowning of a righteous life with "the martyrdom"[114] and the mystical perception of "the ultimate vision."[115] He simply yearns to get rid of a past he has not yet fully conquered and plunge into a purgatorial death so as to acquire salvation. He could only meditate on his "own death and the deaths of those after [him]"[116] without facing any commitment on either side.

In "Animula"[117] we are faced with a type of mind that

Confounds the actual and the fanciful,[118]

and thus lays a "heavy burden"[119] on "the growing soul."[120] It is troubled by "a flat world of changing lights and noise"[121] that handicaps it from mystical progression. "Retreating to the corner"[122] of the room, Animula naively takes pleasure "In the fragrant brilliance of the Christmas tree."[123] The meditative mind goes to the Nativity but it is unable to form any pattern behind the "fragrant brilliance" of the miraculous birth.

Animula sometimes takes to learning not in the consistent way of a scholar but in the fragmentary and rather confused approach of a Tiresias who lacks the concentratedness of a psychically integrated personality. This life of irritations and diversions reacts disastrously on "the simple soul" which becomes

> misshapen, lame
> Unable to fare forward or retreat,
> Fearing the warm reality.[124]

It is a state of quasi-paralysis which is the result of Animula's fear of "the warm reality." It is submerged in that state which is akin to a "spectre in its own gloom."[125] Henceforward, it awaits "the silence after the viaticum"[126] so as to end its life in utter seclusion.

Even in "Marina" (1930) which is written after *Ash Wednesday*, the same theme is still relevant in the oscillations of the protagonist who is Pericles, Marina's father, between the two psychic states of consciousness and somnambulism.[127] They give vent to the state of recognition between the lost Marina and her father who has not fully recovered from his subconscious fit. The daughter was lost at sea, but through the "grey rocks"[128] of patience and "the glory of the hummingbird"[129] announcing the departure of appearance and the coming of revelation, she underwent the purgatorial suffering that is essential for rebirth. This scene of recognition marks an ecstatic vision that brings to mind the climax of the whole dramatic effect of Shakespeare's *Pericles*.[130]

The arrival of Marina has thus driven away the spectre of doubt, but the father is still bewildered between the dream and the reality. The "shining" face of his daughter is to him "less clear and clearer"[131] and her illuminative vision is "more distant than stars and nearer than the eye."[132] Pericles is unable to perceive fully the state of grace and mystical bliss which his daughter enjoys because he has not undergone her purificatory pains. To him this state of visionary elation is "more distant than stars"; yet it is "nearer that the eye" through the presence of his daughter.

Obviously the theme of conflict runs through all these interior monologues. Strife is a marked characteristic of the self that is unable to verify any mode of conviction. In the "Journey of the Magi," for instance, the narrator is suffering from inner and outer schism between the past reverie of "voices singing"[133] in his ears "saying/That this was all folly"[134] and the present that will bring him deliverance. He himself "should be glad of another death"[135] that might bring with it the needed conviction in mystical rebirth. In "Animula" too

> The pain of living and the drug of dreams
> Curl up the small soul in the window seat,[136]

and take full hold of it till it is completely crippled. With the increase of mental tension, the meek soul finds itself enveloped in a "shadow of its own shadows"[137] which is obviously the creation of its illusion.

In *Ash Wednesday* strife is evident from the outset between the attractions of the world and the insistent call to proceed on the way to perfection.[138] It is the antagonism between "the infirm glory"[139] of worldly pomp and the humbleness of "the one veritable"[140] power of blessedness, between the unsatiated desire of "this man's gift and that man's scope"[141] and the earnest yearning of the soul to quench its thirst from "the fountains"[142] of spirituality and "the springs"[143] of rebirth. This state of restlessness is thus the result of the warring claims of the flesh and the spirit, the earthly trivialities and "the unread vision."[144] It covers an austere period termed by St. John of the Cross as one of "spiritual aridity"[145] during which the soul is exposed to different types of wayward attractions that encumber it against its mystical progression. Eliot uses the image of the "desert" to symbolize this dryness and develops it through its association with the "garden," symbol of spiritual revival. He then locates "the desert in the garden"[146] which is an act of invasion denoting that parching drought is invading the growing trees or rather hampering the budding soul from full growth. It needs the abolition of sensuality which has created this state of stagnation, and the perpetual struggle across a Purgatorio rather than an Inferno as far as *Ash Wednesday* is concerned, so as to come to the realization of "the garden in the desert"[147] which is the state of mystical bliss enjoyed by those who have known the way to purgation even among the "dry" trammels of this world.

This period too, though basically one of struggle, may be accompanied at times with lapses of energy or even inactivity:

I no longer strive to strive towards such things
(Why should the agèd eagle stretch its wings?)[148]

. . . .

Because these wings are no longer wings to fly
But merely vans to beat the air.[149]

Mr. Wilson remarks that he is made "a little tired at hearing Eliot, only in his early forties, present himself as an 'agèd eagle' who asks why he should make the effort to stretch his wings."[150] But, in a more scrupulous and objective approach to the poem, Mr. Martin reminds us of

the tradition that in its old age, the eagle flew up into the circle of fire, burnt off its feathers, and fell blinded into a fountain of water, from which it issued with its youth renewed. New life issues from death; regeneration from the grave; restoration from penitence.[151]

In *The Dark Night of the Soul* too we read that

> God makes it [the soul] to die to all that is not naturally God,
> so that, once it is stripped and denuded of its former skin, He
> may begin to clothe it anew. And thus its youth is renewed
> like the eagle's and it is clothed with the new man.[152]

The matter is then not completely bereft of hope but there are
certainly special moments of regression.

Even in "Marina" traces of this turmoil are not lacking and
they are supported by the epigraph to the poem. It is taken
from Seneca's *Hercules Furens*[153] and it reveals the maddening
strife in Hercules' mind. In a state of elation coupled with
frenzy, he slaughtered his children by directing poisoned arrows
at them. Awakening from his fit, he recognizes—in ironic contrast to the recognition scene of Pericles—the ferocity of his
crime and is bewildered by his inhumanity.

The real problem with these figures is their practical inability to conquer the past and live in the present moment. They
are associated with Gerontion in his loss of passion, his isolation
in his rented house, the distractions and confusions irked from
"A dull head among windy spaces,"[154] and with Tiresias in his
wavering between a state of Baudelairian *ennui* and acceptance
of purgatorial suffering. They all fear the present situation
that calls for action and, in this way, they suffer from a
bitter state of maladjustment in which they are all living. It is
no wonder that they have set the reins of hallucinations loose
and have thus tied themselves up with the Hollow Men. Their
flight too at times into an unpredictable future is an extension
of the same theme of escape from facing any form of reality.

In this sense, the transitional poems bear, more or less,
thematic and imagistic affinities with the previous period that
culminated in *The Waste Land*. "Marina" may be linked with
Ash Wednesday not so much because it was written after it[155]
but because they have an inherent similarity in poetic images
that unfold certain mystical implications. The yearnings of the
soul in *Ash Wednesday* to redeem "The empty forms between the
ivory gates"[156] and the lives of those who are moving "in the
time between sleep and waking,"[157] anticipate the wavering
state of Pericles and his nostalgia for mystical redemption. The
expanded "conceit"[158] of a marinal voyage that used to symbolize
for medieval theologians the infernal and purgatorial passage
of the soul, stresses these cravings. The ship's arrival at the har-

bor of rebirth represents Marina's state of restoration at which her
father aspires:

> let me
> Resign my life for this life, my speech for that unspoken,
> The awakened, lips parted, the hope, the new ships.[159]

The awakening condition means resignation of one's life for
the sake of the redeemed "unspoken" vision. Obviously Pericles
is unable to reach this state of transcendence where speech is
inadequate. He simply reiterates:

> What seas what shores what granite islands towards my timbers
> And woodthrush calling through the fog
> My daughter.[160]

Toward the "granite islands" of the envisaged revelation, he
hopes to set sail after gathering his disjointed timbers that were
cast asunder with "ice," "heat," and the waywardness of "the fog."
That his guidance toward this vision will be left to "the woodthrush," gives us a tone not so much of assurance as the possibility of regeneration through painstaking effort. Pericles could
only hope to be awakened as he recoils and identifies himself
with a sailor in an old ship of rotten canvas sailing across the
waters of the "unknowing, half conscious, unknown"[161] and
looks for transformation as he comes to "the new ship."

But this theme of nostalgia and passive hopefulness gains
further development in *Ash Wednesday* through its association with self-renunciation and the ensuing effect of the protagonist's inability to reach a state of resignation. The peace
he was looking for at the end of *The Waste Land* is disturbed here by distractions that agitate the mind and render
his submission to the external authority or the Will of God a
difficult task. His awareness of his unworthiness "Lord, I am not
worthy"[162] drives him farther still. At any rate, this state is the
first step toward humility which is essential for the repentance
of the protagonist before he proceeds along the spiral ascension
of Purgatory. At each "turning" he comes to realize the difficulty
of the full recognition of faith and submission to divine will.
He is haunted by the deceitful face of the devil and earnestly
asks "the veiled sister" to pray for those who "are terrified and
cannot surrender/And affirm before the world and deny between
the rocks."[163] She is his guide in much the same way as Beatrice
was the spiritual guide of Dante; but "the veiled sister" has

guided the protagonist of *Ash Wednesday* along the stages of Purgatory, whereas Beatrice's guidance is basically limited to the *Paradiso* when Virgil's reason was no more needed. This is not exactly the same state, as the protagonist's interest in "the veiled sister" is for the sole purpose of salvation. In the case of Dante love is the animating power behind the whole pilgrimage and it is Platonic rather than sexual love that has attracted the poet to his angelic guide who led him through the sublimities of Paradise. Both Beatrice and "the veiled sister," however, symbolize the mystical state of beatitude toward which the aspirations of Dante and the protagonist of *Ash Wednesday* are gradually directed. Both ladies too represent the supremacy of intuitive revelation over the reasoning ability in seeking truth as far as it derives its power from the solidity of dogma and the affirmation of mystical religion.

But the difference between "the white sister" and Beatrice is the silence of the former and the reproaches that the latter raised against Dante along their procession in the terrestrial and heavenly Paradises. Having perceived that his mind is clouded with the cares and worries of the world, she rebukes him:

> I see thy mind turned to stone and,
> stonelike, such in hue that the light of my
> word dazes thee.[164]

But the stern reproach against Dante was raised by his fair guide when she perceived that he still relied on the deception of fancy even in the *Paradiso:*

> Thou thyself makest thyself dense with false imagining,
> and so thou seest not what thou wouldst see, if
> thou hadst cast it off.[165]

She warns him against indulgence in materialistic philosophy for it will keep him farther still from divine truth and turn him to the vacuity and vanity of the world. She is looking forward to draw his attention to "the eternal light"[166] of Truth based on the intuitive apprehension of reality.

The sister of *Ash Wednesday*, in this sense, represents the contemplative side in mystics, whereas Beatrice is affirmative in her approach by taking an active part in the spiritual re-orientation of the poet. But one should also bear in mind that in Dante's time sanctity was deeply inhaled by the most devout souls; whereas Eliot who lived in an agnostic age which is hostile enough to the concerns of the "spirit," had to rely upon the validity of liturgy and the traditional scheme of values to support his themes.

III *Thematic and Imagistic Echoes of Hinduism and Buddhism in the Structural Mysticism of* Ash Wednesday

The structure displayed through the choice of images and the development of themes is basically mystical. Though the structure is mainly built upon a Christian foundation, affinities with Oriental types of mysticism are not lacking. Apart from the symbolism of the Church, the major themes of *Ash Wednesday* re-echo the mystical philosophy of the East. The identity is striking in considering the concept of renunciation to be the basis upon which the purgatorial efficacy of the soul in the three religions (that is, Hinduism, Buddhism and Christianity) rests. In *Ash Wednesday* it is already accomplished from the outset by giving up "man's gift" and scope. The Buddha himself renounced all family links, all heredity, and limitation of mental horizon and did not tie himself down to the hard and fast rules of materiality. In the *Buddhist Suttas,* he said: "Full of hindrances is household life, a path defiled by passion: free as the air is the life of him who has renounced all worldly things."[167]

These religions agree also on the validity of meditation as a preliminary step along the Mystic Way. In *Ash Wednesday* the Lady "honours the Virgin in meditation,"[168] and "is withdrawn/ In a white gown, to contemplation, in a white gown."[169] Buddha, also, after roaming in the Pavarika mango grove, addressed his brethren saying:

Great is the fruit, great the advantage of intellect when set round with earnest contemplation. The mind set round with intelligence is freed from the great evils, that is to say, from sensuality, from individuality, from delusion, and from ignorance.[170]

This freedom from evil as a concomitant of contemplation is a development of Eliot's theme.

Associated with this view is the element of mystical concentratedness. In the Second Section of *Ash Wednesday* the protagonist says: "I would forget/Thus devoted, concentrated in purpose."[171] This "purpose" is elucidated in the following words from the Twenty-Ninth Lecture of the *Gaina Sutras:*

> By concentration of his thought he [the devotee] obtains stability
> of the mind . . .
> By austerities he cuts off the Karman [and] obtains . . . freedom
> from actions, by doing no actions he will obtain perfection, en-
> lightenment, deliverance, and final beatitude, and will put an
> end to all misery.[172]

The "final beatitude" is the exact equivalent to the intended
"purpose" of Eliot's protagonist and to the attainment of the
Buddhist Nirvana.

Along this Way effort is exerted for the checking of "desire"
and restraint of one's ambitions: "I do not wish to wish these
things,"[173] is the claim of the protagonist in *Ash Wednesday*
to put away with everything that binds him with the cravings
of the carnal self. In *The Sutrakritanga* we read that

> He who knows the pursuit of pleasures, must sooner or later give
> up their enjoyment [lest they drag him down] . . . Being in-
> structed in the creed of the Lord, exert yourself in the truth
> [i.e., in control]![174]

This concept of "desire" as a power dragging us down unless
it is abandoned through control, received further development
in the Aitareya-Aranyaka (Upanishad) by associating it with
mental and verbal desires:

> All desires dwell in the mind, for with the mind he [i.e., who
> knows this] conceives all desires. . . . Speech yields all desires,
> for with speech he declares all his desires.[175]

Here lies the real reason why Eliot's "veiled sister" is silent. She
simply "bent her head and signed but/spoke no word."[176] Buddha also remained silent when his disciples asked him about
crucial matters dealing with the eternity of "being" and the state
of the soul after the nirvanic exaltation.

It would be futile to try to find analogies between the sacra-
ments and religious beliefs expounded in *Ash Wednesday* either
with Hinduism or Buddhism; for they are, in this sense, far removed. Buddhism in particular has gone far in denouncing
any type of sacrament or personal adoration. The Buddha himself
is not God; Buddhism is the practice of wisdom and inner purification; Buddhahood is the enlightenment we may attain through
the Noble Eightfold Path.[177]

A consistent theme, moreover, that runs through *Ash Wednesday* and which has no echo in the Indian religions, is that of

intercession. In the First Section the protagonist asks the "Lady of silences" to "Pray for us sinners now and at the hour of our death."[178] In the Fifth Section he appeals to "the veiled sister" to "Pray for those who chose and oppose,"[179] and in the Sixth one he earnestly begs her who merges into the figure of the "holy mother" to "Suffer us not to mock ourselves with false-hood."[180] It is worth remarking that the idea of intercession in Hinduism, which was a prominent feature of the Vidas,[181] was given up toward the end of the Vedic period (2500-600 B.C.) with the appearance of the Upanishads. In these metaphysical tracts we have, above all, the most unfailing record Indian philosophy of mysticism has ever achieved. Their thesis of elaboration is the "direct" revelation of the luminous and universal Self which is

> the footstep of everything, for through it one knows everything. And as one can find again by footsteps what was lost, thus he who knows this finds glory and praise[182]

without the help of any intermediary power.

In Buddhism too there is no place for worshiping the "immediate" attributes of a personal Deity and consequently of either Sister or Holy Mother. It mainly seeks ethical well-being and spiritual regeneration through the individual's commitment to righteousness, having as his ideal the "Bodhisattva" or the one whose inclination is to attain the mystical state of enlightenment and release from conflict.

From this theme spring in *Ash Wednesday* the concepts of confession: "[Bless me father],"[183] of repentance: "Lord, I am not worthy,"[184] and of forgiveness: "And pray to God to have mercy upon us."[185] But in the Indian religions there is no room for salvation through these media. The rule of Karma[186] is hard and binding and there is no possibility for escape. In the words of Buddha

> beings as they pass from one state of existence and take form in others ... according to the karma they inherit, ... have been reborn, on the dissolution of the body after death, in some unhappy state of suffering or woe.[187]

The only way advisable is to be devoted "to that quietude of heart which springs from within"[188] and through training in "uprightness in life"[189] the influence of the karmic particles is lessened and emancipation ensues. Hence, Indian mysticism

avows the reliance on one's own effort and considers self-discipline essential for the sublimation of consciousness and the
merging of the depossessive self into the absoluteness of the
Universal Whole.

In this sense, Hinduist and Buddhist mysticism is mainly concerned with the life of man on earth, whereas the Christian
quest for salvation which is the major theme of *Ash Wednesday*
is fundamentally based on faith and readiness to proceed to the
"next" world.

IV

Ash Wednesday is thus a record of the spiritual drama of the
soul and the struggle toward quiescence which is rarely achieved.
The poem abounds with moments of strife against the attractions
of life which are naturally followed by complete resignation
to a superior power. There is a sense of deprivation when
the protagonist feels that he is forsaken and thus appeals to
"the veiled sister" to intercede for those who are mocking
themselves with falsehood and those who are dejected and weak
in spirit.

This period of loss and turmoil is essential for the mystical
development of the soul and is stressed in *The Dark Night of
the Soul* as one of spiritual aridity and in *The Cloud of Unknowing* as a moment of forgetfulness. It is necessary for a further
purging of the soul which is now prepared to experience the
timelessness of the mystical moment by transcending time
and peeping through the Garden of Eden.

In this sense, Eliot's preoccupation with the problems of mysticism runs throughout all his poems. Even in the period between "The Hollow Men" (1925) and the *Four Quartets* (1934-
42), though prominence is given to Christian mysticism, the
parallel types of mysticism are still lurking at the back of the
poet's mind and will be treated more elaborately in the *Four
Quartets*. The evocation of certain "common" images is in itself indicative of the perpetuation of the major themes of mystical philosophy whether applied to the East or the West.

Par sa nature cette poésie [d'Eliot] tend à la forme
pur, à l'abstrait et au mysticisme: dans ses sujets
préférés qui sont la condition malheureuse de
l'homme pècheur, les possibilités de sauver l'âme,
les rapports du monde où nous vivons, celui que nos
sens nous révèlent, avec le monde réel qui est celui
de Dieu.[1]

H. W. HÄUSERMANN

CHAPTER SIX

The Mystico-Symbolical Connotations of the "Four Quartets"

The poet in the *Quartets* gives a glimpse of reality, a mystical moment of peeping into the "heart of light," and relates it to the time-movement and to the eternal flux of the four elements of existence that used to busy the minds of the Greek philosophers in the pre-Christian era. He uses for his location places that are reminiscent of childhood (the Gloucestershire Garden of Burnt Norton), of ancestry (the village of East Coker from which the poet's ancestors emigrated to America in 1627), of craggy shores (the rocks of the Dry Salvages at Massachusetts) and of religious devotion (Little Gidding of Nicholas Ferrar). They introduce the theme of history as servitude—means serving certain ends—and as freedom—timeless moments.

I *The Mysticism of Time in* Burnt Norton

The main theme of *Four Quartets* is the human relationship to time and eternity, to the flux of time that operates on all created objects of the world and to the timelessness of "the still point." The idea is cited in the second epigraph to the poem which is based on the Heraclitean concept of elemental transmutations: "Though the Word governs everything, most people trust in their own wisdom."[2] In the *Quartets* "the Word" of Heraclitus[3] becomes the divine

> Word or Logos, as the origin and root of all things [for] Christians believe that this Word became flesh and was subject to the tension of life in time which words suffer.[4]

The flux is motivated by the partiality of our private wisdom; here it takes the form of a revolving pattern at the center of which all movement comes to a stoppage and all contradictory elements are reconciled.

The "time" of the flux in the world of "becoming" is governed by causation and judged by effect:

> Time present and time past
> Are both perhaps present in time future,
> And time future contained in time past.[5]

Eliot bases this concept of time on the Sankarene mysticism of the Advaita Vedanta.[6] The simultaneity of time makes it "eternally present." Human activities, in this sense, are associated with what happened in the past and what is to come in the future. This does not mean that "all time is unredeemable"[7] as Eliot puts it, for in reshaping the present, both the past and the future are transformed and viewed with fresh perspective. Time as succession of "What might have been and what has been"[8] is potent in "a world of speculation."[9]

The time of the prospective moment links the soul with the absoluteness of Being, the "eternal blessedness," and with "a future which transcends time and becomes the eschatological aim of all human desire."[10] This concept of time as spiritual transformation transcends the traditional view of time as "the recurrence of the same events."[11] Eliot takes as his media for the realization of this mystical metamorphosis the "footfalls"[12] that naturally exist and "echo in the memory,"[13] leading us

> Down the passage which we did not take
> Towards the door we never opened
> Into the rose-garden.[14]

Everything that leads to "the rose-garden" of reality marks a fresh experience for us. It is reminiscent of St. Augustine's mystical experience of ecstatic rapture that brings the soul into closer contact with the beatific vision.[15] With Eliot we pass "through the first gate"[16] and then come to "our first world"[17] as we follow "the deception of the thrush"[18] which implicitly refers to the relationship between this vision and the organic world that might lead us astray.

In the garden the "unheard music"[19] is hidden from the human eye "in the shrubbery"[20] and the roses of love "Had the look of flowers."[21] We pass "Along the empty alley"[22] to "the box circle"[23] which is the turning point in the whole vision. It looks over a "drained pool"[24] that is sometimes filled "with water out of sunlight"[25] amidst which a lotus[26] is blooming. Here we come to the apex of the mystical vision where the point of intersection between time and eternity is represented by the lotus. Mr. Melchiori takes the whole vision to be representational of

> the deep instantaneous intuition of all time concentrated in [this] single luminous point. It is the basis of a new conception of time and its relation to eternity. It is the real theme of the "Four Quartets."[27]

Though the pool's "surface glittered out of heart of light"[28] in mystical transcendence, the "single luminous point" of the vision is instantaneous for "They were behind us, reflected in the pool—"[29] our egoistic carnal selves were at our back, reminding us that "human kind/Cannot bear very much reality."[30] The cloud of practical existence passed and the vision was blotted out, and we were unable to perceive the leaves that "were full of children"[31] who enjoyed a Blakean-like innocence.

After the visionary experience of reality in the rose-garden, the Second Movement introduces the mystical symbolism of the wheel and the concept of movement. As the world of "sense" accounts for the distraction from the sublimity of the vision, it is also the major cause of the "contradiction" of the Wheel. "The deception of the thrush"[32] in the First Movement becomes here the "sapphires in the mud"[33] that are associated with the Shakespearian "gilded tombs."[34] The distraction of the flesh originates in "The trilling wire in the blood"[35] that "Sings below inveterate scars/Appeasing long forgotten wars."[36] The "inveterate scars" of sinfulness are reminiscent of the "forgotten wars" between the soul and the body. This "trilling wire" is synonymous with "the drift of stars"[37] and all have their reconciliation "At the still point of the turning world."[38] It is "neither arrest nor movement";[39] in it "There would be no dance, and there is only the dance."[40] There is "no dance" but stillness, and "there is only the dance" through its relatedness to the world of movement where we come to know it. It is

> The inner freedom from the practical desire,
> The release from action and suffering, release from the inner
> And the outer compulsion, yet surrounded
> By a grace of sense.[41]

The "still point" is the freedom from attachment and the heightening of sense-consciousness through grace. It is an "Erhebung without motion"[42] or an exaltation but not extension. It is the completeness of the "partial ecstasy"[43] and the resolution of "partial horror."[44] Paradoxically through "the enchainment of past and future,"[45] we have a perception of eternity as exemplified in the vision of the rose-garden; and "Only through time time is conquered."[46] With the mystical transcendence of time, the temporality of our "time" is invaded.

In the Third Movement the poet develops the theme of time by relating it to light and mystical darkness. The association of "Time before and time after"[47] with the "dim light"[48] signifies its link with the transiency of life. It is not purgatorial

> darkness[49] to purify the soul
> Emptying the sensual with deprivation
> Cleansing affection from the temporal,[50]

but the faint light of the fleeting pleasure of sensuality that links our time with temporality and deprives the soul of a possibility for purification. Conceived in this sense, time is

> Only a flicker
> Over the strained time-ridden faces
> Distracted from distraction by distraction.[51]

These strained faces which are distracted by the world of "becoming," suffer the "distraction" of the flickering gleams of time. In "this twittering world"[52]

> Men and bits of paper, whirled by the cold wind[53]

move adrift the passage of time "Into the faded air."[54]
As this is the case in the world of "Tumid apathy,"[55] descent

> Into the world of perpetual solitude,[56]

sounds plausible in view of the peace acquired after the "Desiccation of the world of sense,"[57] in St. John's Dark Night of the Soul.[58] This *Via Negativa* of "solitude"

> is the one way, and the other
> Is the same, not in movement
> But abstention from movement.[59]

The way of purgatorial "darkness" is not one of movement for that would associate it with the physical world, but it is "abstention from movement" where the dance of matter comes to a standstill.

From the "time-ridden faces" that are worn out in the London scene of the Third Movement which is applicable to any urban locality, the poet shifts in the Fourth Movement to the riddle of life and death: "Time and the bell have buried the day/ The black cloud carries the sun away."[60] The death-knell has hushed the distractions of the day and the "black cloud" has bedimmed its brightness. Yet this deadening atmosphere is not bereft of hope as the poet invokes "the sunflower"[61] to turn to us for mystical rebirth. From the "yew" of death, "the kingfisher's wing"[62] will point the direction to the mystical "light." The image is appropriate as it refers to the mysticism of the resurrection. After His conquest of death, Christ came to the world to show us the way to salvation through mystical illumination.

The translation of this illuminative vision into certain levels of existence through the medium of words is the poet's main concern in the last Movement of this Quartet. Usage of words is here related to the mysticism of "time" as "poetry, like the other things of this world, exists in the flow of time and falls under its law of corruption and death."[63] Words as well as music move "Only in time."[64] Yet, after the very act of creation and through the passage of time, verbal and musical media reach "The stillness, as a Chinese jar still/Moves perpetually in its stillness."[65] The "Chinese jar" is synonymous with the Aristotelian unmoved mover. It is the "stillness" where all perpetual movements meet, the state of crystallization after the removal of the unpoetic in phrase and the harsh in music; and, as such, it is a happy example of "the co-existence"[66] of time and timelessness, existence and essence, accident and substance.[67] For the completeness of their thematic actuality, both "the end and the beginning were always there/Before the beginning and after the end."[68] "Co-existence," in this sense, is the simultaneity of "the beginning" and "the end," and both find their vindication in the eternal Now.

But words are inadequate in giving full vent to the eternal Now, as they crack "Under the tension, slip, slide, perish,/Decay with imprecision."[69] The result is an impoverishment of the mystical experience so long as it is invaded by self-begotten "imprecision." "The Word in the desert"[70] too had the same destiny as it was overshadowed by "the disconsolate chimera."[71]

This Movement, in many ways, recapitulates the whole theme of time and flux. The "pattern" used by the poet here is that of St. John of the Cross who pictured the discipline of contemplation in the form of the stairs.[72] At the top of the "ladder" is the Love of God, the motivation of all movement, as "Love is itself unmoving/Only the cause and end of movement."[73] The perfection of divine Love makes of it a "timeless, and undesiring"[74] entity. Human desire "is movement"[75] in time which is characteristic also of the "limitation"[76] of earthly love. In its attachment to life and its aspiration for mystical revelation, human love oscillates "Between un-being and being."[77] It may attain "being" as typified in the mysticism of the rose-garden to which the poet refers again in his finale:

> Sudden in a shaft of sunlight
> Even while the dust moves
> There rises the hidden laughter
> Of children in the foliage.[78]

But the whole vision is only a sudden moment in the "sunlight" of mystical reality; and, with the movement of the dust and the "laughter/Of children" we are back again to the time-movement theme of our life.

II   The Mysticism of the Life-death Cycle and the Purgatorial Darkness in East Coker

After this theme of time in Burnt Norton, Eliot deals with the mysticism of the life-cycle in both animate and inanimate objects, in the "Bone of man and beast, cornstalk and leaf,"[79] and relies for the development of his themes on the element of dust. He takes for his location the village of his English sixteenth-century ancestors in Somersetshire.

The life of the village as anywhere else undergoes a permanent state of flux: "Old fires to ashes, and ashes to the earth."[80] This succession is traceable to the simultaneity of beginning and end,[81] for every moment in this flux is in itself an end and a beginning of a certain process. There is no fixation as the "dark . . . afternoon"[82] points toward the absorption of "the sultry light."[83]

> In an open field in that village one can perceive
> The association of man and woman
> In daunsinge, signifying matrimonie—
> A dignified and commodious sacrament.[84]

The villagers' dance signifies the perpetuation of life which is reminiscent of the primitive fertility ritual. The rhythm of this dance is an example of the rhythm of "the seasons and the constellations"[85] that brings to mind the rhythmic path to ecstasy and perfection along which the soul should labor.

From this rhythmic life-cycle of the First Movement, we come to "the quiet-voiced elders"[86] of the Renaissance. The only "receipt" we have out of their wisdom is the "deceit" of their knowledge. Their "serenity" was but "a deliberate hebetude"[87] and their knowledge had "a limited value"[88] for it was mainly concerned with the accumulation of "dead secrets"[89] that might lead to pedantry and self-imposition. For the poet, the only wisdom he claims "Is the wisdom of humility"[90] which is "endless."

The mysticism of humility is a basic feature of Eastern and Western asceticism for it constitutes a preliminary and indispensable factor in the mystical development of the soul. It is inseparable from detachment which should not be dependent on

> a "distraction fit" or accidental illuminations, but must be practised deliberately and wholemindedly. Our karma[91] follows us always, but it can be controlled by a disciplined observance of the yogas. If this is to be successful, humility is required. The insistence of this virtue in Hinduism[92] and still more in Buddhism[93] reminds us that Eliot does not see it exclusively as a Christian virtue.[94]

In Christianity the ethical value of humility originates in the Incarnation. In Upanishadic mysticism it is essentially the threshold that leads to proper knowledge and wisdom. In Buddhism it is important for the emancipation of the soul from the tyranny of the Karmic Law[95] and the attainment of Nirvana.[96]

Eliot points to the loss of this mystical wisdom by referring to these opening lines of Dante's *Divina Commedia:*

> In the middle of the journey of our life I [came to] myself in a dark wood [where] the straight way was lost.[97]

And with an ironic touch he stresses this loss by mixing it with Conan Doyle's *Hound of the Baskervilles:*

> In the middle, not only in the middle of the way
> But all the way, in a dark wood, in a bramble,
> On the edge of a grimpen, where is no secure foothold,
> And menaced by monsters, fancy lights,
> Risking enchantment.[98]

In much the same view as that of Dr. Watson, life for us is like a

> great Grimpen Mire. . . . with the black loom of the craggy hills around us, and the yellow speck of light burning steadily in the front . . . in the middle of the moor, with no sign of life near it.[99]

It is an atmosphere of insecurity and loss, of fanciful shadows and hauntingly dark woods.

This theme of darkness is manipulated in the Third Movement by echoing Milton's *Samson Agonistes:* "O dark, dark, dark. They all go into the dark,"[100] that ironically recalls the lines:

> O dark, dark, dark, amid the blaze of noon,
> Irrecoverably dark, total Eclipse
> Without all hope of day![101]

Into the darkness of this world, all types of people go; even "The vacant interstellar spaces"[102] are overshadowed by it. We are all gradually led to the "silent funeral"[103] of our social community which is destitute of the mystical revelation of Samson for it lacks his intuitive perception. It is "Nobody's funeral, for there is no one to bury."[104] It is the death-knell of civilization, and, though "there is no one to bury," it is carrying with it the heritage of the past to the grave. It is not far removed from the "vacant" darkness "in a theatre"[105] during the change of scenes, or the stoppage of "an underground train"[106] "too long between stations,"[107] or the deadening darkness that envelops a mind "under ether."[108]

From the emptiness and aimlessness of this darkness, the poet passes to "the darkness of God,"[109] or the Dark Night of the Soul. The transition from the deadening anaesthesia of contemporary "darkness" to the divine darkness of the soul, denotes the emergence from a state of sense-attachment to the mystic illumination of suprarational knowledge. It marks also the ascent of the soul on its mystical ladder from the *errata* of sense-perception to the *accurata* of the intuitive vision, and from a chaotic incomprehensibility of "appearance" to an ecstatic recognition of Divine Truth.

For St. John of the Cross the way to God is a way of purgatorial darkness based on renunciation, for "In order to possess what you do not possess/You must go by the way of dispossession."[110] We begin our way to Him in a spirit of depossessiveness for in Him we possess everything; and "In order to arrive at what you do not know/You must go by a way which is the way of ignorance."[111] After freeing the mind from its obsession with "matter," the mystical revelation of "what you do not know," of knowledge and divine wisdom, is ascertained if only one follows the way of detachment from terrestrial "desire." In its "devouring" concept as a craving passion,

> all desire imposes a "limit" to our knowledge, possession, existence. [And], in order to escape from every limitation, we must cast off that which ties us down. . . . It narrows and closes the soul, imprisons it within its own limitations, and makes it incapable of perfect communion with the Infinite.[112]

To overcome all these limitations, "desire" should be discarded if ever we aim at the blooming of the mystical life in the domain of asceticism.

Thus, in order to plunge into the Purgatorio of "darkness," one should get rid of all material possessiveness which is a process of mortifying "desire" and a mystical avowal to the life of renunciation. This way of life culminates in the final conviction that "the darkness shall be the light, and the stillness the dancing."[113] It is the "light" of mystical illumination that is coupled here with "the dancing" at the still point which is "neither arrest nor movement."[114]

The Fourth Movement is an extension of the previous one; worldly darkness corresponds to physical death and purgatorial darkness to spiritual death and rebirth. The former state is exemplified in the expanded image of the hospital. In the words of Sir Thomas Browne: "For the World, I count it not an inn, but an Hospital; and a place not to live, but to dye in."[115] With Eliot the Renaissance image is developed into a "wounded surgeon"[116] operating with "bleeding hands."[117] His bleeding is reminiscent of the dripping blood of the crucifixion; and thus it is easy to perceive that the theme of the Movement moves backward and forward between physical and spiritual death. It is also "The bloody flesh"[118] of the holy communion which "sound" rationality is unable to acquiesce; and, from another point of view, it is "The trilling wire in the blood"[119] which is the source of sinfulness.

In a further development of the original simple image, "the healer's art"[120] becomes the mysticism of divine love, and "the fever chart"[121] the upward and downward movement of the soul on the mystical "ladder." The descent of the soul to the "frigid purgatorial fires/Of which the flame is roses, and the smoke is briars,"[122] symbolizes the burial of Christ; its ascent from the darkness of death to the light of mystical rebirth is the resurrection. Though the mysticism of purgatorial suffering (symbolized by the briars of Christ's crown) together with the unitive and constructive efficacy of its flames in the very act of love (symbolized by the roses), are unknown to a world "Endowed by the ruined millionaire,"[123] still "we call this Friday good."[124]

The mysticism of love as expounded by St. Augustine,[125] St. Teresa of Avila,[126] and St. John of the Cross[127] is based upon faith. It speaks of a firm belief in the mysticism of suffering and the possibility of salvation. Yet this hope is no better than that of "the dying nurse"[128] who represents the declining Church, and

> Whose constant care is not to please
> But to remind of our, and Adam's curse,
> And that, to be restored, our sickness must grow worse.[129]

The message of the Church is not one of pleasure but to remind us of our sinfulness and "Adam's curse." Even then, our spiritual restoration might be attained when "our sickness" grows worse.

Continuing the theme of the rhythmic use of language in its relatedness to the time-succession mysticism of *Burnt Norton,* in this last Movement of *East Coker,* Eliot recalls the subject of his art and tells us that he is still "in the middle way,"[130] "Trying to learn to use words."[131] He is still far from the perfection of words and musical notes when they reach the state of "stillness." For him one had to embark on a serious "succession" of endeavors for

> each venture
> Is a new beginning, a raid on the inarticulate
> With shabby equipment always deteriorating
> In the general mess of imprecision of feeling
> Undisciplined squads of emotion.[132]

The "imprecision of feeling" and the chaos in which our emotional life finds expression, speak of the deterioration of our "shabby equipment." Obviously the poet is here

> deeply aware of the process of banalization that has overtaken the traditional language . . . in our time and of the consequent necessity of discovering a new language through which the transcendent meaning of reality may appear to-day as it once did in ages past.[133]

This absence of the "transcendent meaning of reality" in our language in addition to a general lack of reducing our "squads of emotion" to any formulated discipline or organization, account for our inability to engage in "a raid on the inarticulate." But one had "to recover what has been lost/And found and lost again and again,"[134] in conformity with tradition.

The finale of this Quartet elaborates this theme of tradition which goes back to the "old stones that cannot be deciphered."[135] The philosophical aspect of its history is not only "the pattern"[136] "Of dead and living,"[137] but the mystical creativeness of "the intense moment."[138] It is the attainment of the bewildering "stillness" through "strength and submission,"[139] struggle and humility, not only in "a lifetime burning,"[140] but in the whole mystical tradition of humanity. The perpetuation of its unitive process does not come by way of "the dark cold"[141] of physical death and "the empty desolation"[142] of a decaying civilization, but across "the vast waters/Of the petrel and the porpoise."[143] With this spiritual voyage across the vast seas of "time," the poet aims at rehabilitating its mystical connotation through different levels of exploration that range from the lowest depths of an Inferno to the highest sublimities of a Paradiso— from the darkness of death to the mystical "light" of the rose-garden.

III   *Incarnation and the Mystical Detachment of Self in* The Dry Salvages

The mysticism of the time-succession takes here the Heraclitean element of water as emblematic of its eternal flux. The major principle of life is the rhythmic flow of the individual's blood and the universal sea of humanity: "The river is within us, the sea is all about us."[144] The river (the Mississippi of the poet's childhood)[145] "Is a strong brown god"[146] that links man with his primitive ancestry. This symbol as the perpetuation of life is also its destroyer—the "problem confronting the builder of bridges."[147] Once the problem is solved, "the dwellers in cities"[148] have missed its significance though the "rhythm was present in the nursery bedroom"[149] and felt by children but unknown to the adults of the Blakean "experience."

The sea of humanity "is the land's edge"[150] that associates it with experience and activity. It is

> the granite
> Into which it reaches, the beaches where it tosses
> Its hints of earlier and other creation.[151]

It is "the granite" on which human, animal and inorganic histories of the world are inscribed. They are the "hints" that review the crises of human civilization. In tossing "up our losses,"[152] it "howls" and "yelps" in the menacing tone of "many gods."[153] The "wailing warning"[154] of sailors is the cry of Truth re-echoed by every generation, but it is inaudible to ours which is precipitating toward its final doom.

Mixed with "The sea howl"[155] is the tolling of the bell that

> Measures time not our time, rung by the unhurried
> Ground swell.[156]

It is the eternal time that is measured by the waves and the death-knell of those who are swelling the ground with their worries and miseries. It is the time which "is never ending,"[157] "that is and was from the beginning."[158]

This passage of time is marked also by the lifelessness of "The silent withering of autumn flowers/Dropping their petals and remaining motionless."[159] On the other hand, the "drifting wreckage"[160] of civilization is coming to "no end, but addition"[161] of "further days and hours."[162] Instead of the earnest appeal of sailors for safety from the devouring hurricane, there is "the failing/Pride or resentment at failing powers."[163] It is the unpardonable resentment to reiterate "the unprayable/Prayer"[164] that accounts for a new addition of blind obstinacy. The "final addition"[165] is "The silent listening to the undeniable/Clamour of the bell of the last annunciation."[166] This flat indifference becomes "the hardly, barely prayable/Prayer of the one Annunciation."[167] Our hope here rests on the significance of "the one Annunciation" to us—the meeting of time and the timeless, the human and the divine, temporality and eternity. Mr.

Smidt rightly remarks that in clinging to this doctrine, "Eliot finds it possible to believe in Redemption through the realization of timelessness without alienating himself from Christianity."[168] This gives vent to the poet's mystical exploration in "meaning." The pastness of the past should neither be discarded nor "Encouraged by superficial notions of evolution,"[169] which compose, "in the popular mind,"[170] the media of "disowning the past."[171] The recovery of the past is an act of "sudden illumination."[172] From its wisdom, we gathered only "the experience but missed the meaning."[173] A sound

> approach to the meaning restores the experience
> In a different form, beyond any meaning
> We can assign to happiness.[174]

Happiness becomes meaningful through the right intelligibility of approach which will inevitably bring forth the restoration of experience.

Yet the "backward look"[175] at the "recorded history"[176] is not so much of happiness as of "primitive terror."[177] Both terror and "moments of agony"[178] are permanent as "the ragged rock in the restless waters"[179] of humanity. In their self-possessiveness, the people of "the restless waters" have become insensitive to the agonies of one another. They "change, and smile: but the agony abides."[180] It originates in "The bitter apple and the bite in the apple."[181] Adam's sin has been deeply rooted in man's nature but through the right approach to the mysticism "of the one Annunciation"[182] the "drifting wreckage"[183] of humanity might be saved.

To denote the mystical progress of the soul throughout this process of recovery, the poet uses the vehicular journey by train and in an ocean liner. To those who live in the illusion of the future, it is only "a faded song";[184] the past as well could not be revived through our "time of chronometers,"[185] but through "the still point" in which all opposites are reconciled. The drift of time is only a "Fare forward, travellers! not escaping from the past/Into different lives, or into any future."[186] The advice of Krishna (an avatar of Vishnu, the Preserver of the world) to Prince Arjuna who hesitated to take action in war is to fare forward. Wise action on the spur of the moment solves the hesitation of Arjuna; but in conformity with Krishna's advice in the Bhagavad-Gita (the Song of the Blessed), "do not think of the fruit of action."[187] The main thesis of Krishna's doctrine is detachment from "the fruit of action" or the cultivation of a sense of disinterestedness.[188] Disinterested action by way of detachment leads to the luminosity ("sattva") of self. In the case of Buddhist mysticism, it paves the way for the release ("moksa") of the soul from suffering, or from the series of reincarnations, and leads to enlightenment.[189]

The mystical theme of detachment is relevant to the Third Movement of the poem as "(the time of death is every moment)."[190] It is, then, in the existing present, the eternal Now, the actual conscientious duty that is performed in a spirit of disregard to any form of possessiveness, the keeping of an eye on "the moment which is not of action or inaction"[191] that the mysticism of Krishna's "fare forward" is driven home. It signifies the "forward" alienation of self from all forms of superimpositions. Our time is no healer to the scars that are left on the soul but purgatorial detachment through which

> the work of our spirit is to be directed neither upward nor downward, neither to one side nor to the other, neither forward nor backward, as it would be with a physical thing,[192]

for

> to go down is to go up, and to go up, to go down, for he that humbles himself is exalted, and he that exalts himself is humbled.[193]

It is also a manifestation of a Heraclitean dictum that "the way up and the way down are one and the same."[194]

These three images of "cloud," "night," and "flux" are used respectively by the poet to visualize a state of mystical sameness in which the upward or downward, backward or forward movement is of no significance. What matters is the state of consciousness that accompanies the act. The spirit in which it is performed gives it meaning and ethical import.

For the salvation of "all those who are in ships,"[195] the people launched adrift the sea of humanity, and those who are concerned "with every lawful traffic,"[169] the sojourners in the flux of time, the poet appeals in the Fourth Movement to the "Queen of Heaven,"[197] the Holy Virgin, for intercession. God had his human substance to intercede for those who are "Setting forth, and not returning"[198] and those who ended their life "in the dark throat which will not reject them,"[199]—not like Jonah[200] who remained inside the whale for three days and came to life again.

In this sense, the function of this Movement is very similar to that of a prayer given on behalf of those who struggled with the waves and "Ended their voyage"[201] at the bottom of the sea without hearing "the sound of the sea bell's/Perpetual angelus,—"[202] the utterance of "the one Annunciation"[203] to the Virgin which is set against the sea's annunciation of fear and devouring doom.

Contrary to the theme of intercession in the previous Movement, the poet in the fifth one falls heavily upon those who believe that they are able "To communicate with Mars, converse with spirits,/To report the behaviour of the sea monster."[204] The belief in superstition goes back to man's restless anxiety about the future. People's "curiosity searches past and future/And clings to that dimension."[205] Within the range of time, people have used their ratiocinative abilities to dissect "The current image into pre-conscious terrors—/To explore the womb, or tomb, or dreams,"[206] which are the concern of biology and psychology. Their clinging "to that dimension" has by far removed them from the more enduring and everlasting domain of the "spirit." In the sea of life, men have busied themselves with what it tosses, with

> the torn seine,
> The shattered lobsterpot, the broken oar
> And the gear of foreign dead men,[207]

but the Permanence of "the ragged rock" has become less significant.

> On the spiritual plane
>   to apprehend
> The point of intersection of the timeless
> With time, is an occupation for the saint.[208]

This is the point that is "in and out of time,"[209] the dwelling of the saintly mystic, the preoccupation of a mind oriented toward the mysticism of transcendence and its bearing on the time of this world. It is the fruitful struggle of "a lifetime's death in love,/Ardour and selflessness and self-surrender."[210] With sacrifice as the essence of love, the carnal self is conquered, and the true Self, the real Hinduistic or, more specifically, the Upanishadic "Atman,"[211] emerges in a spirit of self-submission.

Apart from this ascetic life, the majority of people are dominated by

The distraction fit, lost in a shaft of sunlight,
The wild thyme unseen, or the winter lightning
Or the waterfall.[212]

The suddenness of the "distraction fit" that is lost in the "sunlight" "shaft" might betray a flash of immortality. Yet it will
remain unseen to a world in which the "wild thyme," the
"winter lightning" and the "waterfall" are understood as the
final realities.

These views on the time-cycle of the world

are only hints and guesses,
Hints followed by guesses; and the rest
Is prayer, observance, discipline, thought and action.
The hint half guessed, the gift half understood, is
Incarnation.[213]

Here we have the major theme of the *Quartets*: Eliot's "hints"
are the landmarks in the succession of time, his "prayer" for
time-sojourners, his "observance" of their chaotic life, his
"thought" of the prospect of humanity and the possibility of
salvation through the mysticism of "action" crystallized in Krishna's dictum "fare forward," are the poet's main concern in these
poems. But the reconciliation of this time-cycle with timelessness
in the mysticism of the Incarnation, is the "gift" that is "half
understood" by the voyagers in time. It symbolizes "the impossible union"[214] of the divine and the human, of eternity and time,
which Miss Gardner takes to be "the subject of the poem"[215] in
"the mystical sense."[216] It gives full realization to our conception
of the conquest of "past and future,"[217] as it also marks the
totality of Being. In it the antagonistic opposites are wedded
happily for it gives vent to the activity that is accomplished in
a spirit of non-attachment. In this sense, "right action is freedom/
From past and future also."[218] It is the release from the hard
and binding rules of purposeful deeds which have driven us to
the "daemonic, chthonic/Powers"[219] of an Inferno; but

For most of us, this is the aim
Never here to be realized.[220]

Even then, we should go on trying and be

content at the last
If our temporal reversion nourish
(Not too far from the yew-tree)
The life of significant soil.[221]

Our temporary journey across the world is not bereft of "reversion" to the past. It is measured by the "yew-tree" of our death and nourished by the "significant soil" of rebirth.

IV   *The Pentecostal Flames and the Crowned Knot of* Little Gidding[222]

The mysticism of *Little Gidding* is that of the *illuminatio,* of the "brief sun"[223] that "flames the ice,"[224] and of the "pentecostal fire/In the dark time of the year."[225] With the prophetic flames the "soul's sap quivers."[226] The "Midwinter spring"[227] of the opening scene becomes "the unimaginable"[228] summer, the season of "intersection"[229] that has pierced "the dark time" of humanity with its radiating light.

As this time is favorable for the mystical pilgrimage of the soul, its destination is, in this part of the poem, toward Little Gidding. But the time of the visit is unimportant whether it is accomplished secretly "at night"[230] like King Charles I or "by day"[231] when the mind is engaged in thinking of "the dull facade/And the tombstone."[232] It is not only the purpose of the visit for that might be "beyond the end you figured/And is altered in fulfilment,"[233] but the "meaning" behind the whole experience is what matters. We should put off "sense and notion,"[234] as one comes "here to kneel/Where prayer has been valid."[235] The validity of prayer is in "the communication"[236] with the "spirit divine" that "is tongued with fire beyond the language of the living."[237] With these "tongues of flames" the Disciples were capable of attaining "the intersection of the timeless moment"[238] through the efficacy of the purgatorial fire and the revelation of the mystical vision "that is beyond the language of the living."

Though the mystical journey takes place in England, it is also identical with "nowhere"[239]—all places of pilgrimage that link time and eternity.

In the Second Movement the poet is concerned with the elemental metamorphoses which the soul encounters in this pilgrimage. The Heraclitean philosophy of succession which serves the poet's purpose, is expounded here in relation to the element of fire. Eliot uses, moreover, the theme of death in all aspects of existence as a correlative "catalyist" between physical death and the mysticism of time.

The roses of *Burnt Norton* are here reduced to ashes "on an old man's sleeve"[240] denoting "The death of hope and despair."[241] Water too, the life-giving and perpetuation symbol of *The Dry Salvages,* is lacking in the enveloping "drouth"; and the productive earth becomes "The parched eviscerate soil."[242] It is the loss of creativeness in man; but there is the underlying possibility of mystical rebirth.

The death of "Water and fire"[243] follows because of

The sacrifice that we denied.[244]

Our denial of the significance of sacrificial action ended in the loss of an integral factor in mysticism. This element together with the other factors of cleansing "the doors of perception" and the possibilities of spiritual revival have become the "marred foundations"[245] of our past.

To give expression to the existence of this past in our life, the poet imagines that he has encountered "a familiar compound ghost"[246] of ancestry and mastery in the poetic tradition of which he is a part. The coming of the ghost from the cleansing fire[247] is set against the smoky atmosphere after an air raid "Before the urban dawn"[248] in World War II. Instead of the white dove of peace, there is "the dark dove"[249] that causes conflagration and loss of many victims with its bombs.

In a semi-dramatic dialogue the poet converses with this ghost and both come to a "concord at this intersection time/Of meeting nowhere, no before and after."[250] Time "before" and time "after," the place "here" and the place "nowhere," are insignificant if we consider time as a composite whole uniting both time and place in a universal simultaneity. This view is made possible through the combination of time and the timeless, the here-ness and nowhere-ness, in the point of intersection where opposites are reconciled. It has rendered our dissection of time and division of place illusory and superficial.

With their agreement on the falsity of these demarcations, the poet's conversation with the ghost shifts to their concern with learning "to get the better of words."[251] Their common aim is "To purify the dialect of the tribe"[252] and the poet's further intention is to disclose "the gifts reserved for old age"[253] and "set a crown"[254] upon a "lifetime's effort"[255] for the revival of the poetic tradition.

The persistent thought that dwells in people's minds when

they reach old age is "the rending pain"[256] of their youthful reckless life,

> offering no promise
> But bitter tastelessness of shadow fruit
> As body and soul begin to fall asunder.[257]

Instead of exhausting the mind with "the cold friction of expiring sense,"[258] of death and physical disintegration, of bitterness in tasting the "fruit" of action, the poet is ironically preoccupied with dialectal purification as much as he has been concerned with the purgation of "the exasperated spirit"[259] in the "refining fire."[260]

Mystical detachment from the fruits of action does not mean inactivity but abstention from results that normally vanish instantaneously. It is also the non-attachment to the previous errors or to any haunting prospect, the "liberation/From the future as well as the past."[261] To be associated with "desire" is to be baffled in love and disappointed in value. The love of one's "own field of action"[262] begins with attachment and shifts toward the right detachment without belittling one's activity. Viewed in this sense, the past as it exists in the present is not servitude but freedom. The "faces and places"[263] of history— "with the self"[264] that extolled them—are renewed, "transfigured, in another pattern."[265] The self has benefited out of considering the phases of history objectively, not as "an eternal repetition of the same events"[266] but as "a sequence of creative moments in which something new enters the world and determines the future";[267] and, instead of involving itself in the blind alley of personal prejudices that lead nowhere, it ponders the past too in a meaningful retrospection.

The Little Gidding of the seventeenth century with its religious Anglicanism and its Civil War is associated in the poet's mind with the "king at nightfall,"[268] King Charles I (1600-49), with those who died "here and abroad,"[269] like Nicholas Ferrar (1592-1637) and Richard Crashaw (1612-49), and with John Milton, the "one who died blind and quiet."[270] Shall we celebrate "These dead men more than the dying?"[271] The past does not exist in ringing "the bell backward"[272] for this is an artificial attempt to awaken our memories. It is the "silence" of death that has brought all contradictions to a harmonious unison and has brought the meaning behind the strife of those seventeenth-century figures to a perfection, that is, the constructive life that follows the schism is what matters. The life of reasonable and sound activity naturally comes after the struggle with the elements of evil, as

> Sin is Behovely, but
> All shall be well, and
> All manner of thing shall be well.[273]

In the words of Dame Julian of Norwich:

> It behoved that there should be sin; but all shall be well, and all shall be well, and all manner of thing shall be well.[274]

"Sin is behovely" because it is the preliminary step in the building up of personalities. It has rendered discipline meaningful and resistance of temptation more comprehensive; and, both are essential for the right conformity to society. "All shall be well" through the power and effect of "divine love."[275]

The lyric Fourth Movement is the manifestation of the mysticism of this love in the descent of the dove (the Holy Ghost)

> Of which the tongues declare
> The one discharge from sin and error.[276]

The "tongues" of flame that inspired the Disciples are meant to discharge the human race from an idulgence in "sin and error" through purgatorial fire. The flame links this lyric with "the dark dove"[277] and "the flickering tongue"[278] of bombardment. For the poet,

> The only hope, or else despair
>   Lies in the choice of pyre or pyre—
>   To be redeemed from fire by fire.[279]

The "choice" which may come after a state of "despair," lies between the consuming fire of destruction and the "refining fire"[280] of a Purgatorio.

The driving force that motivates the sacrificial process of purification is Love,

> the unfamiliar Name
> Behind the hands that wove
> The intolerable shirt of flame
> Which human power cannot remove.[281]

The poisoned Nessus-shirt[282] was given to Hercules by his wife Deianira to prove his love to her. Being deeply embittered by the intolerable pain that the shirt caused, he ascended to Olympus on a burning pyre that consumed his body. The presence of the shirt and the inability of human power to remove it are indicative of the necessity of suffering in life for "We only live, only suspire/Consumed by either fire or fire."[283] We are either emaciated by the fire of grudge or consumed by the fire of rapturous love that gives spice to our life and changes its disillusionment into creativeness.

In the final Movement all the threads of thought are recapitulated, and all thematic development of the mystical symbolism of the *Quartets* is brought to the climax of "the crowned knot of fire"[284] which is the resting spot of all the movements and levels on which the poem operates. The mystical themes of the poem move backward and forward composing a pattern of "time" in which "beginnings" and "ends" are inseparable and indivisible wholes. In this sense,

> What we call the beginning is often the end
> And to make an end is to make a beginning.
> The end is where we start from.[285]

It is also the same case with language as "Every phrase and every sentence is an end and a beginning,"[286] provided that the word is "neither diffident nor ostentatious"[287] but forming an integral part in a well-balanced and composite totality in which the "complete consort"[288] of individual components is achieved.

Each moment in the stream of "time" is both death and mystical rebirth, as

> We die with the dying:
> See, they depart, and we go with them.
> We are born with the dead:
> See, they return, and bring us with them.[289]

In this "consort" the dead are revived partly through "the use of memory,"[290] and partly through the continuation and development of their actions. This simultaneity of time is exemplified in the revisitation of the "compound ghost" which is highly significant not only from the mystical view of the necessity for purgation and abstention from attachment, but for the purification of the tribal dialect.

As these moments, from the historical point of view, are co-existent, history is then "a pattern/Of timeless moments,"[291] which we can relive and reexperience through the multiplicity of our activities. Its time is the eternal "now" and its place is England which is associated with Little Gidding and "With the drawing of this Love and the voice of this Calling."[292] Following the enlightening treatise of *The Cloud of Unknowing*, mysticism has shifted to the side of practicability, to "the voice of this Calling" which is applicable to Eliot's poetic vocation. According to fourteenth-century mysticism, the "draught [drawʒt]" of Love[293] is the divine breath that revives the mystic who is undergoing a state of unawareness or rather a "cloud of unknowing."[294]

The Eliotesque "rose" is symbolic of this divine love typified in the lotus of *Burnt Norton*, the briars of the crucifixion in *East Coker*, the apex of the saintly preoccupation of "a lifetime's death in love"[295] in *The Dry Salvages* and the decisive moment in the pattern of history in *Little Gidding*. It is also the same token that merges in the end "Into the crowned knot"[296] where "the fire and the rose are one."[297] This fusion of the "fire" and the "rose" into the oneness of being, is significant partly in removing the shadows of despair[298] and partly in harmonizing the foregoing elements: the purgatorial fire of suffering and the rose of divine love are here linked together. For the apprehension of their unity in "the crowned knot," we must turn once more to the illuminating treatise *The Cloud of Unknowing* in which the anonymous mystic advised the young man saying "I would hope ultimately to help you tie the spiritual knot of burning love between you and your God in spiritual unity and harmony of will."[299] With this all-inclusiveness of the "knot," the symbol has gained universality by tying up all the versatile elements of the human and the divine will in a harmonious whole.

V

Commenting on these poems as a whole, Mr. D. S. Savage praises them as "they bear the marks of deep sincerity, of a mature intelligence and of experienced and conscientious craftsmanship."[300] He then changes his attitude and censures them "as imperfectly realized summaries of experience, [and] as poetic failures."[301] He builds his accusation on a comparison between the earlier and the later poems and says that the dominant emotions conveyed by the early poems are those of weariness, boredom, frustration, self-doubt and dissatisfaction [which] are brought within the crystallizing range of the poet's craftsmanship and are thereby mastered and transformed, made truly significant;[302]

whereas

the air of aridity, of weariness, which is exhaled by these later poems is marginal, is not part of the substance of the poetry itself, but is unintentional, arising from qualities which the poet has failed to bring in subjection to his inspiration.[303]

Mr. Savage considers the crystallization of emotion which is "dominant" in the early poems, lacking in the *Quartets* as he fails to recognize an insistent theme of an "objective correlative" —to use Eliot's own epithet—that runs through the later as well as the earlier poems. They may betray certain limited personal touches which are inevitable in writing poetry,[304] but Mr. Savage seems to have missed the relation between the "situation"[305] or the external "set of objects"[306] and the very texture of the poems. The attitude here is one of perpetual struggle that gives vent to the mystical philosophy of suffering which Mr. Savage has completely severed from the "tissues" of the poems by considering them as

little more than loosely connected philosophizings about the nature of reality and the value of experience, of which the poetry is ornamental rather than essential.[307]

This is the exact reverse of Eliot's theory of the relation between poetry and philosophy which he has expounded in his essay on "Dante" and of which he was obviously quite aware in the *Quartets*. Considering too the relationship between the different parts and the wholeness of perception experienced in these poems, it becomes evident that they are not "loosely connected philosophizings," as Mr. Savage assumes, for the parts are related to one another in as much as they are intimately related to the whole. These "philosophizings," moreover, are functional rather than ornamental as they have played consistent roles in thematic developments and in enriching the poetic experience expounded in these poems, for example, the vision of the rose-garden in *Burnt Norton*, the theme of mystical renunciation of St. John of the Cross in *East Coker*, the theme of Krishna's depossessiveness in *The Dry Salvages*, and the peace-

ful vision of Dame Julian of Norwich in *Little Gidding*. The
Quartets, in this sense, do not constitute

> patches of imagery [which] are stuck on, as it were from out-
> side, to give poetic verisimilitude to a skeleton of abstract intel-
> lectualism,[308]

as Mr. Savage puts it, for the imagery veils behind it a long
train of mystico-symbolical connotations that emanate from the
inside. They abound with the Heraclitean symbolism of elemental
flux and transmutation, and with the recurrence of highly ac-
centuated spiritual moments that symbolize the mystical insight of looking into the heart of things. These moments mark
not only specific developments in the emotive-intellectual or
physico-spiritual life of the individual but purgatorial stages
in his mystical progression too. In the endless metamorphoses of
the water-imagery—to take only one example—the poet in
The Dry Salvages relates the river of life to the vast seas of
eternity associating the former with the life-death cycle or series
of beginnings and ends, and the latter with the everlastingness of
"the granite"[309] or the permanence of "the rock"[310] in the oceans
of humanity. In its eternal reality, "the granite" points to the
Bergsonian "durée,"[311] the Spenglerian "time-sensation"[312] which
is an "image of eternity"[313] and the Bradleyan "absoluteness."[314]
The "granite teeth"[315] and the "ragged rock"[316] which are
scattered across "the restless waters"[317] of purification are
those of agony and terror, of "torment" and "sudden fury."[318]
"There is no end"[319] in this "trial and judgment of the sea"[320]
of suffering for "People change, and smile: but the agony
abides."[321] Its abiding takes place in "the dark cold and the
empty desolation"[322] of the physical and social decay of *East
Coker* where "the wave cry"[323] and "the wind cry"[324] across
"the vast waters"[325] of purgatory, are reminiscent of the same
theme of affliction. Its perpetuation is essential for "there are
other places"[326] of valuable experience along the way to Little
Gidding, "some at the sea jaws,/Or over a dark lake,"[327] either at
the menacing and haunting "jaws" or the infernal darkness
that presides over the lake of torture. In this sense, "We shall
not cease from exploration";[328] "here and now cease to matter"[329] for this purpose, as

> We must be still and still moving
> Into another intensity
> For a further union, a deeper communion,[330]

till we gain perception of "the drained pool"[331] of *Burnt Norton* that "was filled with water out of sunlight"[332] in a state of insight and mystical ecstasy.

Obviously these images which support the structural symbolism of the *Quartets* are not the disjointed unsymmetrical "patches" which are attached to a worn-out bulk of the poems as Mr. Savage claims, for they constitute a constructivist, robust and an arterial organism. The "skeleton" that holds the body of the poems together is not only one "of abstract intellectualism" but also of an objectified emotionalism upon which the validity of the intuitive perception of the previous visions rests. The sense of objectification here relies upon the embodiment of thought in the image which is the essence of mystico-philosophical poetry.

Thus the role played by imagery in the *Quartets* is predominantly architectonic partly in the visualization of the mystical experience and partly in associating it with the plane of actuality. It is not then one of "poetic verisimilitude" but the portrayal of reality has become here poetically potential. The imagistic function in these poems is one of nearness and clarification in relating the super-conscious experience to the level of consciousness and in elucidating the vagueness of the ineffable.

Eliot's aim behind this theme of interrelatedness is the rehabilitation of "time before and time after,"[333] of history as "freedom"[334] (of detached moments) and "co-existence"[335] (in relation to other planes of life), partly through a pattern that includes both time and timelessness and partly through experiencing the past in our present activities.[336] The riddle of time is solved in this way through its recognition

as history, personal and family history: time as suffering: time as the "still centre", the timeless moment when past, present and future are joined and compressed into one moment of vision.[337]

Eliot seems to be rather Bergsonian[338] only in relating these aspects of time to the concept of "duration" and succession; but he is basically mystic in considering "time as suffering" and in taking it to be the crystallization of the visionary moment. In this mysticism of "the still point" temporality and eternity are reconciled in "The point of intersection of the timeless/With time,"[339] which is "an occupation for the saint"[340] and a dwelling for the mystic after "a lifetime's death in love."[341] It is the crescendo of concentratedness that brings forth the relief from the worries, miseries and tumultuous attractions of the world. It speaks of the reality that has marked the spiritual quest in all ages of mysticism, though it has existed under a multiplicity of nomenclature. It is the Hindu "Atman" (the real Self), the Buddhist Be-ness of the ultimate Reality, the Platonic "Idea," and the Plotinian One or the Absolute. It is also the Eliotesque "rose-garden," the source of love or mystical illumination, and "the crowned knot"[342] in which suffering is mated with love.

Through this mystical philosophy we read the "essence" of eternality in the Thomistic formulation of "existence"[343] and perceive the purity of Being in the vagaries of time and place. Our notion of "time" has thus acquired new meaning by relating it to eternity; and the visible world has become more intelligible by imbuing it with the essence of Being. The Movements of the *Quartets,* reviewed separately, point to this ultimate end which may be the liberation from the bondage of time. In *Burnt Norton* the act of liberating the soul is viewed in terms of insight or looking into the "heart of light,"[344] which is normally considered by mystics to be the sole way of accession to the loveliness of the Divine. The notion is driven home in an unpublished MS. that throws light on the foregoing theme of divine illumination. The anonymous writer assertingly commences:

> I say þat asoule touched in affeasñ by þe sensible pleusr of god as he is in hý self: is aparfite soule illimund in þe zeson by þe cloze Beme of eulaʒtyng liʒt . . . forto se and for to fele þe louelines of god in hý self say for þat tyme and for þat moment lost alle þe mynde of any good nes or of any kind nes þat en god did to him ī þis luf.[345]

> [I say that a soul touched in affection by the sensible pleasure of God as He is in himself, is a perfect soul illumined in the season[346] by the close beam of everlasting light . . . for to see and for to feel the loveliness of God in himself say for that time and for that moment, is lost all the mind of any goodness or of any kindness that in God did to him in this life.]

The MS. is highly charged with mystical meaning as it speaks of the perfection of the soul through "the close beam" of divine light. It is significant too in directing our attention to the end of the Mystic Way which is the complete absorption of the mind in the Creator.

In *East Coker* the theme of liberation shifts from this illuminative vision and takes the form of "dancing around the bonfire,"[347] the happy "association of man and woman"[348] who are

> keeping time,
> Keeping the rhythm in their dancing
> As in their living in the living seasons[349]

of their rustic lives that are reminiscent of the eternal cycle of growth and decay; in *The Dry Salvages* it is a perilous sea voyage, a "fare forward"[350] rather than a farewell that frees consciousness from "the menace and caress of wave"[351] and "the oppression of the silent fog,"[352] a relaxation "from grief into relief";[353] and in *Little Gidding* it is the spiritual exploration of the way to the "secluded chapel,"[354] the mystical recognition of the "timeless moments"[355] of history,[356] which are experienced "here" in the Huntingdonshire village of Nicholas Ferrar in the eternal Now[357] that is free "from the future as well as the past."[358]

This major theme links the world of time to eternity by piercing through "the unattended/Moment"[359] that is "in and out of time"[360]—the demarcation between ordinary consciousness and super-awareness, immanence and transcendence, spatialization and simultaneity. It is the moment of full maturity that is rarely experienced in our lives. It speaks of the completeness of "being" and the totality of the mystical perception which appear to us as fragmentary because of the distractions of "this twittering world"[361] and the presence of "Garlic and sapphires in the mud"[362] that exemplify the modes of irreconciliation and the pairs of opposites which are the source of conflict. The muddy sapphires too denote the deception of the sensuous world and the illusion in which we are living. They do not allow for any possibility of the clarity of perception which is here bedimmed and screened behind our muddled knowledge. It is a happy example of the type of world in which the majority of people are living and from which they are in most cases unwilling to seek deliverance.

These themes of mystical philosophy are woven together in a network characterized by integrity that at times betrays certain inconsistencies, for example,

> Do not let me hear
> Of the wisdom of old men, but rather of their folly,[363]

or

> The serenity only a deliberate hebetude
> The wisdom only the knowledge of dead secrets,[364]

or

> the past is all deception,
> The future futureless.[365]

The folly of "old men" and the wisdom of "dead secrets" do not conform to the poet's notion of the mystical rehabilitation of history and the consistency of tradition. The "deception" of "the past" falls short in illustrating the idea that

> the past experience revived in the meaning
> Is not the experience of one life only
> But of many generations.[366]

With the revivification of "the past," the futurelessness of "the future" sounds inaccurate as the poet in the opening lines of *Burnt Norton* states that "time future"[367] is contained "in time past"[368] and both are intimately related to each other.

The *Quartets,* at any rate, have exhibited the way of loosening the age-old fetters of "time" by giving a glimpse of eternity as portrayed in the rose-garden, but the partial relief from worldly chaos which we may attain is not based on a fully fledged synthesis between worldliness and otherworldliness. These poems, reviewed collectively, have offered no solution to the monstrous acts and evils that disturb the world. The poet, in Mr. Harding's view,

> besides displaying little faith in a revolt against anything outside himself, . . . in his recent work[369] [he] never invites you to believe that everything undesirable in you is due to outside influences that can be blamed for tampering with your original rightness.[370]

Eliot has concentrated upon the inward world of the soul and has obviously worked out its progression along the way to Perfection at the expense of disregarding the "outside influences" that handicap it. And though he himself confesses in *The Idea of a Christian Society* that

> a negative culture has ceased to be efficient in a world where economic as well as spiritual forces are proving the efficiency of cultures which, even when pagan, are positive,[371]

his *Quartets* work on the negative side and have left the practicability of a positivistic experience untouched. They offer no possibility for a reconstruction of the trammels that beset our existence. They have provided only the constant stress on the theme of suffering and the possibility of struggle, but there are no traces of a final reconciliation between meditation and experience,[372] passivity and activity,[373] negation and affirmation.[374]

The way the poet has chosen is the negative way of renunciation:

> I said to my soul, be still, and wait without hope
> For hope would be hope for the wrong thing; wait without love
> For love would be love of the wrong thing; there is yet faith
> But the faith and the love and the hope are all in the waiting.[375]

Eliot's *Via Negativa* is not only Dantean in character but the Dark Night of the Soul plays a fundamental role in accomplishing the effect of purification. With St. John of the Cross mystical "darkness" is essentially purgatorial and it results in the ascent of the soul to Mount Carmel, symbol of perfection, whence it is united with the Absolute and attains divine wisdom and salvation. With Eliot, in agreement with the Spanish mystic, the soul takes the mystical "ladder" for its progression; but its development after the refining process is left incomplete. After the attainment of wisdom or perfection, the return to the ordinary conditions of life for sociological and spiritual amelioration sounds plausible. We hear only the appeal to the "Queen of Heaven"[376] for intercession and salvation of those who are bound to the wheel of time. For the completeness of the cycle, suffering should be followed by activity. Inward purification, therefore, is of little value unless it is given expression on a wide scale in the bigger community, otherwise it will remain individualistic.

Conclusion

The early poems depict the soul in a state of scrutiny and discovery of all its surroundings. The poet has taken individual cases like the neurotic Prufrock, the sarcastic Mr. Apollinax, the introvert Gerontion, and the reckless Sweeney to portray aspects of modern life which hamper mystical development insofar as they are symptomatic of desolation and regression toward an unpredictable doom.

These phases of psychic malady are only epitomes of the general all-encompassing degeneration that characterizes the years which followed World War I. Only images of decay and anarchy could visualize the state of a land laid waste and a virility lost through an abuse of sex. It is the decline of "belief" that has led to the vacuity of life.

From this inward and outward sterility, the soul had to seek deliverance and thus we get the theme of oscillation between the claims of the flesh and the spirit in the *Ariel Poems*. It is not armed yet with faith and still gives heed to worldly attractions even in *Ash Wednesday* when ritual and dogma give hope for the possibility of revivification.

But the hope is still ambivalent and the agony that characterizes the bitter struggle of *Ash Wednesday* gives vent to the backward and forward travels of the soul in the *Four Quartets* with the view of gaining fresh experience and coming to terms with reality partly through an attempt to solve the riddle of "time" and partly through the realization of the creativeness of the eternal moments of history. The mystical journey as Eliot envisaged it will take us to the saintly point of intersection which is the crystallization of impersonality and simultaneity. I take it to be the focalization of all the experienced activities portrayed in the previous poems. They were all driving to this ultimate end and were working for its full realization. They are to be interpreted, moreover, with the view of throwing light on the *Quartets;* and, in a sense, the earlier poems compose the foundation upon which the edifice of the later poems takes shape. Not only are the beginning and the end symmetrical but one may find in the *Quartets* themes and images that have undergone certain changes, as "experience" throughout the whole of the poems deepens and meaning consequently gains profundity.

The poems that appeared before *The Waste Land* are more or less characterized by egocentricity and the naiveté of a marginal life that seeks its own selfish ends. Baffled by their practical inability to attain what they are craving for, Prufrock and his compeers revert to dreamful projections of past experiences on which they relish.

On the other hand, the theme of an egocentric life diminishes gradually in *The Waste Land* and the poems that follow it. The poet himself claimed that

the end of the enjoyment of poetry is a pure contemplation from which all the accidents of personal emotion are removed; thus we aim to see the object as it really is.[1]

This trend of impersonality is exemplified in the happy choice of Tiresias, the blind Greek seer of visions, who was able to predict the loss of chastity and the chaos of the "new" life. The protagonists of *Ash Wednesday* and the *Four Quartets* are following the same lines of this legendary figure in their distrust and suspicion of anything that may lead the soul astray.

Behind all the poems, however, there is an insistent theme that binds the whole of their bulk together—the soul that seeks salvation. In the early poems, it is handicapped by the "hundred indecisions"[2] of a Prufrock, the "self-possession"[3] of a lady that has passed the prime of life, the shaking of memory at midnight that throws up "a crowd of twisted things"[4] (like the mutterings of a streetlamp and the smell of cocktails in bars), the craving for lust in *The Waste Land,* and the meaningless hope of "The Hollow Men." But the soul is unable to proceed toward "divine union, until it has divested itself of the love of created beings."[5] It had to pass not through the damned state of darkness toward which the early figures of Eliot are inevitably doomed, that is, the smoky atmosphere that envelops their urban lives or the sepulchral darkness which "covers" them, but through the mystical darkness which is necessary for purgation: "I said to my soul, be still, and let the dark come upon you/Which shall be the darkness of God."[6] This cleansing darkness is "not here"[7] in "this twittering world,"[8] but in the world of visionary perception. It is not even where you exist, for, as St. John of the Cross puts it in Eliot's quotation: "Where you are is where you

are not,"[9] in the mystic-poet's presumption that one is still
farther away from "the still point of the turning world";[10] and "in
order to arrive there,"[11] as Eliot tells us, "You must go by a way
wherein there is no ecstasy"[12] for the ecstatic vision comes only
where the way terminates. Hence, "the darkness shall be the
light"[13] of revelation and the period of struggle and aridity
is crowned with the blessedness of divine love.

Another factor that contributes to this act of purification is
the element of fire which may operate on two different levels.
It is the fire of dusk that buries a day in the miserable life of
Prufrock; the fire of the "four wax candles in the darkened
room"[14] of a lady who feels that her life will be soon blown
out after her friend's departure; the conflagration that has burnt
out the "smoky days"[15] of a suffocating life; the consuming
element in the licentious life of the barbarous king and
Philomel,[16] Sweeney and Mrs. Porter,[17] the clerk of the house
agent and the typist;[18] and the smashing power behind the
parade of "triumphal March." Against this victimizing force is
the image of fire that "eats up" our sins and is inevitably
linked with mystical suffering and Platonic love. It is the refining fire of "the penitential gates"[19]

> Where the souls of the devout
> Burn invisible and dim,[20]

and it is also the cleansing fire of the Crucifixion which re-
flects its torchlight redness on the "sweaty faces"[21] of the gathering soldiers and mob near Golgotha.

But the two levels of the fire-symbolism as a destructive and
creative force are mixed together in the mythological image of
Nessus' "intolerable shirt of flame"[22] and in Hercules' "choice
of pyre or pyre"[23] which will lead to his redemption "from
fire by fire."[24] As the motivating power behind the hands that
wove the shirt is love, the resultant image operates on a third
level to imply love in its possessiveness. In a further and more
elaborate development, the redeeming fire may be mated
with celestial love in the mystical image of the "crowned knot"[25]
where the fire of purgatory and the rose of divine love are in-
folded in this multiple image.

Even the image of the ghost has received certain startling
alterations in the very process of its development so as to be
imbued in the *Quartets* with mystical connotations that have

their purgatorial significance. In *The Waste Land* the inhabitants are haunted by the Baudelairian "spectre" which appears at midday. In *Ash Wednesday* the protagonist's bewilderment is mixed with pity for those mortals who are "struggling with the devil of the stairs"[26] whose deceit tyrannizes them. But these haunting traits are eclipsed with the appearance of the "Woodthrush singing through the fog"[27] giving Pericles hope for mystical revival, with the hovering too of the bird that led the protagonist of *Burnt Norton* to the ecstasy of the rose-garden, with the unfelt presence of Christ on the way to Emmaus, and with the dove of the Holy Ghost that "breaks the air/With flame of incandescent terror"[28] in its descent upon the Disciples. It is the white dove of the Pentecost that "is tongued with fire"[29] for the resurrection of humanity in contradistinction of "the dark dove"[30] that causes destruction and loss of victims with its "flickering tongue."[31] This image has developed also to the "familiar compound ghost"[32] who left Purgatory to join the poet in his "raid on the inarticulate"[33] so as "to get the better of words."[34] The coming of this familiar ghost during the air raid with the poet as warden is not an accident. They are both armed with poetic tradition and their common concern is "to conquer"[35] the "shabby equipment"[36] and "the general mess"[37] of language in order to attain "the complete consort"[38] of preciseness and perfectibility.

Eliot has used all these images in order to portray certain aspects of the psychic and the spiritual life in relation to different modes of experience. They have helped him elaborate a further thematic study of a soul not only seeking salvation through purgatorial efficacy but obsessed with the very idea of truth and perfection. This theme originates in *The Waste Land* in the restlessness of the soul which is unable to find satisfaction in any real ideology. In *Ash Wednesday* the problem is partly solved through the protagonist's acquiescence of the validity of dogma, but his conviction is neither wholehearted nor is it the result of a deeply felt "belief." His renunciation is partial and his hope for the "wisdom of humility" is disturbed by many physical and worldly distractions. In the *Four Quartets* this theme of perfectibility gains a firm foothold when the protagonist is exposed to nearly all the sublimities of mystic revelation with the experience of the *Rosa Mystica* (the illuminative vision of divine love) and the stillness of the eternal moment. His self-scrutiny has shifted here to a completely different level, obviously giving way to a serious engagement with eternal verities and wisdom.

In this sense, if satire dominates the earlier poems, the insistent theme in the later ones is the soul's quest for the absoluteness of Being. Its search for Truth could be interpreted in terms of a psychological satisfaction for it will provide her with a shelter against the waywardness of the world. But we are asked to understand that this final abode is difficult to attain mainly because it is not easy to acquire a true sense of submission.

Again, in the light of the foregoing discussion, it is difficult to say that the "early Eliot" is an agnostic whereas Eliot of the later poems is religious for that would result in a dichotomy from which the poet is obviously free. This line of thought, at any rate, does not constitute a major trend in the criticism of the poetic output of Eliot. In my interview with the poet on October 19, 1961, I raised this matter saying that "some critics separate the early poems from the later ones and place a sharp line of demarcation between 'The Hollow Men' and *Ash Wednesday*. To what extent do you agree?" He answered that "there is obviously a line after 'The Hollow Men,' but this does not break the integrity of the whole thing." Both the earlier and the later poems are in many ways intimately related to each other, and the homogeneity of the whole bulk is maintained by the consistency of thematic and imagistic developments which are marked throughout the individual components. The only exception—the single example of abrupt transition—is the unbridgeable gulf that separates the *Ariel Poems* and *Ash Wednesday* where the divorce between form and content leaves certain motifs underdeveloped. Had the poet traced them to maturity, no such vacuum would have been the dominant feature of such a period.

The religious nature of the later poems, moreover, has its counterpart in the earlier ones and both are linked through reference to certain mystically eschatological themes which are stressed from the very outset. Obsession with "matter" is death to the "spirit" and engagement in modes of transiency is the barrier that screens eternal realities. From "Whispers of Immortality" in which we witness Webster who

was much possessed by death
And saw the skull beneath the skin,[39]

and

knew that thought clings round dead limbs,[40]

we pass to the physical and spiritual death of *The Waste Land*. The atmosphere is peopled here with various embodiments of lust, abortion and moral anarchy which are relentlessly carried away to a predetermined doom in the "empty" desolation of the tumbling graves. Yet, "The awful daring of a moment's surrender"[41] of those who have gone throughout the Inferno of Self and "responded/Gaily"[42]

To controlling hands[43]

and to a thundering wisdom coming from the East, will inevitably snatch them from the horrors of life without "belief." Instead of passing to vacuity as the Hollow Men do, they enjoy the company of the "violent souls"[44] of those who have crossed peacefully "to death's other Kingdom."[45] Their peaceful death is indicative of a firm conviction which is still inexperienced by the Magi who have witnessed the Birth of Christ. To them it is a "Hard and bitter agony."[46] For Simeon "death" is primarily sacrificial for he says:

I am dying in my own death and the deaths of those after me,[47]

but he is unable to mount "the saints' stair"[48]

Not for me the martyrdom, the ecstasy of thought and prayer,
Not for me the ultimate vision.[49]

In these words of Simeon the two themes of death and ecstatic vision are brought together; the former has developed from corporeal to psychological and spiritual death, the latter from the hallucinatory reminiscences of Prufrock or an elderly woman in "Portrait of a Lady" or Gerontion on the departure of youth to the visions of Tiresias in *The Waste Land* concerning the "unreal City"[50] and its inhabitants. Here a new element is added and this is the prophecy of the protagonist about the collapse of the whole edifice of civilization, the ruins of time, and the possibility of lightning and rain bringing forth spiritual rebirth.

But this theme of visionary perception parts company again with the corollary one of the macabre pronouncements. And in "Animula" the image is limited to "the fragrant brilliance of the Christmas tree,"[51] or the outward sensuous implication of "a flat world of changing lights and noise."[52] In the often-neglected or little known poem *The Cultivation of Christmas Trees* the image shifts to the child who

> wonders at the Christmas tree:
> Let him continue in the spirit of wonder
>
> .   .   .   .
>
> So that the reverence and the gaiety
> May not be forgotten in later experience,
> In the bored habituation, the fatigue, the tedium,
> The wareness of death.[53]

Here the image of death is partly linked with the boredom of life and partly with the pleasurable experience of reminiscence.

For the inner significance and the hidden meaning of a vision, we had to go to *Ash Wednesday* where the soul, though still disturbed by the waywardness of the egoistic self, exerts certain efforts for concentration on righteousness and the Mystic Way to it. Images range from the mundane to the sublime, from life pictured as a valley full of broken bones to prayer for a "silent" death (and here again the two themes are associated). The image of the protagonist's struggle for spiritual revivification gains profundity through its linkage with the distractions and torments that agitate his soul at every turning of his spiral ascent. It is also imbued with holiness in its association with the Services of the Mass, with contemplative devotion, and the figures of the veiled Sister and the Virgin Mother.

In the *Four Quartets* mystical visions of the highest order have given these poems richness in connotation, depth in meaning and, at the same time, complexity in understanding. Some of them have their echoes in previous poems, as "The surface glittered out of heart of light"[54] which refers to the "drained pool" of *Burnt Norton* that recalls the words of *The Waste Land:* "I knew nothing/Looking into the heart of light, the silence."[55] And the image of the "wheel," symbol of the ever-going pattern of suffering, which occurs in the Heraclitean epigraph to the *Four Quartets* (that is, of the sameness of the upward and downward movements) recalls

> O you who turn the wheel and look to windward,
> Consider Phlebas, who was once handsome and tall as you[56]

in "Death by Water" with the implication not only of suffering
but of predestination; also the turning "round the prickly pear"[57]
of "The Hollow Men" signifying attachment to a "thorny"
destiny; and

> the light shone in darkness and
> Against the World the unstilled world still whirled
> About the centre of the silent Word[58]

of *Ash Wednesday* denoting the worldly movement against the
symbol of the Incarnation.

At the center of the wheel there is the "still point" which is
a predominant image in Eliot's poetry for it marks the culmination of the foregoing theme of visionary perception. It is also
the meeting center of most of the other themes and images for it
is related to the world of movement and stillness: "There would
be no dance, and there is only the dance."[59] It is the pattern
where images of life and death, time and eternity, become
meaningful. Through it we come to understand "The release
from action and suffering,"[60] that is, the purposeless action
of the early poems and the sufferings of an Inferno and a
Purgatorio which are characteristic of the poems that appeared
after the group *Ara Vos Prec* (1920). It helps us also get to
know the

> release from the inner
> And the outer compulsion—[61]

that is, the strife that causes our disturbance. Evidently it is a
"cosmic image" insofar as it interprets the universe and its
realities which is the major concern of mystical philosophy.

The theme of death, moreover, is associated with mystical
rebirth of which the figures of *The Waste Land* are deprived.
Of all the *Ariel Poems,* it is only in "Marina" that we witness
the daughter in a regenerate state: "This form, this face, this life/
Living to live in a world of time beyond me,"[62] which are the
words of her father (Pericles) after her revival. In *Ash Wednesday* it is "The dreamcrossed twilight between birth and dying"[63]
which is no more than the hope of the protagonist for a moment
of insight. In the *Four Quartets* the laughter of the children
in the shrubbery points

> to the agony
> Of death and birth[64]

and to the "distraction fit"[65] which is

> Only a flicker
> Over the strained time-ridden faces,[66]

of those who are still "Caught in the form of limitation"[67] to "the waste sad time."[68] It is also the glimpse of "light" betrayed from "the kingfisher's wing."[69] After this point, however, our theme reaches its climax in the poet's emphasis that in order to be "born with the dead"[70] we had to consider that "the time of death is every moment"[71] in matter of readiness, and that mystical rebirth is "a lifetime's death in love"[72] which associates this theme with selfless benevolent action.

This cross-fertilization between mystic imagery and philosophical theme has given the poet a wider scope of expression. Scenic enrichment is the legitimate offspring of their growth; and their embellishment with ethical verities has given us a deeper interpretation of the permanent "universals" behind existence. They have, in this sense, added to our experience of reality and have thrown some light on our visualization of eternity.

In conclusion, I am inclined to stress the fact that there is a degree of philosophical reciprocity among all these various components which have enlivened the "meaning" of the universe. Though the ensuing concept is one of organic completion, the impression conveyed is that of a biased outlook (for example, in the *Quartets*). The imagery works for the communication of completeness and transcendence, but the resultant effect is what one might call an "envisaged partiality."

The Eliotesque image is, in this sense, an amalgam of visibility and unknowability, possibility and ineffability—a comparatively rare unit that has precisely interpreted the realm of suprarationality. And, with its involvement in the spatially and temporally symbolic in its relatedness to the visionary eternal, his poetic image can easily fit in with the mystic vision. The idea is hinted at even shortly after the publication of the *Quartets* in one volume with the reviewer's remark:

> Since the Inarticulate that Eliot has raided, and raided with complete success, is the realm of mystic vision, one has to be diffident in criticising, or even discussing, his content.[73]

The critic takes for granted the verbal medium whereby the visionary perception is rendered possible. The whole raid is directed against the inadequacy of our syntactical media in interpreting a sublime vision. The affinities, in fact, between the poetic non-secular image and the mystic vision,[74] as far as the *Quartets* are concerned, depend so much on the emotional and intellectual resoluteness with which we approach the poems. That the images of the poet have struck a deeper chord of the awareness of time and eternity and freedom from the fatalistic world bear sufficient evidence that the resemblance is not only striking but intensifying for both. They are drawn together, neither by way of yoking nor obliqueness, but through a grafting process that enlivens their audo-tactility and their eclecticism.

The poems, particularly the later ones, thus reveal certain traces of the mystic image, but the visionary perception with which they are imbued never develops to a state of union with the Absolute. Obviously the *Quartets* have given us some touches of the illuminative vision of the mystic, but these poems, on the whole, do not sanction the unification with God as the consummation of the Mystic Way. Though we have certain glimpses of Dante's Paradiso like the "Multifoliate rose" of "The Hollow Men," the "veiled sister" of the Terrestrial Paradise of *Ash Wednesday,* the garden of *Burnt Norton* and the Queen of Heaven of *The Dry Salvages,* the experience projected is mainly that of a Purgatorio.

In this way, the poems depict the stages of the spiritual development along the Mystic Way up to the perception of visions.[75] It seems that Eliot was aware of the fact that

> Words strain,
> Crack and sometimes break, under the burden,
> Under the tension,[76]

and thus left the more sublime experience of union and extinction[77] to the orthodox mystics.

Psychologically Eliot could not give us an exact picture of the saintly experience as portrayed by true mystics. He mused on the theme of "time," but not with the same ardor of the deeply rooted and inborn "faith" of St. Augustine who associates it with the notion of expectation and redemption;[78] he deals with "the dark night," but he lacks the scrupulous power of dissection as St. John of the Cross takes us from one division to another through a series of pictorial images; he refers also to the sublimity of "divine love," but the penetrating vision of the anonymous mystic who manages to associate contemplation with everyday practicability in *The Cloud of Unknowing* is beyond his reach. The "silent sister" of his *Ash Wednesday* too lacks the initiative of a St. Teresa or the dynamism of a Beatrice.

It is obvious that Eliot in his mystical philosophy is influenced by the modern trends of thought. His references to the various types of mysticism are accomplished through the projection of certain representational figures that are cited to suit his purpose. But his attempt at developing the themes which they invoke is not sufficiently evidenced in his later poems. Apart from the misunderstanding and gaps with which the reader is left, the relationships among his themes exist only in sharp contrasts. But the two camps, so to speak, of contemporaneity and antiquity, of undecipherable vagueness and formulated classicism, neither fall into combat nor come to an agreement. The result is the sense of "hesitant approach" that characterizes the later poems. Had the poet applied his theory of the consistency of tradition to the entire body of his works and then traced these themes to the end of the journey, that is, envisaging an issue whether by way of reconciliation or separateness but within a clear-cut view or a worked-out framework, no such obstructions would have been raised, against which we had to grapple for an integral appreciation of the poems.

Eliot, however, sought a way out of this dilemma through flight into dogmatic and mystical religion. It is as if he has grown impatient with common mundane existence and finds refuge from the waves of doubt and anxiety that characterize the early poems in an institutional Church. His attitude, in this sense, is quasi-similar to George Herbert, for the latter was still distracted by worldly pleasures even after taking orders in 1626:

> Recover all thy sigh-blown-age
> On double pleasures, leave thy cold dispute
> of What is fit, and not.[79]

Eliot's development is the more consistent and one feels that the poet was on his guard against this theme of regression as he paves the way for man's spiritual development. The chain of distractions which continued to disturb him as far as *Ash*

Wednesday was loosened in the *Four Quartets* with the passage of the soul through purgatorial darkness.

On the whole, his poems after *The Waste Land* give an open expression to a lurking spiritual nostalgia at which he has been driving from the start. The subject-matter and a great deal of his symbolism are drawn from the liturgy of the Church (*Ash Wednesday*), from the Gospel ("A Song for Simeon") and from Hindu and Spanish mysticism (*Four Quartets*). Even the ritualist themes of the ancient cults in *The Waste Land*—let alone the Buddha and St. Augustine—do not only give evidence of the mystical connotations of the poems but help to stress the spiritual trend against which their whole bulk could be interpreted.

In no place are we left with the impression that the poet is trying to extol the spiritual value of any mystical religion at the expense of the other. From the outset and most particularly in *The Waste Land* and the poems that appeared after it, Christian mysticism is noticeable side by side with either Hinduist or Buddhist mysticism and the theme of parallelism runs throughout the whole of the poems, in spite of the doctrinal differences that separate them. Both Hinduism and Buddhism seek the dissolution of the false self and even the annihilation of the ego, whereas Christianity looks for the beatific vision of the purified ego as an assessment of saintly life. The one runs after self-effacement and considers it essential before any approach is made toward true knowledge; the other approaches the mystical state of transcendence through cleansing "the doors of perception" without abolishing them.

But there are common grounds on which these religions meet. In my interview with the poet, he gave me the following answer to my question: "Do you think that Buddhism, Hinduism and Christianity work for the same purpose irrespective of the sacramental differences among them, at least from the mystical point of view?" "Yes. One can't believe in them all. One should have 'a' faith. I think Christianity has more in common with the Buddhist Sutra which states that Buddha will come back for the salvation of others. These religions are in common in love, in charity and in seeking salvation." They are notably alike too in the fields of detachment from "matter" and renunciation of all types of possessiveness. These features play fundamental roles in bringing about the necessary redemption which may ensue in the rescue of mortals from imminent loss. It is no wonder, then, that this major theme is given full vent in a life imaged as an Inferno (in the early poems together with *The Waste Land* and "The Hollow Men"), a spiral ascent of a Purgatorio (in *Ash Wednesday*) and a mystical "ladder" that may take the agonized soul upward to the source of peace and divine love (in *Burnt Norton*).

It is difficult and even impossible for this theme of renunciation to operate unless it is coupled with the subduing of our self-will. Its absence has led to the perplexity of a Prufrock, to the incompetence of a Gerontion, the wayward strife of a Tiresias, the unregenerate death of a Phoenician Sailor and to the vacuity of a Hollow Man. Without the control ("Damyata") preached by the Upanishad sages when it is mated with Christian humility and love, "time" will remain unredeemed because the souls that are launched adrift its seas have missed the "rock" and only cling to any floating wreckage.

The necessary submission that is associated with this *Via Negativa* does not end in sheer meekness but it aims at the regaining of the lost Eden of *Burnt Norton,* the recovery of the desolate self of *The Waste Land,* and the revivification of the "dry bones" of *Ash Wednesday.* Eliot has, in fact, left the matter at this point without giving it the necessary development. Again, in my interview with him, he confessed in his usually humble way that his "solution is not final, but it is as far as [he] can go."[80] The yearning for regeneration or the passage from despair to hope, needs the orientation of mysticism toward socially constructivist channels.

Here lies the main reason why the poems of Eliot particularly the later ones appeal only to a limited number of the intelligentsia. Although he himself confesses that a poet "would like to convey the pleasures of poetry, not only to a larger audience, but to larger groups of people collectively,"[81] one is persuaded to stress the fact that most of his poems convey their message only to a small minority and as such they are isolated from the sociological concern of the majority of people. The poet, as Mr. Hamilton has rightly pointed out, "is out of touch with the active virtue and strength which even to-day survive in ordinary men, and which make the drama of their life worth while."[82] As early as 1930 we come across the following words in a review of J. Middleton Murry's *'God: Being an Introduction to the Science of Metabiology':* "I am quite in accord [with Mr. Murry] that no mystical experience in and by itself can be for human beings the guarantee of anything, as it must itself be verified in daily life."[83] But it seems that Eliot has abandoned this attitude as one feels that the gulf between "mystical experience" and "daily life" has been broadened in the later poems. In the *Four Quartets* he does not attempt to solve the issues that he partly tackled in *The Waste Land* and "The Hollow Men." He is not concerned—as Mr. Spender puts it—

> with saving the world: reformers seem to him as irrelevant as anything else in the objects that surround him. His poetry simply develops from an original position in which it questions the possibility even of damnation, to a firm belief, in his most recent poetry, in the possibility of personal salvation.[84]

Thus the riddle of existence, the cleavage of society, the restlessness of humanity, the haunting awe of annihilation, are all left without giving us the necessary relief in the form of a satisfactory solution. This does not mean that the poet should be a sociologist nor does it imply a restatement of existing ideological pronouncements. At the same time, he is not completely severed from all of them for it is through his poetic medium that he seeks order in chaos and everlastingness in the transitoriness of contemporaneity.

In his essay on *The Social Function of Poetry*, Eliot states that "the business of a poet is to express the culture in which he lives, and to which he belongs."[85] This—he continues—is not meant

> to imply that the poet has to approve the society in which he lives: to express an actual culture, and to approve a social situation, are two quite different things. This expression of his culture, indeed, may set the poet into violent opposition to a social situation which violates that culture.[86]

Although "expression" may lead to disapproval and sometimes to violation, the process would undoubtedly appear incomplete. We only destroy in order to rebuild, and the reconstruction of the previous problems, whether they are psychological or sociological, on positivistic levels, sounds laudable after the demolishing act. Applying this view to the poems of Eliot and bearing in mind their mystical interpretation, one is inclined to conclude that the soul which has been exposed to the Purgatorio of *Ash Wednesday* and the *Four Quartets,* should emerge from the cleansing experience armed with faith and ready to enlighten the numberless masses who are driven headlong to material captivity.

Consequently, I hold the *Via Negativa* not to be the ultimate end of mysticism. It is only a means that leads to the unitive experience which in its turn should blossom in sociological benevolence. The mystically purified soul that has experienced the beatific vision is the one that reacts spontaneously even on the most infertile soil.

To grasp the meaning of this trend which is termed "mysticism in activity," I refer by way of comparison to the mystico-ethical practicability of Albert Schweitzer in whom we get a type of renunciation that is coupled with what I may call the *Via Affirmativa.* In his devotion to the service of humanity and in taking an active part to relieve others from misery, he was putting into practice the theories he used to preach in the Church of St. Nicholas, Strasbourg. His approach is the exact reverse of Eliot's passivity and it is with the help of the German theologian that sociological mysticism bears its blossoms.

The theme of love that we witnessed in the *Quartets* of Eliot is brought here to maturity through Schweitzer's preoccupation with the elements of evil and suffering in human life and his firm resolution to mitigate pain through his medical services. His colossal efforts in this field speak of a philanthropy of the highest order.

Eliot's meditation on the eternal moments of history is re-molded by Schweitzer not into a mystifying system of speculation but into a humane identity with the pains and agonies of his fellowmen. The aim of the German scholar is to reinterpret the contemporaneity of history insofar as it is intimately related to the social and ethical dilemmas of our time. And so he affirms that

> we must reconcile ourselves to the fact that Jesus' religion of love made its appearance as part of a system of thought that anticipated a speedy end of the world. We cannot make it our own through the concepts in which he proclaimed it but must rather translate it into those of our modern view of the world.[87]

It is this penetration into the present world and its problems, which is left either vague or incomplete by Eliot, that enables us to approximate the otherworldliness. Schweitzer begins with the rational and soon shifts to elevated planes of experience because the ethical with him "surpasses the rational and enters the sphere of the supra-rational which is the spiritual, the mystical."[88] But this transition from rationality to ethical mysticism is left undefined by him save the usage of his favorite terminology of the "will-to-live" which marks volition and "life-affirmation" which indicates morally serviceable deeds.

In agreement with his views, however, the drawback of old and modern "mysticism"

> is that of becoming supra-ethical, that is to say, of making the spirituality associated with the being-in-eternity an end in itself . . . Its efforts are directed only towards attaining for the individual man, through initiation, the assurance of immortality. It does not urge the man, born again to new life, to live as a new person an ethical life in the world.[89]

From this view the whole trend of "seclusion" that is related to the subject, has evolved. Its shortcomings have been mostly felt in the field of theology and ethics whence the mystical experience has been limited to quietistical piety irrespective of the claims of the community. The result is a quasi-moral system that encourages spiritual exercises at the expense of communal relief.

But it is worth remarking at this point that Schweitzer's mysticism is positivistic in character, although his Christian "belief" is not the orthodox type. He does not countenance ascetic and visionary pursuits as ends in themselves and here he stands in striking opposition to T. S. Eliot. The German theologian too does not consider transcendentalism essential in his moral gospel, but takes righteousness to be the core of his ethical theory.

Schweitzer basically aims at the regeneration of humanity and his optimistic outlook is inextricably intermingled with his belief that "decadence changes into renaissance as soon as ethical activities are set to work again in our convictions and in the ideas which we undertake to stamp upon reality."[90] This pronouncement applies to the *Quartets* of Eliot who has undertaken the task of stamping the necessity of inward purification if ever we aim at the mystical revelation of reality and live in "peace" with the eternal verities of the universe; but he has left the process open. Here the cycle is brought to completion through the "ethical activities" of Schweitzer which are the outward manifestation of our deep convictions.

In this sense, it is futile to spray the leaves as Eliot has done in his later poems, when bacteria are multiplying among the withering subterranean tumors. To unearth the evils that haunt humanity particularly today, a reestablishment of moral values sounds plausible. Both illusion and tyranny that are eating up the body of the human community will never be fully eradicated unless we realize that the great masses of mortals need both ethical and spiritual guidance and are capable of improving. The poet himself announced that

> we must believe, first, that the human race can, if it will, improve indefinitely; that it can improve both its material well-being and its spiritual capacities. We must also have a conception of a perfect society attainable on earth.[91]

In fact, not only has automatic material "happiness" generated jealousy among human beings but it has also become an incentive of strife and friction. Any perpetuation of this short-sighted policy is a momentary inoculation that keeps the dying body alive for a short while, but it is bound, sooner or later, to collapse. For its survival, economic as well as ethical "nurture" is substantial not only for the physique of the individual but for that of civilization too. Upon the degree of reciprocity between both, in my view, rests the well-being of the world and the assurance of a fearless prospective.

These statements are not hostile to mysticism, for any theory of mystical philosophy—however sound it may appear—that disregards the claims of the community, is incomplete and is bound to exist only in abstraction. Sociological mysticism continues the same route that commences with passive meditation. Bias and indifference are the major causes of the shrinkage that is marked in both literary and philosophical circles in dealing with the problem in its totality.

The *Quartets* of Eliot have elaborately expressed this attitude of indifference in relation to the spiritual well-being of the individual who sought his salvation in a Purgatorio passing through a "dark night" and a "cloud of unknowing." But the supreme issue of communal delivery from the ever-persistent awe that disturbs our very existence is left untouched. The attitude of neutrality which they extol has perpetuated the meaningful "quest" after many vital problems. As they become deeply rooted through the passage of time, it is difficult to disentangle them. The waves of doubt and atheism that have beset the world of ethics have also left their impress on the economic as well as the material flourishing of the society. This is why it is difficult to seek deliverance in a chaotic society and to claim for salvation in a community where individuals are divided against themselves.

In this sense, it is essential to drive away the phantom of "fear" through a genuine realization of common fellowship not only in one's own land but in the world at large. This is a natural and logical step after creating an awareness of the previous factors and building up a scheme of values based on ethical and sociological mysticism. Loosening the fetters of individuality and breaking the chains that tie the self up are indispensable as media toward the attainment of this goal. The marks of isolation that we encounter every now and then whether in economic monopolizing, intellectual theorizing, or religious doctrinizing have kept civilization lagging behind and dropped many enlightened views in the fathomless depths of oblivion. With mutual understanding, goodwill and the creation of a real sense of likemindedness, the problems of ethics and religion, of economics and sociology, will no more trouble us. Their solution rests on the degree of realizing the significance of this prospectus. It will not be the outcome of a passive nostalgia for the "Peace which passeth understanding" but the active endeavor to emancipate humanity from the snares of greed and doubt that have ever disturbed its social as well as its spiritual growth.

With these points in view, one may conclude that Eliot, the poet, has a remarkable mystical bent of mind. Both theories and practice of mysticism, in the East and the West, in pre-Christianity and post-Renaissance, have contributed a great deal to enliven the interest in the poems and to direct our attention to the unusual note of spirituality which we have heard since the very beginning. That certain mystical "assets" have not been satisfactorily lodged is indicative that the poet's success in this respect is undeniably limited.

It is worth illustrating that this problem, at whatever level of experience we approach it, allows room for conviction that the motivation behind the whole quest is the feeling of spiritual insecurity. It is easy for the modern society to part with religion, but it is not easy for its members to find a secure shelter where they could harbor the insoluble conflicts that are devastating their inner selves. The envisaged equilibrium is neither within easy reach nor accessible to those who have given way to modes of psychic tensions and introversions.

It follows that the problem is not so much of a willing "suspension of disbelief" as the readiness of the free and enlightened thinker to heighten people's awareness of the pressing necessity of moral reform. But the recurrence of repudiations as a result of our preoccupation with transitory pursuits and obsession with the satieties of the ego will inevitably alienate us from the right "path."

It is only fair to add too that Eliot has cleared the way for further investigation in this field by devoting himself wholeheartedly to the "voice of this Calling."[92] His efforts are evidenced in many situations particularly in the *Four Quartets*. The meeting of the poet, for instance, with the Compound Ghost whose attempt is to disclose "the gifts reserved for age/To set a crown upon your lifetime's effort,"[93] speaks of a full life's devotion to the study of Letters in order to draw out certain modes of experience, both poetic and mystical, to fit in with the "tradition" of world thought.

In conformity to the mystical tradition, the poet has achieved certain success in creating an awareness of this out-of-the-ordinary range of spirituality. But it often happens that the reputations of writers suffer some sort of fluctuations and it is difficult, in this respect, to predict the "star" of Eliot. That his has been in the ascendancy is indicative that his work will continue to rank high among those of the leading figures in the mystical poetry of the world at least in the remaining years of our century. The genre of the present critical trend, at any rate, has shifted from the poet to "what the poem is." A sound assessment of the poems on psycho-metaphysical bases will not only rejuvenate the interest in their study but will reveal essential features with which one should be armed before proceeding to the intricate themes that appeared after 1920.

To round out the picture, the mystically philosophical study of the poems will not only help to fill a certain gap that was lacking, but will link contemporary English poetry with the modern trends of thought that are prevalent in Europe. If we compare Eliot, for example, with Laforgue, Gautier, Baudelaire and Rilke,[94] it will be easy for us to note that the French influence is marked in the early poems that appeared before

The Waste Land, whereas the Germano-Austrian affinity is mostly evident in the later poems particularly the *Four Quartets.* But the Italian (that is, Dante), the purely Christian, Hindu and Buddhist themes do not only cover the period between both but almost run on parallel lines throughout the entire bulk of the poetic output, giving eminence at times to either one or the other. The pre-Christian influence of anthropology appears in *The Waste Land* and dies soon after it.

In this sense, the satirically French reactions of the early period have paved the way to the more complex mystico-philosophical themes of the later one. There is obviously sufficient justification for plunging into the range of mystification which is not only the result of a major concern with mystical religion but is also the natural concomitant of the bafflement experienced in the early works. Undoubtedly one comes across certain correlations between the later and earlier poems in the way developed in the foregoing pages which bring forth the conclusion that they all compose a homogeneous work of art, organically compact though it allows for certain gaps, abrupt transitions and subjective reminiscences which are inevitable in the very process of creation. That the poet showed, moreover, a certain inability to give expression in his poetry to what he preaches in critical theory[95] is a conviction evidenced in the previously discussed cases. But one should beware of pushing the last conclusion too far. The poet himself confessed that "in one's prose reflexions one may be legitimately occupied with ideals, whereas in the writing of verse one can only deal with actuality,"[96] which speaks of the difficulty in achieving a full-fledged consistency between theory and practice.

Appendix

Rainer M. Rilke and Eliot's Four Quartets

Both Rilke and Eliot relied upon various levels of mystical experience in their attempt to interpret the human quest after reality and the mystery of "being." This vogue with the Austrian poet took the form of a system of mythology (e.g., "Sonnets to Orpheus"); with Eliot, it is the allusion to the body of tradition. Both poets join hands in their preoccupation with "the dilemma of man, with his intuition of space, confined within the dimension of time."[1] The Elegies of Rilke express this confinement and the earnest desire of the soul to experience the unseen world not by way of abandonment but through an Eliotesque reconciliation of time with the timeless. Eliot's rose-vision in *Burnt Norton* is a moment of experience that overlaps this imprisonment by peeping into the heart of reality. With Rilke

> round this
> centre the spectatorial rose
> blooms and unblossoms.[2]

The "spectatorial rose" is reminiscent of Eliot's "lotus rose"; both symbolize the mystical moments of revelation, and, though they are blooming with illuminative visions, they have not blossomed to maturity for humanity is unable to bear "very much reality"[3] in the case of Eliot, and is caught "by its own/dust-pollen"[4] and reduced to "a sham-fruit of boredom"[5] through its attachment to material and moody desires, as Rilke puts it.

Obviously both Rilke and Eliot busied themselves with the time-space binding of temporality from which no escape is possible. Even the perception of reality could only be interpreted in terms of time,

> because being here amounts to so much, because all this
> Here and Now, so fleeting, seems to require us and
> strangely
> concern us.[6]

Our concern with space and time has crystallized in the case
of Rilke into "Here and Now." With Eliot the mysticism of
space is "here and everywhere," England of the Little Gidding and the Holy Land of Jerusalem, and the mysticism of
"time" has been reduced to the eternal Now, the present moment in the garden of Burnt Norton, the time of revelation and
unfolding of reality.

The Rilkean mysticism of perception is revealed through
images of struggle: "O painful labour/Labour beyond all
strength"[7] that is borne heroically by the soul in its mystical
voyage across a "whole expanse of . . . broad watercourses"[8]
and an Eliotesque sea of agonies. In much the same way as
Eliot, Rilke associates human cares with the succession of time:

> now you were in time, and time is long,
> and time goes by, and time goes on, and time
> is like relapsing after some long illness.[9]

And, musing on this theme, he concludes that

> we keep on slipping backwards from our progress
> into some unintended thing, and there
> we get ourselves involved as in a stream,
> and there at last we die without awakening.[10]

Instead of progressing along the stream of time, we "slip"
backward into the nightmarish region of personal reverie where
we perish without acquiring this awakening of Self that we
have long been looking for.

But Rilke did not leave the matter at this unhappy ending;
he mixes this theme of time along which the soul develops with
spatial symbols that do not only represent seasonal transmutations but specific phases in the life of human beings. Speaking
of a "Bowl of Roses," he says that it is

> Living in silence, endless opening out,
> space being used, but without space being taken
> from that space which the things around diminish.[11]

Obviously the Austrian poet is going on parallel lines with those
of Eliot. The silence of the roses is the period of meditation
that ends in "opening out" endless vistas of "space" and aspects
of life.

But the two poets part company when we are faced with
Rilke's besetting anguish that disturbs his soul, rather "a sinn

of feare"[12] that used to haunt John Donne, or the "consuming agues"[13] that "swelt in ev'ry vein"[14] of Herbert urging him to put away the clerical gown and "forsake [his] cage."[15] He shares with these metaphysical poets their sense of guilt which has so much tormented their souls[16] that the growing conflict finds an outlet in rebellion. Though there are traces of this conflict in the transitional period of Eliot's *Ariel Poems,* we have never encountered a rebellious state. Turmoil with him which is the result of a dichotomy between the two worlds of phenomenality and revelation usually boils down either to a state of seclusion as in "Animula" or to spiritual nostalgia as in the "Journey of the Magi" and "Marina." With Rilke "the eternal torrent [that] whirls all the ages"[17] and "the storm of [this] roaring world,"[18] are his symbols of this strife. Their consuming force may "override us"[19] and create a perpetual tension that may lead to disastrous results.

Rilke was, above all, obsessed with the conflict between body and soul which originates in what he calls the "hidden guilty river-god of the blood"[20] that recalls to mind "the trilling wire in the blood"[21] in the *Quartets* of Eliot. The notion is not far removed from the soul's complaint of being

> hung up, as 'twere, in Chains
> Of Nerves, and Arteries, and Veins[22]

in Marvell's "Dialogue between Soul and Body." This duality with Rilke was only a prototype of the antagonism between Self and the outer communal existence. It has become more manifest in *The Book of Hours* (*Das Studen-Buch* 1899-1903) with the division of its protagonist, who is here a Russian monk, between modernity in religion and the adherence to traditional values. With this sense of ambivalence that is typical of the three parts: "The Book of Monkish Life" (1899),[23] "The Book of Pilgrimage" (1901), and "The Book of Poverty and Death" (1903) which compose this poem, the monk seeks refuge in the art of Michelangelo

> who always reappears
> when any age, to mark its closing years,
> strives yet once more to recapitulate,[24]

and derives from his paintings a wealth of aesthetic values. Again, in his search for the sublime power of God,[25] the pilgrimage of his soul is set this time toward the inward world of intuition and feeling where we listen to him speaking of the devout in terms of sensation:

> They'll feel you: as though fragrant exhalations
> were rising from some garden's presentness;
> and, as an invalid his prized possessions,
> will love you with divining tenderness.[26]

The fragrance of this intuitive world will awaken the invalidated soul to modes of refined sensibility, tenderness, and divine love. But the issue of this restraint comes in poverty that is coupled with humility, the endless wisdom of humility advocated in Eliot's *Burnt Norton,* and in an Eliotesque regenerate death of which Rilke deplores our unawareness:

> when our time has come, the dead abortion
> of our own death is all we labour for;
> that twisted, miserable embryo
> which (as in terror of some dread surprise)
> has covered with its hands its budding eyes.[27]

The poet laments the "drooping" of youth before the attainment of spiritual revivification. This is why the working out of a tapestry of illuminative visions becomes the poet's major concern in "The Book of Images" (1902-6). Figures of children and angels and scenes of landscape supply him with the envisaged state of illumination which is set against the appalling condition of Paris when he visited it in the winter of 1902-3:[28]

> Houses behind us fall upon their knees,
> alleys cringe crookedly before our train,
> squares break in flight: we summon and we seize:
> we ride, and our great horses rush like rain.[29]

The last image of fertility gives vent to the spiritual equipoise which we encounter toward the end of these poems with the protagonist's ability to loosen the fetters of this imprisonment and go "forth upright and resurrected."[30]

This poise is not achieved at the expense of the outside world. In fact, it is the result of a "mystical unison of self and the all, [a] merging of the inner and outer world"[31] through which "Rilke achieves for a while a new, childlike freedom from . . . the distressing intellectual distractions of [the] earlier years."[32] In his poems and lyrics, the Austrian poet sought the glorification of the inner self insofar as it bears relevance to

human task and man's endeavor to understand the mystery
of existence. The processes of life were for him symbolically
significant in relating the external world to ordinary morality.
With Eliot, on the contrary,

> The task of life, and of his poetry, is to enter into and con-
> form with an already existing pattern which has nothing to do
> with self. You have to go by the way of dispossession (which
> means, above all, dispossession of the self) in order to arrive
> at the place where you started, that is to say, at the point in
> the pattern which existed before you were born.[33]

The difference between Rilke and Eliot, in this respect, is one
of personal first-hand experience and that of depersonalization
in Eliot's sense. Speaking of "les conceptions religieuses du
Livre de la vie monastique," M. Angelloz describes them as

> subjectives et affectives, nées d'une tension passagère de l'âme,
> devaient avoir toute la fragilité de l'homme, et un être dont
> le moi était si peu centré encore, si instable, courait au devant
> d'une crise douloureuse.[34]

The religious views of Rilke are the result of certain sensations
that have influenced the soul, took so strong a possession of it
that they have moved the ego (i.e., *le moi*) on which they are
gradually concentrated. They usually come to life in moments
of great emotional crisis which shudder the whole being of
the poet, but they are ephemeral and can be easily eradicated.
In the case of Eliot, we had to give up subjective pursuits
so as to respond properly to preconceived patterns and eternal
values which have been "there"

> Before the beginning and after the end,[35]

and, in this sense, are not susceptible to human moods and
momentary fluctuations.

Eliot has, moreover, a religious bent of mind, and, in his
poetry, he develops a theme of mystical philosophy which he
uses as a medium in his search for the permanent and abiding
realities. Rilke, on the other hand, expounds in his works certain aesthetic values, and it seems that his association with
Rodin and his deep appreciation of his art (i.e., sculpture)
have left certain imprints on the sensibility of the poet. "Instead of living among dreams," as Sir Maurice Bowra tells
us, "he lived among works of visual art until, by a natural

process, he wished to make his own poems like them—self-sufficient, perfectly wrought and rich in content."[36] This is why his poems and lyrics abound with the sensational image:

> oh, we
> breathe ourselves out and away; from ember to ember
> yielding a fainter scent,[37]

and the pictorial image:

> this span of life might be fleeted away
> as laurel, a little darker than all
> the surrounding green, with tiny waves on the border
> of every leaf (like the smile of a wind).[38]

With Eliot, it is the auditory-elliptical image that is most striking:

> Someone frames upon the keys
> That exquisite nocturne, with which we explain
> The night and moonshine; music which we seize
> To body forth our own vacuity.[39]

The images of Rilke are thus intimately related to the work-a-day life whereas those of Eliot are transcendental in leading us to the other-worldliness.

Apart from the diversity of these views, the two poets share the same concept in their reliance upon the time-space theme in dealing with the composite wholeness of reality. For both of them, mystical experience is the ultimate realization of a close approximation between temporality and eternity which they consider essential in the unveiling process that culminates in the revelation of the essence of existence and the meaning of life. The significance of this experience, in the case of Rilke, is derived from his mysticism of "inwardness." To him "Nowhere . . . can world exist but within."[40] With Eliot it is the reality of the intuitive vision. Inwardness for Rilke, moreover, is synonymous with the primitivism of feeling; for Eliot, it is the realization of "being" in a moment of detachment. Though the approach may seem different, the two poets have in common a serious desire to apprehend Being in its totality and to unfold the mysterious meaning behind the creative processes of the world.

Notes

Notes to Chapter One

1. *The Physical Phenomena of Mysticism* (London, 1950), p. 24.
2. Dom Cuthbert Butler, *Western Mysticism: Neglected Chapters in the History of Religion* (London, 1922), p. 2.
3. "Pantheism" is the doctrine which holds that the universe is God. According to this doctrine, neither God nor anything in the universe has an independent identity distinguishable from the other. This view obviously denies personality to God and makes Him responsible for evil in the world.
4. "Transcendence" means the view that God is beyond the world. God as an essence is beyond the world for in His wholeness and over-all integrity, He is greater than it.
5. "Immanence" means the presence of God in the world. It may be complete or partial identification: absolute "immanence" of God in the universe is "pantheism"; "immanence" of God in the world but not exhausted in it is "transcendence"; absolute independence of God from the world is "deism."
6. William Ralph Inge, *Christian Mysticism*—the Bampton Lectures (London, 1899), p. 343.
7. R. C. Zehner, *Mysticism: Sacred and Profane—An Inquiry into some Varieties of Praeternatural Experience* (Oxford, 1957), p. 32.
8. Edward Gall, *Mysticism Throughout the Ages* (London, 1934), p. 15.
9. *Ibid.*, p. 17.
10. Jane (Miller) Fisher, *Mystic Gnosis* (Letchworth, 1922), p. 4.
11. *Ibid.*
12. *Ibid.*, pp. 4-5.
13. E. Holmes, *Experience and Reality* (London, 1928), p. 13.
14. Nicolas Berdyaev, *Spirit and Reality*, trans. from Russian by George Reavey (London, 1939), p. 131.
15. "Emanation" means the doctrine that all existing things have issued from the Supreme Reality or Being.
16. Evelyn Underhill, *Mysticism: A Study in the Nature and Development of Man's Spiritual Consciousness* (London, First Published 1911—Twelfth Revised Edition, 1930), p. 75.
17. A Franciscan of the thirteenth century who has been entitled the "Prince of Mystical Theologians" owing to his pious meditations on Passion and Asceticism. In his view, mystical experience is an open way to all people and not limited to an exceptional or privileged minority.

18. Summers, p. 52.

19. Fisher, p. 13.

20. Berdyaev, p. 136.

21. *Ibid.*, p. 137.

22. *Ibid.*, p. 142.

23. St. Athanasius fought heroically against the Arian doctrine, that the Son is a creation out of nothing and that He is foreign to the Divine.

24. James Hastings (ed.), *Encyclopaedia of Religion and Ethics*, Vol. VIII (Edinburgh, 1915), p. 784.

25. Felix Vernet, *Medieval Spirituality*, trans. by the Benedictines of Talacre (London, 1930), p. 215.

26. In the "Deuxième Partie" of his "discours," Descartes refers to the reasoning steps as "ces longues chaines de raisons" (p. 19) on which syllogism is based. They obviously fall short in supporting the philosophical certitude which is the main guiding theme throughout this treatise. "Certitude métaphisique" (p. 36) for him is corollary to "[les] démonstrations mathématiques" (p. 47) the apprehension of which is not far removed from intuition.

René Descartes, *Discours de la Méthode* (Manchester 1941–Reprinted 1949).

27. W. H. Walsh, *Reason and Experience* (Oxford, 1947), p. 17.

28. The term "rationalist" is "a good deal wider and looser than 'empiricist,' and while rationalist philosophers are often agreed in what they deny, they are by no means united in what they affirm." *Ibid.*

29. "Sensation is always the registration of feeling, something primary and essential; perception always testifies of something objective and external; sensation follows temporally and logically the impression made on the brain; perception follows the sensation."

Olin M. Jones, *Empiricism and Intuitionism in Reid's Common Sense Philosophy* (Princeton, 1927), p. 32.

30. Albert Einstein, "Remarks on Bertrand Russell's Theory of Knowledge," *The Philosophy of Bertrand Russell*, ed. by Paul A. Schilpp. Vol. V (Evanston & Chicago, 1944), p. 287.

31. Walsh, p. 63.

32. W. E. Hocking, *Types of Philosophy* (London, 1929), p. 184.

33. George Santayana, *The Realm of Spirit* (London, 1940), p. 93.

34. B. Spinoza, "Proof to the Second Corollary of Proposition XLIV," *Ethics and De Intellectus Emendatione* (London, 1955), p. 72.

35. Studies on the subject:

Arthur Schopenhauer, *The World as Will and Idea*, trans. from the German by R. B. Haldane and J. Kemp (London, 1883-86), 3 Vols.

Walter Jekill (select. ed. & trans.), *The Wisdom of Schopenhauer* (London, 1911).

Thomas Mann, *The Living Thoughts of Schopenhauer* (London, 1939).

36. Bertrand Russell, *History of Western Philosophy* (London, 1946), p. 783.

37. *Ibid.*

38. See Henri Bergson's *Durée et Simultanéité: A Propos de la Théorie d'Einstein* (Paris, 1922).

John Joseph Kelley in *Bergson's Mysticism* (Fribourg—Switzerland, 1954).

39. Russell, p. 823.

40. *Ibid.*, p. 824.

41. Fisher, p. 116.

42. T. M. Watt, *The Intuition of God* (Edinburgh, 1929), p. 13.

43. *Ibid.*

44. W. R. Inge, *Mysticism in Religion* (London, 1947), p. 22.

45. *Ibid.*

46. *Ibid.*

47. Nicolas Berdyaev, *Freedom and the Spirit* (London, 1935), p. 8.

48. It is essential for the appreciation of Eliot's *Ash Wednesday*.

49. The Mystic Way is supposed to be the cornerstone in both Eastern and Western mysticism.

50. *The Mystical Element of Religion as Studied in Saint Catherine of Genoa and her Friends,* Vol. I (London, 1923), p. 105.

51. See Alexander GilChrist's *Life of William Blake* (London, 1942).

52. His proper name is Titus Flavius Clemens. Though Athenian by birth, he became the Head of the School of Theology at Alexandria in the year A.D. 190. Origen was his most distinguished pupil.

53. Clement of Alexandria, "On Spiritual Perfection," *Alexandrian Christianity*, trans. by J. E. L. Oulton and H. Chadwick, Vol. II (London, 1954), p. 114.

54. Origen, "Exhortation to Martyrdom," *ibid.*, p. 418.

55. Dante Alighieri, *The Purgatorio*, ed. by Gollancz, 11. 124-26 (London: The Temple Classics, 1901), p. 319.

56. Inge, *Christian Mysticism*, p. 10.

57. *Ibid.*, p. 11.

58. Jean Descola, *Quintessence de Saint Jean de la Croix* (Paris, 1952), p. 70.

59. The word "soul" is now used to cover certain states of consciousness, psycho-physical relations, and certain spiritual activities of distinctive quality. Its development throughout these states and its kinship with God are of particular interest to the mystic. It is the superrational soul that develops and unites with God.

60. She was called "the mother of thousands of souls." Equilibrium between the meditative and outward life reaches perfection in Catherine. Though she received little education, she was able in her *Divine Dialogue* to throw light on Italian religious history.

61. Rabia El-Adawia is an Arabian mystic. She is one of the most

important founders of Sufism in Islamic mysticism in the eighth century.

62. It is the main theme of the First, Third, and Fifth Sections of *Ash Wednesday* and the Fifth Movement of *Burnt Norton*. In the Third Movement of *East Coker* the theme of elaboration is based on *The Ascent of Mount Carmel* which is a companion treatise of the "Dark Night."

63. Underhill, p. 73.

64. St. John of the Cross, "The Ascent of Mount Carmel," *The Complete Works,* trans. and ed. by E. Allison Peers, Vol. I (London, 1935–Reprinted 1957), pp. 23-24.

65. Descola, p. 43.

66. This idea is stressed in *Ash Wednesday* through the protagonist's reiteration: "Lord, I am not worthy."

T. S. Eliot, "Ash Wednesday," *Collected Poems: 1909-1935* (London, 1958), p. 97.

67. Underhill, p. 402.

68. According to the Platonic system "the soul of man is conceived as trapped in the body, in the sensible world, and Eros is the force which drives the soul upward to the super-sensible world."

J. R. Horne, "Bergson's Mysticism Compared with Agape and Eros," *The Hibbert Journal,* Vol. LV (July, 1957), p. 363.

69. Descola, p. 20.

Notes to Chapter Two

1. In this vast area of Oriental and Occidental mysticism, a great deal had to be left out, for my study in this chapter is not meant to be exhaustive. I had to concentrate only on the topics that bear relevance to the development of Eliot's themes.

2. *La Litterature et L'Occultisme: Etudes sur la Poésie Philosophique Moderne* (Paris, 1939), p. 181.

3. "The national form of Indian religion is Hinduism. The term 'Hindu' was first used under the foreign domination of the Mohammedans to mean unconverted native Indians . . . The term 'Brahmanism' refers to the fact that a definite type of priest, the [Brahmin], was the leader of religion."

Max Weber, *The Religion of India,* trans. and ed. by Hans H. Gerth and Don Martindale (Illinois, 1958), p. 4.

4. Heinrich Zimmer, *Philosophies of India* (London, 1951), p. 3.

5. He is the national hero-god of the Aryan invaders.

6. "The figure of Varuna, the god of the sky, is progressively transformed and idealized into the moral overseer of the world. It becomes Varuna's function to punish evildoers and reward the good."

J. R. Everett, *Religion in Human Experience* (London, 1952), p. 54.

7. He is concerned with the Triple Law (i.e., "give, sympathize and control") with which Eliot's *Waste Land* closes.

166   THE MYSTICAL PHILOSOPHY OF T. S. ELIOT

8. S. Radhakrishnan, *Indian Philosophy*, Vol. I (London, 1927), p. 92.

9. F. Max Müller, *Three Lectures on the Vedanta Philosophy* (London, 1894), p. 8.

10. *Ibid.*, First Adhyaya, Second Valli, "The Upanishads," *The Sacred Books of the East*, ed. by F. Max Müller, Vol. XV (Oxford, 1884), p. 11.

11. Radhakrishnan, Vol. I, p. 173.

12. Albert Schweitzer, *Indian Thought and its Development*, trans. by Mrs. C. E. B. Russell (London, 1936), p. 42.

13. The effects of action on the Self and the ties that actions involve are the very causes of its transmigration from one life to another in a process of perpetual rebirth known as "Samsara" or the round of births. According to the Karmic Law, each individual reaps the fruit of his action whether in his lifetime or in a future reincarnation.

Actions which are characterized by sheer ignorance tie us to the world of misery. Enlightened actions (i.e., of non-attached character) bring forth the release from suffering through the emancipation of Self from material and sensuous domination.

14. It is the main theme of the Third Movement of T. S. Eliot's *Dry Salvages*.

15. Purohit Swami, *The Geeta: The Gospel of the Lord Shri Krishna*, trans. from the original Sanskrit (London, 1935), p. 11.

16. Kashinath Trimbak Telang (trans.), "The Bhagavadgita," *The Sacred Books of the East*, Vol. III, *op. cit.*, p. 40.

17. "Krishna [that is to say the Black One], the son of Vasudeva and Devaki, is probably a deified tribal hero, later held to be an avatar of the God Vishnu."

Schweitzer, p. 175.

18. Zimmer, p. 381.

19. Kashinath Trimbak Telang (trans.), p. 44.

20. Schweitzer, p. 188.

21. Vedantic theories concerning the reality and simultaneity of Being, the pairs of opposites, and the modes of reconciliation have exercised remarkable influence on the development of the philosophical themes of Eliot's *Four Quartets*.

22. "Sankaracharya (A.D. 788-850) is India's supreme philosopher . . . He interprets the Upanishads as teaching a strict monism: God alone exists; the whole visible world is illusion ['maya']; the human soul is actually identical with God: 'Tat tvam asi' ['Thou art That']. His influence over thinking Hindus is unchallenged."

J. N. Farquhar, "Achievements of the Indian Mind," *The Hibbert Journal*, Vol. XXVI (October, 1927), p. 111.

23. Oliver Lacombe, *L'Absolu Selon le Vedanta*, Tome XIXL (Paris, 1937), p. 35.

24. Annie Besant, *The Wisdom of the Upanishads* (Benares and London, 1907), p. 31.

25. This theory is relevant to the choice of the mystic images in Eliot's *Four Quartets*. They are linked with certain locations in "space" and aspects of "time" only to reveal an intimate relationship to the transcendent sphere of Being.

26. The state of absorption without distinction which Indian mysticism avows is alien to Christian mysticism that stresses the element of distinction in the very act of union between the mystic's soul and the absolute Reality or God. Arabian mysticism typified in the Sufi School follows the same lines of Indian mysticism in this respect.

27. T. S. Eliot, "The Dry Salvages," *Four Quartets* (London, First Published 1944—Ninth Impression 1952), p. 30.

28. *Ibid., Little Gidding*, p. 42.

29. Schweitzer, p. 97.

30. T. W. Rhys Davids (trans. from Pali), "The Foundation of the Kingdom of Righteousness or Dhamma-Kakka-Ppavattana-Sutta, Buddhist Suttas," *The Sacred Books of the East*, Vol. XI, *op. cit.*, p. 148.

31. Schweitzer, p. 107.

32. J. Caird, "Religions of India," *The Faith of the World* (Edinburgh, 1882), p. 52.

33. James Allen, "The Noble Eightfold Path," *An Illustrated Quarterly Review*, Vol. I, No. 2 (September, 1903), p. 218.

34. *The Flowering of Mysticism* (New York, 1939), p. 28.

35. The Nous is the "spirit" or "divine mind" as manifestation of the One.

36. A. H. Armstrong, "Platonic Mysticism," *The Dublin Review*, Vol. CCXVI (April, 1945), p. 137.

37. Plotinus, *Physic and Physical Treatises; Comprising the Second and Third Enneads*, trans. from the Greek by Stephen Mackenna, Vol. II (London, 1921), p. 134.

38. John Watson, "The Philosophy of Plotinus," *The Philosophical Review*, Vol. XXXVII (September, 1928), p. 498.

39. An "anonymous personage, probably a Syrian monk (A.D. 500) . . . Though himself an orthodox Christian, Dionysius adopted many of the Neoplatonic conceptions. . . . [Whereas] for Augustine the Christian may attain to a momentary glimpse of uncreated light, with Dionysius he may, but only rarely and briefly, experience the ecstatic Plotinian going forth to the divine."

David Knowles, *The English Mystical Tradition* (London, 1961), pp. 29-30.

40. *History and Literature of Christianity from Tertullian to Boethius*, trans. from French by Herbert Wilson (London, 1924), p. 392.

41. In "Burnt Norton" Eliot gives us the poetic equivalent to this illuminative vision with the soul peeping through

> the passage which we did not take
> Towards the door we never opened
> Into the rose-garden.
>
> Eliot, *Four Quartets*, p. 7.

42. St. Augustine, *The Confessions*, trans. by William Watts, Vol. II, Bk X, Chap. XXVII (London: The Loeb Edition, 1912—Reprinted 1931), p. 147.

43. Martin Grabmann, *Thomas Aquinas: His Personality and Thought*, trans. by Virgil Michel (New York-London, 1928), p. 129.

44. St. Thomas went even further in asking his friend, William of Moerbeke, to undertake a more accurate translation of Aristotelian metaphysics from Greek texts.

45. *The Summa Contra Gentiles of Saint Thomas Aquinas*, literally trans. by the English Dominican Fathers from the latest Leonine Edition, Vol. I (London, 1924), p. 155.

46. *Dante and the Mystics* (London, 1913), p. 5.

47. Henry Osborn Taylor, *The Medieval Mind: A History of the Development of Thought and Emotion in the Middle Ages*, Vol. II (London, 1911), p. 552.

48. Adolf Gaspary, "The Meaning and Character of the Vita Nuova," *Aids to the Study of Dante*, ed. by Charles Allen Dinsmore (Boston & New York, 1903), p. 174.

49. Dante Alighieri, *The Vita Nuova and Canzoniere*, Section II (London: The Temple Classics, 1903), p. 5.

50. The poems of Eliot abound with echoes from the Commedia which are evidenced in *The Waste Land*, "The Hollow Men," *Ash Wednesday* and the *Four Quartets*. In comparison with Shakespeare who "understands a greater extent and variety of human life than Dante," the Italian poet "understands deeper degrees of degradation and higher degrees of exaltation" in Eliot's view.

T. S. Eliot, "Dante," *Selected Essays* (London, First Published 1932—Third Enlarged Edition 1951), p. 252.

51. Dante Alighieri, *The Paradiso*, Canto II, ll. 31-36 (London: The Temple Classics, 1899), p. 17.

52. It is the subject of the Second Section of *Ash Wednesday* and the last Movement of the *Four Quartets*.

The term "Cloud of Unknowing" first appeared in a fourteenth-century mystical treatise written by an anonymous English monk. It denotes a state of unawareness during which the mystic is unable to discern the tangible world around him.

To this anonymous monk, the works of Dionysius the Areopagite "were second only in value and authority to the Bible. As an act of gratitude, he translated Dionysius' *Mystical Theology* into English; he also strove to simplify this work, *The Cloud of Unknowing*."

T. W. Coleman, *English Mystics of the Fourteenth Century* (London, 1938), p. 87.

Professor Hodgson is in favor of placing it "between the works of [Richard] Rolle [of Hampole 1290-1349] and those of [Walter] Hilton [d. 1395]."

Phyllis Hodgson, *The Cloud of Unknowing and the Book of Privy Counselling*, ed. from the MSS. (London, 1944), p. lxxxiv.

53. *Grey Eminence* (London, 1941), p. 50.

54. Ira Progoff (trans.), *The Cloud of Unknowing* (London, 1959), p. 18.

55. *Ibid.*, p. 23.

56. *Ibid.*, Chap. XXI, Text No. 3, pp. 99-100.

57. *Ibid.*, Chap. IV, Text No. 18, p. 64.

58. *Ibid.*, Chap. II, Text No. 1, p. 55.

59. *Ibid.*, Chap. III, Text No. 1, p. 57.

60. *Ibid.*, Chap. IV, Text No. 12, p. 62.

61. *Ibid.*, Text No. 16, p. 63.

62. *Ibid.*, Chap. XXVI, Text No. 5, p. 111.

63. *Ibid.*

64. *Ibid.*, Chap. XLVIII, Text No. 2, p. 152.

65. St. Teresa of Jesus, *The Complete Works*, trans. and ed. by E. Allison Peers, Vol. II (London, 1946), p. 70.

66. *Ibid.*, p. 201.

67. *Ibid.*, p. 227.

68. The effort which is exerted for this renunciation together with the attractions of the world that handicap it, constitute the major theme of Eliot's *Ash Wednesday*.

69. A detailed account of "the Dark Night of the Soul" is expounded in Section III of my first chapter.

70. E. Allison Peers, *Studies of the Spanish Mystics*, Vol. I (London, 1951), p. 204.

71. St. John of the Cross, "The Ascent of Mount Carmel," *The Complete Works*, Vol. I, Bk. II, Chap. XXIV, *op cit.*, pp. 177-78.

72. Jacques Maritain, *The Degrees of Knowledge*, trans. under the supervision of Gerald B. Phelan (London, 1959), p. 325.

73. In the Third Movement of his *Little Gidding*, Eliot refers to her concept of sin and the possibility of righteousness through purification and love.

74. Julian of Norwich, *Revelations of Divine Love*, a version from the MS. in the British Museum, ed. by Grace Warrack (London, 1901–Reprinted 1949), p. 189.

75. E. I. Watkin, *Poets and Mystics* (London, 1953), p. 90.

Notes to Chapter Three

1. Introduction to *The Wheel of Fire* by G. Wilson Knight (London, 1930), p. xiv.

2. The fact that these philosophers are mentioned here does not necessarily mean that Eliot is familiar with them all. He undoubtedly shows familiarity with the philosophies of F. H. Bradley, J. Maritain, and W. Lewis as expounded in the first division of this chapter; with the rest a striking theme of similarity does not only help to round out the picture, but, more specifically, to clarify many parts that would otherwise remain obscure.

3. *Conflict and Dreams,* International Library of Psychology and Scientific Method (London and New York, 1923).

4. J. Henry Bodgener, "Spiritual Life and Literary Trends," *The London Quarterly and Holborn Review,* Vol. CLXX (January, 1945), p. 323.

5. Joseph McCabe, *Outlines of the World's Great 'Isms* (Kansas, 1945), p. 5.

6. While at Harvard (Undergraduate: 1906-09; Graduate: 1909-10; Research Worker: 1911-13; Assistant in Philosophy: 1913-14), Eliot was so much attracted to the philosophy of F. H. Bradley that he wrote his doctoral dissertation on *Experience and Objects of Knowledge in the Philosophy of F. H. Bradley* (1916).

The year 1910-11 was spent in reading French literature and philosophy at the Sorbonne; between 1911 and 1913 he continued his studies in philosophy at Harvard and came in contact with Sanskrit philosophy and Patanjali metaphysics that left him in "a state of enlightened mystification"; and in the winter of 1914-15 he was at Merton College, Oxford, reading Greek philosophy.

7. T. S. Eliot, "Francis Herbert Bradley," *Selected Essays, op. cit.,* p. 453.

8. F. H. Bradley, *Appearance and Reality* (London, 1908), p. 486.

9. *Ibid.,* p. 487.

10. T. S. Eliot, "Tradition and the Individual Talent," *Points of View* (London, 1951), pp. 23-34.

11. "Now [or 'And so'] I pray you," said by Arnaut Daniel.

Dante Alighieri, *The Purgatorio,* Canto XXVI, 1. 145, *op. cit.,* pp. 330-31.

12. C. Fabro, "Actualité et originalité de l'esse thomiste," *Revue Thomiste,* Tome LVI-LXIV (Janvier-Mars, 1956), p. 240.

13. Jacques Maritain, *The Degrees of Knowledge, op. cit.,* p. 36.

14. *Ibid.,* p. 255.

15. J. Maritain, "Le pêche de l'Ange: Essai de re-interprétation de positions thomistes," *Revue Thomiste, op. cit.,* p. 214.

16. Maritain happily differentiates between the processes used in metaphysics and poetry in order to come to terms with reality saying that "metaphysics keeps on the line of 'knowing,' of the contemplation, of truth; poetry keeps on the line of 'making,' of the delight in beauty; an essential difference which cannot be ignored

without loss. The one seizes the spiritual in an idea and by the most abstract intellection; . . . the other finds it at all crossroads of the singular and the contingent; . . . metaphysics hunts down essences and definitions; poetry every form shining as it passes, every reflection of an invisible order."

J. Maritain, "Poetry and Religion," trans. by F. S. Flint, *The New Criterion*, Vol. V (January-June, 1927), pp. 15-16.

17. Marjorie Grene, *Martin Heidegger* (London, 1957), p. 40.

18. Werner Brock, *An Introduction to Contemporary German Philosophy* (Cambridge, 1935), p. 116.

19. Duration for Bergson "is what occurs when we completely telescope the past into the present, and make our life a fiery point 'eating' like an acetylene flame into the future. 'Duration' is inside us, not outside. There is nothing but 'mathematical Time' outside us." Wyndham Lewis, *Time and Western Man* (London, 1927), p. 437.

20. See *The Philosophical Basis of Intuition*, Chap. I, Sec. II, pp. 23-24.

21. Wyndham Lewis, p. 222.

22. *Ibid.*, p. 227.

23. *Ibid.*, p. 232.

24. *Ibid.*, *The Enemy*, Vol. I.

25. *Ibid.*, *Time and Western Man*, p. 419.

26. *Ibid.*, p. 421.

27. *Ibid.*, p. 438.

28. A. E. Taylor, *Elements of Metaphysics* (London, 1952), p. 13.

29. W. H. Auden, "To John Warner, son of Rex and Frances Warner," *The Orators* (London, 1946), p. 101.

30. Stephen Spender, "Without that once clear aim," *Collected Poems 1928-53* (London, 1955), p. 43.

31. Cecil D. Lewis, "The Magnetic Mountain," *Collected Poems* (London, 1954), p. 88.

32. Louis MacNeice, "Prayer Before Birth," *Eighty-Five Poems Selected by the Author* (London, 1959), p. 122.

33. Lawrence Durrell, *Key to Modern Poetry* (London, 1952), p. 161.

34. T. S. Eliot, "The Frontiers of Criticism," *The Sewanee Review*, Vol. LXIV, No. 4 (Autumn, 1956), p. 539.

35. In his childhood Eliot was influenced by Unitarianism—the belief in the Father with the exclusion of the Son and the Holy Ghost. As this belief is outside the proper domain of Christianity, it was abandoned by the poet even before he reached maturity.

36. T. S. Eliot, *The Use of Poetry and the Use of Criticism* (London, 1933—Reprinted 1950), pp. 139-40.

37. Though the *Four Quartets* contain glimpses of the Paradiso, the major theme is still purgatorial.

38. T. S. Eliot, "The Metaphysical Poets," *Selected Essays, op. cit.*, p. 289.

39. *Ibid.*, p. 288.

40. See *Aristotelianism Versus Augustinianism*, Chap. II, Sec. X, pp. 38-39.

41. T. S. Eliot, "Milton," *Annual Lecture on a Master Mind: Henriette Hertz Trust of the British Academy* (London, 1947), p. 7.

42. Jacques Vallette, "Fortunes d'Un Apophtegme," *Mercure de France*, Tome CCCXIV (Janvier-Avril, 1925), p. 151.

43. Frank Kermode, "Dissociation of Sensibility," *The Kenyon Review*, No. 2, Vol. XIX (Spring, 1957), p. 177.

44. T. S. Eliot, "The Love Song of J. Alfred Prufrock," *Collected Poems: 1909-1935* (London, 1958), p. 12.

45. *Ibid.*, p. 14.

46. *Ibid.*, p. 11.

47. *Ibid.*, "Portrait of a Lady," p. 18.

48. *Ibid.*

49. *Ibid.*, "Sweeney Among the Nightingales," p. 57.

50. *Ibid.*

51. *Ibid.*, "The Hippopotamus," p. 50.

52. *Ibid.*, p. 49.

53. Grover Smith, *T. S. Eliot's Poetry and Plays: A Study in Sources and Meaning* (Chicago, 1956), p. 40.

54. T. S. Eliot, "The Hippopotamus," p. 49.

55. *Ibid.*, p. 50.

56. *Ibid.*, p. 49.

57. *Ibid.*, "Mr. Eliot's Sunday Morning Service," p. 55.

58. *Ibid.*, p. 56.

59. *Ibid.*

60. *Ibid.*, "The Hippopotamus," p. 49.

61. *Ibid.*, "Mr. Eliot's Sunday Morning Service," p. 56.

62. *Ibid.*

63. *Ibid.*, p. 55.

64. *Ibid.*, "The Hippopotamus," p. 49.

65. *Ibid.*, "Mr. Eliot's Sunday Morning Service," p. 56.

66. *Ibid.*

67. *Ibid.*, p. 55.

68. *Ibid.*

69. "Eliot's conversion to Anglo-Catholicism [occurred] during 1925-1928 (his leanings go back several years)."
Albert Mordell, *T. S. Eliot—Special Pleader as Book Reviewer and Literary Critic* (Kansas, 1951), p. 37.
It is significant that this period falls between "The Hollow Men" (1925) and *Ash Wednesday* (1930).

70. T. S. Eliot, "Mr. Eliot's Sunday Morning Service," p. 55.

71. St. Luke, III, 22.

72. T. S. Eliot, "Gerontion," *Collected Poems*, p. 37.

73. The passage which Eliot quotes from the Sermons in his essay on "Lancelot Andrewes" does not fully illustrate the themes of "Gerontion." In fact, he traces only the single theme of the "Verbum infans, the Word an infant" and does not seem to have the poem in mind in the rest of the essay.

T. S. Eliot, *For Lancelot Andrewes* (London, 1929), p. 28.

74. Lancelot Andrewes, "The Right Honourable and Reverend Father in God," *XCVI Sermons* (London, 1635), pp. 110-12.

75. T. S. Eliot, "Gerontion," p. 37.

76. *Ibid.*

77. *Ibid.*

78. *Ibid.*

79. *Ibid.*

80. *Ibid.*

81. *Ibid.*

82. *Ibid.*

83. *Ibid.*, p. 38.

84. "The idea that God cannot be angry is by no means a new one, but it is not Biblical. . . . It represents a pagan, not a Christian view of God."

Leon Morris, "The Wrath of God," *The Expository Times*, Vol. LXIII (October, 1951-September, 1952), p. 144.

85. T. S. Eliot, "Gerontion," p. 38.

86. *Ibid.*

87. *Ibid.*, p. 37.

88. *Ibid.*, p. 38.

89. *Ibid.*

90. *Ibid.*

91. *Ibid.*

92. *Ibid.*

93. *Ibid.*

94. *Ibid.*

95. *Ibid.*

96. *Ibid.*, p. 39.

97. *Ibid.*

98. *Ibid.*, "The Love Song of J. Alfred Prufrock," p. 13.

99. *Ibid.*, "Portrait of a Lady," p. 17.

100. *Ibid.*, "La Figlia Che Piange," p. 34.

101. *Ibid.*, "Sweeney Among the Nightingales," p. 57.

102. *Ibid.*

103. Mr. Hyman rightly remarks that "the scene appears to be a bar frequented by prostitutes, and public behavior there is somewhat indecorous."

Stanley Edgar Hyman, "Poetry and Criticism: T. S. Eliot," *The American Scholar*, Vol. XXX, No. 1 (Winter, 1960-61), p. 44.

104. T. S. Eliot, "A Cooking Egg," *Collected Poems*, p. 45.

105. *Ibid.*, "The Love Song of J. Alfred Prufrock," p. 12.

106. *Ibid.*, p. 14.

107. *Ibid.*, p. 15.

108. *Ibid.*

109. *Ibid.*

110. *Ibid.*

The image evoked here is that of a crab.

111. *Ibid.*, "Portrait of a Lady," p. 20.

112. *Ibid.*, "Dans le Restaurant," p. 52.

This theme will appear again in the Fourth Section of *The Waste Land*.

113. *Ibid.*, "Burbank with a Baedeker: Bleistein with a Cigar," p. 41.

114. See Chap. I, Sec. III, Footnote No. 68, p. 28.

115. T. S. Eliot, "The Love Song of J. Alfred Prufrock," p. 11.

116. *Ibid.*

117. *Ibid.*

118. *Ibid.*, "Portrait of a Lady," p. 16.

119. *Ibid.*

120. *Ibid.*

121. *Ibid.*, "Preludes," pp. 22-23.

122. *Ibid.*, p. 22.

123. *Ibid.*, p. 21.

124. *Ibid.*, p. 22.

125. *Ibid.*, p. 23.

126. Symons' book was first published in 1899 but the mood was not ripe yet for its acceptance. It is an after-effect of the Decadence.

127. T. S. Eliot, "A Review of 'Baudelaire and the Symbolists' by Peter Quennell," *The Criterion* (January, 1930), p. 357.

128. Enid Starkie, *From Gautier to Eliot* (London, 1960), p. 163.

129. T. S. Eliot, "Spleen," *Harvard Advocate*—a photostatic copy from the Library of Harvard University, Vol. LXXXVIII (January 26, 1910), p. 114.

130. Jules Laforgue, "Rosace en Vitrail," *Oeuvres Complètes*, Tome I (Paris, 1922), p. 32.

131. *Ibid.*, "Fantasie," p. 29.

132. T. S. Eliot, "Humouresque," *Harvard Advocate*, a photostatic copy, Vol. LXXXVIII (January 12, 1910), p. 103.

133. *Ibid.*

134. Jules Laforgue, "Complaine de la Lune," p. 103.

135. *Ibid.*

136. T. S. Eliot, "On a Portrait," *Harvard Advocate*, Vol. LXXXVI (January 26, 1909), p. 135.

137. Jules Laforgue, "Complainte d'Un Certain Dimanche," pp. 89-91. Cf.

138. *Ibid.*, "Figurez-Vous un Peu," *Des Fleurs de Bonne Volonté* (Paris, 1912), pp. 343-44. Cf.

139. *Ibid.*, "Autre Complainte de Lord Pierrot," *Oeuvres Complètes, op. cit.*, pp. 136-37. Cf.

140. Theophile Gautier, *Poésies Complètes*, Tome Premier (Paris, 1889), p. 344.

141. Eliot confesses that his "early *vers libre* . . . was started under the endeavour to practise the same form as Laforgue. This meant merely rhyming lines of irregular length, with the rhymes coming in irregular places."

Donald Hall, "T. S. Eliot Speaks," *The Poetry Review*, Vol. LI, No. 4 (October-December, 1960), p. 209.

142. Hulme firmly believed in man's original sin and this belief exercised a remarkable influence on Eliot (e.g., "the wrath-bearing tree" in "Gerontion"). His theories dealing with the philosophy of art (i.e., Bergson's) and literary criticism (particularly his essay on "Romanticism and Classicism") are the subject of his *Speculations: Essays on Humanism and the Philosophy of Art*, ed. by Herbert Read, 1936.

143. Andre Lebois, "T. S. Eliot, Les Imagistes et Jean de Boschère," *Revue de Littérature Comparée*, 26ᵉ Année (Juillet, 1952), p. 366.

144. *Ibid.*

145. Jacob Isaacs, *The Background of Modern Poetry* (London, 1951), p. 33.

146. "Is This Poetry?" *The Athenaeum* (January-June, 1919), p. 491.

147. *Ibid.*

148. T. S. Eliot, *The Use of Poetry and the Use of Criticism*, p. 155.

149. *Ibid.*, "The Love Song of J. Alfred Prufrock," p. 13.

150. *Ibid.*, "The Hippopotamus," p. 49.

151. *Ibid.*, "The Love Song of J. Alfred Prufrock," p. 12.

152. Jules de Gautier, "Les Limites de l'Intelligence et de la Croyance," *Mercure de France*, Tome CLXXIX (Avril-Mai, 1925), p. 602.

153. I take the "horse" to be the symbol of sexual power, like the "libido" of Schopenhauer or the "élan vital" of Bergson.

154. "The horses of the dawn race at full speed up from the east [Istria, the peninsula across the Adriatic from Venice]."

Robert F. Goheen, "Burbank with a Baedeker: the Third Stanza," *The Sewanee Review*, Vol. LXI (January, 1953), p. 111.

155. T. S. Eliot, "Burbank with a Baedeker: Bleistein with a Cigar," p. 40.

156. *Ibid.*, pp. 40-41.

157. *Ibid.*, p. 40.

158. The theme of contrast is intensified too by the jagged brokenness of the fourth verse after the lucid flexibility of the first three

verses. The abrupt change of rhythmical effect stresses the concept
of loss and helps in driving it home.

159. T. S. Eliot, "Gerontion," p. 37.

160. *Ibid.*, p. 38.

161. *Ibid.*, "Mr. Eliot's Sunday Morning Service," p. 55.

162. *Ibid.*, "Whispers of Immortality," p. 53.

163. Georges Cattaui, *Trois Poètes: Hopkins, Yeats et Eliot* (Paris, 1947), p. 105.

164. Harold Osborne, *Aesthetics and Criticism* (London, 1955), p. 217.

165. This does not mean that a poem should be didactic; at the same time, the theory of "Art for Art's Sake" is now obsolete; but an inborn message conveyed explicitly or preferably by "oblique" implication, has avowedly been recognized behind all great poetry (e.g., Homer's *Iliad* and *Odyssey*, Dante's *Divine Comedy* and Milton's *Paradise Lost*).

166. T. S. Eliot, "The Hippopotamus," p. 49.

167. In an essay on "Catholicism and International Order," Eliot begins with a conviction of "the vital importance of the reunion of Christendom" and then goes on analyzing the present state of affairs with a habitual bias toward a Catholic outlook. Both method and after-effects of the reunion are deliberately left for us to work out. T. S. Eliot, *Essays Ancient and Modern* (London, 1947), pp. 113-35.

168. T. S. Eliot, "The Hippopotamus," p. 49.

169. *Ibid.*, "Mr. Eliot's Sunday Morning Service," p. 55.

170. "In the mystic experience the World Faiths find the sacred meeting-ground. This is the glorious gospel of the universal to which those of every religion, in all loyalty to their own, can subscribe and do so without losing one jot or tittle of its beauty, its inspiration or its joy . . . [It] can itself become a saving faith for the growing number of those who do not find in any of the traditional moulds that enlightenment, illumination, salvation, for which their souls inescapably seek. Universalism is the shape of religion to come." (Sir) John Stewart-Wallace, "The World Religions One in Mysticism," *The Hibbert Journal*, Vol. L (January, 1952), p. 112.

Notes to Chapter Four

1. To reduce the growing puzzle and obscurity that cluster around this poem, I do not follow the normal ordering of its sections as I have found it more illuminating to rearrange them on a basis of thematic development.

2. *New Bearings in English Poetry* (London, 1932), p. 93.

3. "After Eliot had completed, in the fall or winter of 1921, the draft of what he has described as a 'sprawling chaotic poem,'

he visited Pound in Paris. There he submitted the poem to his friend's inspection and criticism. Following Pound's suggestions, he reduced the poem to about half its original size. These revisions made upon the draft, are now presumably lost."

D. D. Paige (ed.), "Letters of Ezra Pound to T. S. Eliot concerning 'The Waste Land,' " *The Hudson Review*, Vol. III, No. 1 (Spring, 1950), p. 53.

4. T. S. Eliot, "The Burial of the Dead," 11. 2-3, *Collected Poems: 1909-35.*

5. "Not only the title, but the plan and a good deal of the incidental symbolism of the poem were suggested by Miss Jessie L. Weston's book on the Grail legend: *From Ritual to Romance* . . . To another work of anthropology I am indebted in general, one which has influenced our generation profoundly; I mean *The Golden Bough;* I have used especially the two volumes 'Adonis, Attis, Osiris.' Anyone who is acquainted with these works will immediately recognise in the poem certain references to vegetation ceremonies."

Ibid., Notes on the Waste Land, p. 78.

6. *Ibid.*, "The Burial of the Dead," 1. 60.

7. London is only an example of the unreality of modern urbanity:

> Jerusalem Athens Alexandria
> Vienna London
> Unreal.

I take "Jerusalem Athens Alexandria" to be associated with the flourishing of religious belief at the dawn of Christianity, but it was lost throughout the ages among the trammels of urbanism. Hence, the unreality of these cities rests on their artificiality.

Ibid., "What the Thunder said," 11. 374-76.

8. Charles Baudelaire, "Les Sept Vieillards," *Les Fleurs du Mal, Oeuvres Complètes*, Tome I (Paris, 1918), p. 233.

9. Nathan A. Scott, *Rehearsals of Discomposure* (London, 1952), p. 208.

10. Eliot, "The Burial of the Dead," 1. 2.

11. *Ibid.*, 11. 5-6.

12. Geoffrey Bullough, *The Trend of Modern Poetry* (London, 1949), p. 161.

13. "The Burial of the Dead" as a title is significant on various levels of experience. In addition to the burial of the corn-god, it is also the burial of the Redeemer for man's spiritual rebirth; the burial of self in the sepulchral atmosphere of the modern Waste Land; and the burial of reality in the mirage of self-deceit.

14. Sir James Frazer tells us that "the priests [in Egypt] used to bury effigies of Osiris made of earth and corn. When these effigies were taken up again at the end of the year or of a short interval, the

corn would be found to have sprouted from the body of Osiris, and this sprouting of the grain would be hailed as an omen, or rather as the cause, of the growth of the crops."

J. Frazer, "Adonis, Attis, Osiris," *The Golden Bough*, Part IV, Vol. II (London, 1936), p. 90.

15. Stetson is not only modern but rather a universal figure who fought at Mylae in the Punic War "in which the Carthaginians were defeated [against the Romans]."

F. O. Matthiessen, *The Achievement of T. S. Eliot* (New York: First Published, 1935—Third Edition, 1958), p. 37.

Moreover, "it is plain that Eliot in having the protagonist address the friend in a London Street as one who was with him in the Punic War . . . is making the point that all the wars are one war; all experience, one experience."

Cleanth Brooks, *Modern Poetry and the Tradition* (London, 1948), p. 145.

16. Eliot, "The Burial of the Dead," 1. 73.

17. The reason why the Dog is capitalized is that it refers also to "Sirius, the Dog star, which for the Egyptians foretold the coming of the fertilising floods of the Nile."

D. E. S. Maxwell, *The Poetry of T. S. Eliot* (London, 1952), p. 83.

18. But keepe the wolfe far thence, that's foe to men,
    For with his nailes hee'l dig them up agen.

John Webster, "The White Devil," *The Complete Works*, ed. by F. L. Lucas, Vol. I, Act V, Sc. IV, ll. 97-98 (London, 1927), p. 182.

19. George Williamson, "The Structure of 'The Waste Land,'" *Modern Philology*, Vol. XLVII (1949-50), p. 199.

20. Eliot, "The Burial of the Dead," 1. 72.

21. *Ibid.*, 1. 6.

22. Mr. Dobson remarks that the "legendary land that is waste is our land; infertility and aridness are everywhere; especially are the relations of men and women unworthy—they are either sentimental, or fail of their purpose and are sterile, or are mere indulgence and crudity."

E. J. Dobson, "The Hollow Men and the Work of T. S. Eliot," *Some Recent Developments in English Literature* (Sidney, 1935), p. 40.

23. Maxwell, p. 84.

24. Eliot, "A Game of Chess," ll. 147-49.

25. I am referring here to the seduction of the bored typist by the clerk of a small house-agent.

26. Eliot, "The Fire Sermon," ll. 253-56.

Obviously the allusion is to Goldsmith's song after the seduction of Olivia in *The Vicar of Wakefield*:

When lovely Woman stoops to folly,
    And finds too late that men betray,

> What charm can soothe her melancholy,
> What art can wash her guilt away?

In the poet's view, death only would remove her guilt.
Peter Cunningham (ed.), *The Works of Oliver Goldsmith*, Vol. I
(London, 1854), p. 514.

27. Thomas Middleton, Act IV, Sc. IV, 1. 143 (Cambridge, 1929),
p. 103.

28. A. H. Bullen (ed.), *The Works of Thomas Middleton*, Act
II, Sc. II, 1. 280, Vol. VI (London, 1885), p. 283.

29. Eliot, "The Fire Sermon," 11. 197-98.

30. *Ibid.*, 1. 176.

31. It is reminiscent of the nymphs in Spenser's "Prothalamion,"
of the barge in which Queen Elizabeth I used to meet the Earl of
Leicester, and of the Thames-daughters who are connected with the
Rhine-daughters of Wagner's "Gotterdamerung," but the last two
cases speak of violation through deceit.

32. Eliot, "The Burial of the Dead," 1. 62.

33. *The Inferno*, Canto III, 11. 35-36, p. 29.

34. *Ibid.*, 11. 56-57, p. 31.

35. The source of the epigraph to the poem is the Satyricon of
Petronius in which Trimalchio says:

> Nam Sibyllam quiden Cumis ego ipse oculis meis vidi in ampulla
> pendere, et cum illi pueri dicerent: Σίβυλλα τί θέλεις; responde-
> bat illa: ἀποθανεῖν θέλω.

> [Yes, and I myself with my own eyes saw the Sibyl hanging in a
> cage; and when the boys cried at her: "Sibyl, Sibyl, what do you
> want?" "I would that I were dead," she used to answer.]

Petronius, *Satyricon*, trans. by Michael Heseltine, Sec. 48 (London: The Loeb Classical Library, 1925), pp. 84-87.
This famous "Cumaen Sibyl was supposed to be the authoress of
the Sibylline Oracles. Apollo loved her and granted her the gift of
prophecy, and also a life of as many years as she had grains of dust
in her hand; but she forgot to ask for youth, and so gradually with-
ered away almost to nothing."
E. M. Stephenson, *T. S. Eliot and the Lay Reader* (London, 1944),
p. 30.

36. *The Inferno*, Canto IV, 1. 9, p. 37.

37. In his essay on "Hamlet," Eliot states that "the only way of
expressing emotion in the form of art is by finding an 'objective
correlative'; in other words, a set of objects, a situation, a chain of
events which shall be the formula of that particular emotion; such
that when the external facts, which must terminate in sensory experience, are given, the emotion is immediately evoked."
Eliot, *Selected Essays*, p. 145.

38. *Ibid.*, Notes on the Waste Land, p. 80.

39. *Ibid.*

40. *Ibid.*, "The Burial of the Dead," 1. 65.

41. *Ibid.*, 1. 76.

42. Scott, p. 213.

43. E. Sitwell, *Aspects of Modern Poetry* (London, 1934), p. 131.

44. Eliot, "The Burial of the Dead," 1. 43.

45. *Ibid.*, 1. 55.

46. *Ibid.*, 1. 46.
The "original use of the 'Tarot' . . . [was] not to foretell the Future
in general, but to predict the rise and fall of the waters which brought
fertility to the land."
Jessie L. Weston, *From Ritual to Romance* (New York: First
Printed 1920—Reprinted 1957), p. 80.

47. Eliot, "The Burial of the Dead," 1. 45.

48. *Ibid.*, "Death by Water," 1. 312.

49. "Just as the one-eyed [Smyrna] merchant, seller of currants,
melts into the Phoenician Sailor, and the latter is not wholly distinct
from Ferdinand, Prince of Naples, so all the women are one woman,
and the two sexes meet in Tiresias."
Ibid., *Notes on the Waste Land*, p. 80.

50. Frank Kermode (ed.), Shakespeare's *The Tempest*, Act I,
Sc. II, 1. 401 (London: The Arden Edition, 1954), p. 35.

51. *Ibid.*, pp. 35-36.

52. *Ibid.*, Act V, Sc. I, 1. 313, p. 131.

53. "The corn-god [Osiris] produced the corn from himself: he
gave his own body to feed the people: he died that they might live."
Frazer, p. 90.

54. Eliot, *The Waste Land*, 1. 385.

55. *Ibid.*, 1. 396.

56. *Ibid.*, 11. 39-40.

57. *Ibid.*, 11. 115-16.

58. *Ibid.*, 1. 60.

59. *Ibid.*, 1. 315.

60. *Ibid.*, "Dans le Restaurant," *Collected Poems*, p. 51.

61. *Ibid.*

62. *Ibid.*, p. 52.

63. *Ibid.*, "Death by Water," 1. 318.

64. See *Buddhist Mysticism*, Chap. II, Sec. VI, p. 35 ff.

65. Bowra, "The Waste Land," *The Creative Experiment* (London, 1949), p. 168.

66. Eliot, "Death by Water," 1. 320.

67. See *Buddhist Mysticism*, p. 35 ff.

68. Christmas Humphreys, *Buddhism* (Middlesex, 1952), p. 91.

69. Eliot, "Death by Water," 1. 319.

70. "The Mahâvagga, First Khandhaka (the Admission to the
Order of Bhikkhus)," "Vinaya Texts," trans. from the Pali by T. W.
Rhys Davids and Hermann Oldenberg, Pt. I, Vol. XIII, No. 21, *The
Sacred Books of the East*, p. 134.

71. Edward J. H. Greene, *T. S. Eliot et la France* (Paris, 1951), p. 123.

72. See *The Ethical Mysticism of the Buddhist Philosophy*, Chap. II, Sec. VI, p. 35 ff.

73. *Ibid.*

74. Eliot, *Notes on the Waste Land*, p. 82.
In the Loeb Classical Edition of *The Confessions*, the quotation is mentioned in Vol. I, Bk. III, Chap. I, p. 90.

75. The notion of "burning" with St. Augustine is associated with the ardent desire for deliverance.

76. St. Augustine, *The Confessions*, Vol. I, Bk. III, Chap. IV, *op. cit.*, p. 111.

77. *Ibid.*, Chap. VIII, p. 169.

78. *Ibid.*, Vol. II, Bk. X, Pt. XXXIV, p. 173.

79. *Ibid.*, p. 175.

80. Eliot, "The Fire Sermon," 11. 308-10.

81. Zechariah, III, 2.
Of. Amos IV, 11, and Jude verse 23.

82. See *The Mystical Philosophy of St. Augustine*, Chap. II, Sec. IX, p. 37 ff.

83. See *Buddhist Mysticism*, p. 35 ff.

84. Eliot, *Notes on the Waste Land*, p. 82.

85. See *The Components of the Mystic Way*, Chap. I, Sec. III, p. 26 ff.

86. Eliot, "The Fire Sermon," 1. 195.

87. *Ibid.*, "A Game of Chess," 11. 100-3.

88. *Ibid.*, "Gerontion," p. 39.
Tiresias is not only an extension but a development of the character of Gerontion partly because he is bisexual and partly because he possesses the ability of prophecy.
Before printing *The Waste Land*, however, Eliot thought that "Gerontion" might serve as an introduction to its subject. In a letter to Ezra Pound, he puts forward the following question: "Do you advise printing 'Gerontion' as prelude in book or pamphlet form?" Pound answered: "I do not advise printing 'Gerontion' as preface. One don't [*sic*] miss it 'at' all as the thing now stands. To be more lucid still, let me say that I advise you NOT to print 'Gerontion' as prelude."
"A letter from T. S. Eliot to Ezra Pound and vice versa," January, 1922, *The Hudson Review*, Vol. III, No. I (Spring, 1950), pp. 56-57.

89. Eliot, "The Fire Sermon," 1. 243.

90. "Leman" is the old name for Lake Geneva (Chambers' *Encyclopaedia*, Vol. VI, 1959, p. 213, or Chambers' *World Gazetteer and Geographical Dictionary*, 1959, pp. 275-76); but the original text of this allusion is associated with the Jewish exile at Babylon. We read in Psalm CXXXVII:

> By the rivers of Babylon,
> There we sat down, yea, we wept,
> When we remembered Zion.

According to the Prophecy of Ezekiel, moreover, "folk came from far and near with nets to snare him [Joachin of Israel], caught him in their cruel toil and caged him. This one they led off in chains to the King of Babylon; in Babylon he remained a prisoner, and his voice was heard on the hillsides . . . no more."

Ezekiel, Chap. XIX, 8 & 9.

91. Eliot, "The Fire Sermon," 1. 182.

92. In his voluminous study on the growth of the Holy Grail as a legend, Mr. Nutt tells us that its history is one of "gradual transformation of old Celtic folk-tales into a poem charged with Christian symbolism and mysticism. [It] . . . was hastened . . . by the perception that it was a fitting vehicle for certain moral and spiritual ideas."

Alfred Nutt, *Studies on the Legend of the Holy Grail* (London, 1888), p. 227.

93. He is the Supreme Being, the lord of life and death and the recognized symbol of immortality.

See *The Mystification of the Rig-Veda,* Chap. II, Sec. II, p. 31.

94. Second Brahmana, Fifth Adhyâya, "The Upanishads," trans. by F. Max Müller, *The Sacred Books of the East,* Vol. XV, pp. 189-90.

95. *Three Lectures on the Vedanta Philosophy* (London, 1894), pp. 14-15.

96. Eliot, "What the Thunder said," 1. 337.

97. *Ibid.,* "The Burial of the Dead," 11. 23-25.

Eliot had this image from the Thirty-second Chapter of the *Prophecy of Isaiah* (verses 1 & 2). Cf. *The Book of Ecclesiastes,* XII, 8; and the *Prophecy of Ezekiel,* VI, 3-4.

98. *Ibid.,* "What the Thunder said," 11. 328-30.

99. *Ibid.,* 11. 322-23.

100. *Ibid.,* 1. 325.

101. St. John, XIX, 6.

102. Eliot, "What the Thunder said," 1. 324.

103. *Ibid.,* 1. 327.

104. *Ibid.,* 11. 362-63.

The reference here is to the journey to Emmaus and the appearance of Christ to two of the Disciples. See St. Luke, XXIV, 13-16.

105. *Ibid.,* "What the Thunder said," 1. 339.

106. *Ibid.,* 1. 341.

107. *Ibid.,* 1. 339.

108. *Ibid.,* 1. 342.

109. *Ibid.,* 1. 344.

110. *Ibid.,* 11. 344-45.

111. *Ibid.,* 1. 387.

112. Weston, p. 176.

113. T. S. Eliot, "What the Thunder said," 1. 391.

114. *Ibid.*, 1. 393.

115. Originally the "blame bestowed upon the hero [the quester] is solely on account of the prolonged sorrow his silence has inflicted on King and people [and on] a Land laid Waste."
Weston, p. 18.

116. Eliot, "What the Thunder said," 11. 401, 411, 418.

117. "*Damyata,* Subdue yourselves, subdue the passions of the senses, of pride and selfwill; *Datta,* Give, be liberal and charitable to your neighbours; and *Dayadhvam,* Have pity on those who deserve your pity."
Müller, *Three Lectures on the Vedanta Philosophy*, pp. 14-15.

118. Eliot, "What the Thunder said," 1. 409.

119. *Ibid.*, 1. 407.

120. *Ibid.*, 1. 415.

121. *Ibid.*, 1. 413.

Eliot's note on this imprisonment comes from Bradley's *Appearance and Reality:* "[One's] experience falls within [his] own circle, a circle closed on the outside . . . [like] the world for each is peculiar and private to [his] soul."
Eliot, *Notes on the Waste Land*, p. 84.

122. John Peter, "A New Interpretation of 'The Waste Land,'" *Essays in Criticism,* Vol. II, No. 3 (July, 1952), p. 263.

123. Eliot, *Notes on the Waste Land*, p. 82.

124. *Ibid.*, "What the Thunder said," 1. 426.

125. The "bridge" is symbolically used in the poem as the crossing to reality.

126. In Kyd's *Spanish Tragedy* Hieronymo feigned madness in order to avenge the inhuman butchery of Horatio, his son. When Balthazar and Lorenzo asked him to help them in entertaining the King's court by writing a play, he replied promptly:

> *Why then, ile fit you;* say no more.
> When I was yong, I gave my minde
> And Plide my selfe to fruitles Poetrie;
> Which though it profite the professor naught,
> Yet is it passing pleasing to the world.

In his play, Hieronymo tried to fit Balthazar and Lorenzo in his scheme of seeking revenge.
Frederick S. Boas (ed.), *The Works of Thomas Kyd,* Act IV, Sc. I, 11. 69-73 (Oxford, 1955), p. 83.

Like Hieronymo the protagonist of *The Waste Land* (i.e., Tiresias) has come to his scheme in the end by fitting in various layers of Eastern and Western knowledge to suit a complex civilization.

127. Je suis le Ténébreux,—le Veuf,—l'Inconsolé,

Le Prince d'Aquitaine à la Tour abolie:
Ma seule Etoile est morte, et mon luth constellé
Porte le Soleil noir de la Mélancolie.

Gérard de Nerval, *Oeuvres,* Tome I (Paris, 1952), p. 33.
128.   When shall my spring come to me?
When shall I grow as a swallow, and my lips at last be free?
F. L. Lucas (trans.), *The Vigil of Venus,* 11. 88-89 (Cambridge,
1848), pp. 48-49.
129. Eliot, "What the Thunder said," 1. 433.
130. *Ibid., Notes on the Waste Land,* p. 84.
131. George Williamson, *A Reader's Guide to T. S. Eliot* (London,
1955), p. 154.
132. Matthiessen, p. 99.
133. Eliot, "The Hollow Men," *Collected Poems,* p. 88.
134. *Ibid.*
135. *Ibid.*
136. *Ibid.*
137. *Ibid.,* p. 87.
138. *Ibid.*
139. *Ibid.,* p. 89.
140. *Ibid.,* p. 87.
We are like the Old Guy, effigies stuffed with straw, which is the
notion cited in the epigraph to the poem.
141. *Ibid.*
142. *Ibid.,* p. 88.
143. *Ibid.*
144. In his hollowness, he is identified with Kurtz who is referred
to in the epigraph to the poem as "Mistah Kurtz—he dead" which
are the words of the illiterate cabin boy who announced the death
of this ivory hunter.
Mr. Conrad tells us about him (i.e., Kurtz) that "the wastes of
his weary brain were haunted by shadowy images . . . images of
wealth and fame revolving obsequiously round his unextinguishable
gift of noble and lofty expression . . . The shade of the original Kurtz
frequented the bedside of the hollow sham, whose fate it was to be
buried presently in the mould of primeval earth."
Joseph Conrad, *Heart of Darkness,* Chap. III (London, 1956),
p. 147.
Eliot's epigraph comes on page 150 of this book.
145. Eliot, "The Hollow Men," p. 88.
146. *Ibid.*
147. *Ibid.*
148. *Ibid.*
149. *Ibid.*
150. *Ibid.,* p. 89.
151. *Ibid.*

> . . . all of them together, sorely weeping, drew to the accursed
> shore, which awaits every man that fears not God.

The Inferno, Canto III, 11. 106-8, p. 33.

153. The image of the "eyes" occurs again in a minor companion poem *Eyes that last I saw in tears:*

> Here in death's dream kingdom
> The golden vision reappears
> I see the eyes but not the tears
> This is my affliction.

These are not the "sightless eyes" of the Hollow Men, but the "eyes" that stand for divine and eternal Truth. Even in "death's dream kingdom" of this nightmarish world of illusion, the protagonist in this poem is able to perceive "the golden vision." Obviously he has parted company with the "empty men" and has taken a step forward toward Truth, but the vision that "reappears" to him is incomplete as it is not accompanied with the translucence of divine illumination symbolized by the "tears." Hence, the dimness of the perception is the cause of his affliction.

Eliot, *Collected Poems,* p. 143.

"Eyes that last I saw in tears" first appeared in the autumn of 1924 with " 'The Wind sprang up at Four o'clock' and 'This is the Dead Land' . . . in the *Chapbook* under the general title 'Doris Dream Songs.' " Then it was published with "Part II and Part IV of 'The Hollow Men' . . . in the *Criterion* for January, 1925." Part I of "The Hollow Men" appeared previously "with a French translation by St. J. Perse in *Commerce.* Part V was first printed in *Poems: 1909-1925.*"

Smith, p. 100.

154. Eliot, "The Hollow Men," *Collected Poems,* p. 89.

155. *Ibid.*

156. *Ibid.*

157. *The Paradiso,* Canto XXIII, 11. 70-75, p. 285.

158. T. S. Eliot, "The Hollow Men," p. 89.

159. *Ibid.,* pp. 89-90.

160. *Ibid.,* p. 90.

161. Paul Fussell, "A Note on 'The Hollow Men,' " *Modern Language Notes,* Vol. LXV (April, 1950), p. 254.

162. Eliot, "The Hollow Men," p. 90.

163. Smith, p. 109.

164. It is significant that this poem was written in 1925 "during the aftermath of unemployment and discontent which made the years between the Wars a nightmare."

Walker, p. 338.

165. In Professor Knight's view too " 'The Waste Land' is chaotic. But the gaps in its logic may be said to serve a purpose since to fill

them in would show a sequence and relation where the poem would point rather to the absence of any such relation."

G. Wilson Knight, "A Note on the Poetry of T. S. Eliot," *The Christian Renaissance* (Toronto, 1933), p. 371.

Thus in building up relationships among the various parts of the poem and the layers of meaning they invoke, a consistent theme evolves.

166. Bonamy Dobrée, *The Lamp and the Lute: Studies in Six Modern Authors* (Oxford, 1929), pp. 122-23.

167. Dilys Powell, *Descent from Parnassus* (London, 1934), p. 73.

168. Edward J. H. Greene, *T. S. Eliot et la France* (Paris, 1951), p. 108.

169. F. R. Leavis, *New Bearings in English Poetry* (London, 1932), p. 103.

170. *Ibid.*

171. Eliot, "The Burial of the Dead," 1. 61.

172. *Ibid.*, "What the Thunder said," 1. 393.

173. Helen Gardner, *The Art of T. S. Eliot* (London, 1949), p. 97.

174. Eliot, "What the Thunder said," 1. 386.

175. *Ibid.*, 1. 379.

176. *Ibid.*, 1. 393.

177. *The Purgatorio*, Canto XXVI, 11. 145-48, pp. 330-31.

Eliot's translation of the last line makes it clear: "Then dived he back into that fire which refines them."

Eliot, "Dante," *Selected Essays*, p. 256.

178. Grover Smith, p. 76.

(Line 42 of *The Waste Land*).

These are the words of the Shepherd who told the injured lover that Isolde's ship was not at sea. After being deadly wounded by his jealous friend Melot, Tristan was carried to Brittany by his loyal servant, Kurvenal, where he anxiously waited for Isolde.

In the Eulenburg Edition (1932) of Richard Wagner's *Tristan und Isolde,* the above quotation appears on page 725.

179. Eliot, "What the Thunder said," 11. 418-19.

180. *Ibid.*, 1. 388.

181. *Ibid.*, "The Burial of the Dead," 1. 24.

182. *Ibid.*, "What the Thunder said," 11. 393-94.

183. Leavis, p. 114.

184. Eliot, "What the Thunder said," 1. 342.

185. *Ibid.*, 1. 340.

186. Anthony Thwaite, *Contemporary English Poetry* (London, 1959), p. 60.

187. Eliot, "What the Thunder said," 1. 368.

188. *Ibid.*, 11. 368-69.

190. *Ibid.*, 1. 425.

190. *Ibid.*, 1.425.

191. Also the lands that are laid waste through lust.

192. "In the Mahayana scriptures Buddha is referred to as the Fisherman who draws fish from the ocean of Samsara to the light of salvation" (p. 126).

"The Babylonians had the Fish, or Fisher, god Oannes who revealed to them the arts of Writing, Agriculture, etc., and was . . . lord of all wisdom" (p. 127).

"For those who hold that the Grail story is essentially . . . Christian . . . the title is naturally connected with the use of the Fish symbol in early Christianity: the 'Icthys' anagram, as applied to Christ, the title 'Fishers of Men,' . . . though it must be noted that no manipulation of the Christian symbolism avails satisfactorily to account for the lamentable condition into which . . . the title has fallen" (p. 124).

"There is thus little reason to doubt that, if we regard the Fish as a Divine Life symbol, of immemorial antiquity, we shall not go very far astray."

Weston, *op. cit.*

193. *Ibid.*, p. 23.

194. Bowra, p. 164.

195. "Tereus, King of Thrace, having forced Philomela to his will, cut out her tongue that she might not tell her sister Procne of the outrage. But Procne discovered the truth . . . [and] served as a meal to Tereus, her husband, the murdered body of their son. The very barbarity of this myth sharpens its appropriateness to the theme of 'The Waste Land,' and references to it and to the sequel—the metamorphosis of Philomela into a nightingale . . . and of Procne into a swallow—are to appear again."

Hugh Ross Williamson, *The Poetry of T. S. Eliot* (London, 1932), p. 110.

196. Eliot, *The Waste Land*, 11. 99-100.

197. *Ibid.*, 11. 385-87.

198. *Ibid.*, 1. 427.

199. *Ibid.*, 1. 22.

200. *Ibid.*, 1. 23.

201. *Ibid.*, 1. 20.

202. *Ibid.*, 1. 25.

203. *Ibid.*, 1. 339.

204. *Ibid.*, 1. 384.

205. *Ibid.*

206. *Ibid.*, 1. 413.

207. Hans W. Häusermann, *L'Oeuvre Poétique de T. S. Eliot* (Montreux, 1940), pp. 8-9.

208. Smith, p. 97.

209. Georges Cattaui, *Trois Poètes: Hopkins, Yeats et Eliot* (Paris, 1947), pp. 85-86.

210. Miss Fry, for instance, states that "Eliot often comes near to despair, and his philosophy at its best is negative and passive."
Edith M. Fry, "The Poetic Work of T. S. Eliot," *The British Annual of Literature*, Vol. V (London, 1948), p. 8.

211. Bullough, p. 165.

212. Eliot, *The Waste Land*, 11. 401, 411, 418.

213. *Ibid.*, 1. 401.

214. Spartaco Gamberini, *La poesia di T. S. Eliot* (Genoua, 1954), p. 62.

215. That is why the poet has grown impatient with the critics who said that in *The Waste Land* he "had expressed the 'disillusionment of a generation,'" (e.g., Dilys Powell, "The Poetry of T. S. Eliot," *Life and Letters*, Vol. VII, 1931, pp. 386-419; and Edmund Wilson in *Axel's Castle*, 1931, pp. 104-14) and adds that he "may have expressed for them their own illusion of being disillusioned, but that did not form part of [his] intention."
Eliot, "Thoughts After Lambeth," *Selected Essays*, p. 386.

216. Green, p. 112.

217. Dealing with this point, Mr. Moorman remarks that "superficial eccentricities and difficulties do not necessarily point to a central disunity. [They] are merely . . . engendered by the difficulty of writing a poem based on many facets of a single myth."
Charles Moorman, "Myth and Organic Unity in 'The Waste Land,'" *The South Atlantic Quarterly*, Vol. LVII (Spring, 1958), p. 201.

218. Stephen Spender, *The Destructive Element* (London, 1938), p. 145.

219. *Ibid.*

220. I. A. Richards, *Science and Poetry* (London, 1926), pp. 64-65 fn.

221. T. S. Eliot, "A Note on Poetry and Belief," *The Enemy*, Vol. I (January, 1927), p. 16.

222. *Ibid.*, *Selected Essays*, p. 269.

223. *Ibid.*, *The Use of Poetry and the Use of Criticism*, p. 130.

224. *Ibid.*

225. I use the term "belief" here in its wide sense to denote emotional, mystical, literary, and social convictions.

226. F. L. Lucas, "Review of 'The Waste Land,'" *The New Statesman*, Vol. XXII, No. 551 (3 Nov., 1923), p. 116.

227. Kristian Smidt, *Poetry and Belief in the Work of T. S. Eliot* (Oslo, 1949), p. 132.

228. *Ibid.*

229. *Ibid.*

230. G. S. Fraser, *Vision and Rhetoric* (London, 1959), pp. 100-1.

231. The poet reasons that "doubt and uncertainty are merely a variety of unbelief."

Eliot, "A Note on Poetry and Belief," *The Enemy*, p. 16.

232. Eliot, "The Hollow Men," p. 88.

233. *Ibid.*, "Dante," *Selected Essays*, p. 258.

234. *Ibid.*

235. *Ibid.*, p. 259.

236. Though Eliot's main thesis in *Tradition and the Individual Talent* is that "the progress of an artist is a continual self-sacrifice, a continual extinction of personality," he confesses toward the end of his essay on *Dante* that he "cannot, in practice, wholly separate [his] poetic appreciation from [his] personal beliefs."
Eliot, *Selected Essays*, pp. 17, 271.
Obviously the complete extinction of the personal element either in writing or in appreciating poetry is a practical impossibility.

237. Eliot, "The Burial of the Dead," 1. 18.

238. *Ibid.*, "What the Thunder said," 1. 430.

239. *Ibid.*, "Gerontion," p. 38.

240. Spender, p. 144.

241. Maxwell, p. 36.

242. *Ibid.*, p. 37.

243. Bullough, p. 159.

244. Cleanth Brooks, "The Waste Land: Critique of the Myth," *Modern Poetry and the Tradition* (London, 1948), p. 166.

245. Bowra, p. 182.

246. Elizabeth Drew, *T. S. Eliot: The Design of his Poetry* (London, 1950), p. 43.

247. Eliot, "Tradition and the Individual Talent," *Selected Essays*, pp. 13-22.

248. Giorgio Melchiori, *The Tightrope Walkers: Studies of Mannerism in Modern English Literature* (London, 1956), p. 54.

249. Eliot, "The Burial of the Dead," 1. 37.

250. *Ibid.*, 1. 41.

251. David Daiches, *Poetry and the Modern World* (Chicago, 1940), p. 114.

252. Scott, p. 222.

253. Eliot, *The Waste Land*, 11. 54-55.

254. It is significant that Eliot in his Notes refers to the Antarctic explorers who, "at the extremity of their strength, had the constant delusion that there was one more member than could actually be counted."
Eliot, *Notes on the Waste Land*, p. 83.
It is the delusion that governs the lives of the people in the Waste Land.

255. Eliot, *The Waste Land*, 1. 60.

256. *Ibid.*, 1. 367.

257. *Ibid.*, 1. 180.

Notes to Chapter Five

1. "In the service of Ash Wednesday the priest dips his thumb in the ashes of the burnt palm of the previous Palm Sunday and marking the forehead of those who approach, intones these words—'Remember, man, that thou art dust and unto dust thou shalt return.'"

E. M. Stephenson, *T. S. Eliot and the Lay Reader* (London, 1944), p. 24.

2. Though an Anglo-Catholic, Eliot has not confined himself to post-Reformation rites, but has gone back to the original sources of "Catholic" liturgy and Mass. A contextual study of the poem reveals his indebtedness to Roman Catholicism and he obviously had it in mind when he wrote this poem.

3. *Ash Wednesday*, p. 93.

4. Guido Cavalcanti, Dante's greatest friend, "was actively involved in the party feuds of Florence in the late thirteenth century, and after a violent fracas in the streets he was exiled in 1300 to Sarzana, where he caught the fever of which he soon died. In this place of exile, from which there appeared no expectation of return [although in fact, probably through the good offices of Dante, he was later recalled], he wrote the ballad beginning:

> Perch'io non spero di tornar gia mai,
> Ballatetta, in Toscana,
> 'because I do not hope to turn again,
> Ballatetta, to Tuscany.'"

Philip M. Martin, *Mastery and Mercy: A Study of Two Religious Poems, 'The Wreck of the Deutschland' by G. M. Hopkins and 'Ash Wednesday' by T. S. Eliot* (London, 1957), pp. 96-97.

A complete translation of the ballad is found in Ezra Pound's *Umbra* which is a collection of the early poems of Guido Cavalcanti and Arnaut Daniel (London, 1920), pp. 105-6.

5. *Ash Wednesday*, p. 93.

6. *Ibid.*

7. See *The Mysticism of the Dark Night*, Chap. I, Sec. III, pp. 28-29 and Chap. II, Sec. XIV, p. 43.

8. *Ibid.*

9. *Ash Wednesday*, p. 93.

10. *Ibid.*

11. *Ibid.*

12. *Ibid.*

13. *Ibid.*

14. *Ibid.*, p. 94.

15. This Lady might be identified with St. Teresa or with any other woman Saint who fits in with this spiritual function in the poem, i.e., of adoration and intercession.

16. *Ash Wednesday,* p. 95.

17. *Ibid.*

18. *Ibid.*

19. The image of the dry bones comes from the Prophecy of Ezekiel, Chap. XXXVII, 1-5.

20. *Ash Wednesday,* p. 95.

21. ". . . just as this cloud of unknowing is above you and between you and your God, it will be necessary for you to put in the same way a cloud of forgetting beneath you, between you and all the creatures that have ever been made."

Ira Progoff (trans.), *The Cloud of Unknowing,* Chap. V, Sec. I, p. 65.

22. *Ash Wednesday,* p. 96.

23. It is reminiscent of the Divine Rose (i.e., the Virgin in the *Paradiso,* Canto XXIII, 1. 73), the Heavenly Rose (i.e., the Angels and the Saints—Canto XXX, 11. 115-17), and the Eternal Rose (i.e., the divine love of God—11. 124-32).

24. *Ash Wednesday,* p. 96.

25. *Ibid.*

26. *Ibid.*

27. *Ibid.*

28. *Ibid.*

29. *The Purgatorio,* Canto IX, 11. 76-77, p. 109.

The three steps are interpreted allegorically "as sincerity, contrition and love, and analogically as contrition, confession and expiation by the blood of Christ."

Gardner, *The Art of T. S. Eliot,* p. 119.

30. ". . . the mind can by no means be directed to the spiritual presentation and contemplation of the Celestial Hierarchies unless it use[s] the material guidance suited to it . . . so that we might be guided through the sensible to the intelligible, and from sacred symbols to the Primal Source of the Celestial hierarchies."

Dionysius the Areopagite, *The Celestial Hierarchies,* trans. from the Greek by the editors of "The Shrine of Wisdom," Manual No. 15 (London, 1935), pp. 10, 19.

31. *Infra,* Chap. VI, Sec. I, p. 112.

32. Unpublished MS. bearing the title *A ladder to heaven of twelve staves,* kept in the British Museum under Royal 17.c.XIII (fol. 23). The MS. is dated at the beginning of the seventeenth century.

33. *Ash Wednesday,* p. 97.

34. Matthiessen, p. 66.

35. *Ibid.*

36. *Ash Wednesday,* p. 97.

37. *Ibid.*

38. *Ibid.*

39. See *The Mysticism of the Dark Night,* Chap. I, Sec. III, pp. 28-29.

192 THE MYSTICAL PHILOSOPHY OF T. S. ELIOT

40. *Ash Wednesday,* p. 97.

41. *Ibid.*

42. *Ibid.*

43. *Ibid.*

44. *Ibid.*

45. *Ibid.*

46. *Ibid.*

47. *Ibid.*

48. *Ibid.,* "The Love Song of J. Alfred Prufrock," p. 15.

49. *Ibid.*

50. *Ibid., Ash Wednesday,* p. 97.

51. *Ibid.*

52. Striking his breast three times, the priest says:

> Domine, non sum dignus ut intres sub tectum meum:
> sed tantum dic verbo, et sanabitur anima mea.
> [*Lord, I am not worthy* that thou shouldst enter under
> my roof: *say but the word* and my soul shall be healed.]

After receiving Holy Communion, the priest repeats the same words before the Communion of the people.

The Ordinary of the Mass (London, 1958), p. 37.

The words are taken from the Biblical text of St. Matthew, Chap. VIII, 8.

Concerning this prayer, Professor Jungmann remarks that the oldest texts which were found "in the Sacramentary of Amiens" (ninth century) contain two preparatory prayers: "Domine Jesu Christi, Fili Dei Vivi" and "Perceptio." But "a series of other formulations of a prayer of preparation appear here and there." Some of them "are marked entirely by a tone of humble petition. Others have a hymnic character." Joseph A. Jungmann, *The Mass of the Roman Rite,* trans. by Francis A. Brunner (London, 1951), p. 492.

53. *Ash Wednesday,* p. 98.

This Lady of *Ash Wednesday* brings to mind the angelic figure of Matilda

> who went along singing, and culling flower after
> flower, wherewith all her path was painted.

The Purgatorio, Canto XXVIII, ll. 40-42, p. 351.

54. *Ash Wednesday,* p. 98.

55. *Ibid.*

56. *Ibid.*

57. *Ibid.*

58. *Ibid.*

59. *Ibid.*

In his *Thoughts After Lambeth,* Eliot closes his argument on the Report of the Lambeth Conference (1930) saying that "the World is trying the experiment of attempting to form a civilized but non-Christian mentality. The experiment will fail; but we must be very patient in awaiting its collapse; meanwhile redeeming the time: so that the Faith may be preserved alive through the dark ages before us; to renew and rebuild civilization, and save the World from suicide."

Eliot, *Selected Essays*, p. 387.

60. *Ash Wednesday*, p. 98.
61. *Ibid.*
62. *Ibid.*, p. 99.
63. *Ibid.*
64. C. C. Martindale (trans.), *The Office of Compline*, Prayer IV (London, 1954), pp. 30-31.
65. *Ibid.*
66. *Ash Wednesday*, p. 100.
67. *Ibid.*
68. *Ibid.*
69. *Ibid.*
70. *Ibid.*, p. 101.

These words come from *The Reproaches* which are sung on Good Friday:

> Popule meus, quid feci tibi? aut in quo contristavi te? responde mihi.
> Quia eduxi te de terra Aegypti: parasti crucem Salvatori tuo.
> [*O my people, what have I done to thee? or wherein have I aggrieved thee? answer me.*
> Because I led thee out of the land of Egypt, thou hast prepared a Cross for thy Saviour].

Monsignor Ronald A. Knox (trans.), *Holy Week Manual* (London, 1956), p. 128.

71. *Ash Wednesday*, p. 100.
72. *Ibid.*
73. Leonard Unger, ed., *"Ash Wednesday," T. S. Eliot: A Selected Critique* (New York, 1948), p. 369.
74. *Ash Wednesday*, p. 101.
75. *Ibid.*
76. *Ibid.*, p. 102.
77. *Ibid.*
78. *Ibid.*, p. 97.
79. *Ibid.*, p. 102.
80. *Ibid.*
81. *Ibid.*
82. *Ibid.*
83. *Ibid.*
84. *Ibid.*
85. *Ibid.*
86. *Ibid.*, p. 103.

87. *Ibid.*

88. Unpublished MS. entitled *Thomas Aquinas of the Angelical Salutation,* trans. by Henry P. Lord Morley, kept in the British Museum under Royal 17.c.XVI (fol. 10). The MS. is dated between A.D. 1528 and 1547.

89. *Ash Wednesday,* p. 103.

90. *Ibid.*

91. *The Paradiso,* Canto III, 11. 69-74, 85-87, p. 31.

92. *Ash Wednesday,* p. 103.

93. *Breviarum Romanum: Gratianum Actio Post Missam:* Thanksgiving After Mass (Rome, 1936), p. 20.

94. *Ash Wednesday,* p. 103.

95. *The Forty Hours* (London, 1960), p. 37.

96. Granville Hicks, *The Great Tradition* (New York, 1935), p. 270.

97. See Wilson, p. 130 and Daiches, p. 126.

98. Allen Tate, *Reactionary Essays on Poetry and Ideas* (New York, 1936), p. 212.

99. *Ibid.,* pp. 212-13.

100. *Ibid.,* p. 213.

101. Eliot, "Dante," *Selected Essays,* p. 271.

102. Tate, p. 214.

103. Bullough, p. 150.

104. *Ibid.*

105. *The Waste Land,* 1. 425.

106. "Gerontion," p. 37.

107. "Journey of the Magi," *Collected Poems,* p. 108.

108. "Used by the Greeks . . . 'magia' signified originally the religion, learning and occult practices of the Eastern magi.

"They were distinguished in many ways from other men . . . the Magi penetrated into Greece, India and some say even into China; and throughout the ancient world their power was recognized. . . . however strange their rites might appear to Herodotus and later to Plutarch, this did not subtract from their value as the great magicians of antiquity, the professional readers of dreams and diviners by the stars."

E. M. Butler, *The Myth of the Magus* (Cambridge, 1948), pp. 15, 19.

109. "Journey of the Magi," p. 107.

110. *Ibid.,* p. 108.

111. It derives its title from *Nunc Dimittis* or "Song of Simeon" in the Book of Common Prayer.

112. "A Song for Simeon," *Collected Poems,* p. 109.

113. *Ibid.,* p. 110.

114. *Ibid.*

115. *Ibid.*

116. *Ibid.*
117. Reference to "Animula" as a little soul enjoying the innocence of childhood, is suggested by Dante's *Purgatorio*, Canto XVI, ll. 85-90, p. 197.
118. "Animula," *Collected Poems*, p. 111.
119. *Ibid.*
120. *Ibid.*
121. *Ibid.*
122. *Ibid.*
123. *Ibid.*
124. *Ibid.*
125. *Ibid.*
126. *Ibid.*, p. 112.
127. Pericles: Most heavenly music!
　　　　　　　It nips me unto listening, and thick slumber
　　　　　　　Hangs upon mine eyes; let me rest.
William Shakespeare, *Pericles*, ed. by K. Deighton, Act V, Sc. I, ll. 230-32 (London: The Arden Shakespeare, 1907), p. 139.
128. "Marina," *Collected Poems*, p. 113.
129. *Ibid.*
130. Per.　　　　　　　O! come
　　　　　hither,
　　Thou that begett'st him that did thee beget;
　　Thou that wast born at sea, buried at Tarsus,
　　And found at sea again. O Helicanus!
　　Down on thy knees, thank the holy gods as loud
　　as thunder threatens us; this is Marina.

Shakespeare, *Pericles*, ll. 193-98, p. 137.
It is noteworthy that Shakespeare's Pericles enjoys a state of complete wakefulness after his slumber; whereas in Eliot's poem, he is still attached to his dreamy world.
131. "Marina," p. 113.
132. *Ibid.*
133. "Journey of the Magi," p. 107.
134. *Ibid.*
135. *Ibid.*, p. 108.
136. "Animula," p. 111.
137. *Ibid.*
138. See *Spanish Mysticism*, Chap. II, Sec. XIV, pp. 42-43.
139. *Ash Wednesday*, p. 93.
140. *Ibid.*
141. *Ibid.*
Eliot has substituted "man's art" for "man's gift." Shakespeare's line reads: "Desiring this man's art and that man's scope."
William Shakespeare, *The Sonnets*, ed. by C. Knox Pooler, No. XXIX, l. 7 (London: The Arden Shakespeare, 1918), p. 34.
142. *Ash Wednesday*, p. 98.

143. *Ibid.*

144. *Ibid.*

145. See *The Mysticism of the Dark Night*, Chap. I, Sec. III, pp. 28-29.

146. *Ash Wednesday* p. 101.

147. *Ibid.*

148. *Ibid.*, p. 93.

149. *Ibid.*, p. 94.

150. Wilson, p. 130.

151. Martin, p. 100.

152. St. John of the Cross, *The Complete Works*, Vol. I, Bk. II, Chap. XIII, p. 418.

Mr. Unger coincidently mentions the above passage but does not state its location. He refers only to the fact that "the term 'old man' is often used for the unpurged condition of the soul."

Unger, pp. 353-54.

153. *"What place is this? What region, what quarter of the world?* Where am I? Beneath the sun's rising or beneath the wheeling course of the frozen Bear?"

Lucius Annaeus Seneca, "Hercules Furens," *The Tragedies* (trans. by F. J. Miller), Vol. I, ll. 1138-40 (London, 1916), pp. 99, 101.

Cf.   "De Bailhache, Fresca, Mrs. Cammel, whirled
           Beyond the circuit of *the shuddering Bear*
           In fractured atoms."   ("Gerontion," p. 39).

154. "Gerontion," p. 37.

155. "Ash Wednesday" was first published "on April 24, 1930." Two thousand copies of "Marina" appeared "on September 25, 1930."

Donald Gallup, *A Bibliographical Check-List of the Writings of T. S. Eliot* (New Haven, 1947), pp. 20, 22.

156. *Ash Wednesday*, p. 102.

157. *Ibid.*, p. 98.

158. Mr. Williamson differentiates between the "expanded conceit, which is the exposition of an extended comparison, and the 'condensed conceit,' which is a telescoped image that develops the thought by rapid association or sudden contrast." He takes the famous pair of compasses in the "Valediction" and the "bracelet of bright haire about the bone" in "The Relique" of Donne as respective examples.

George Williamson, *The Donne Tradition: A Study in English Poetry from Donne to the Death of Cowley* (New York, First Published 1930—Reprinted 1958), p. 31.

159. "Marina," p. 114.

160. *Ibid.*

161. *Ash Wednesday*, p. 97.

162. *Ibid.*

163. *Ibid.*, p. 101.

164. *The Purgatorio*, Canto XXXIII, ll. 73-75 (London: The Temple Classics, 1901), p. 423.

165. *The Paradiso,* Canto I, 11. 88-90, p. 9.

166. *Ibid.,* Canto V, 1. 8, p. 49.

167. "Tevigga Sutta," Buddhist Suttas, *The Sacred Books of the East,* trans. from Pali by T. W. Rhys Davids, Vol. XI, p. 187.

168. *Ash Wednesday,* p. 95.

169. *Ibid.*

170. "Maha-Parinibbana-Sutta," *Buddhist Suttas,* p. 15.

171. *Ash Wednesday,* p. 95.

172. *The Sacred Books of the East,* trans. from Prakrit by Hermann Jacobi, Vol. XLV, p. 166.

173. *Ash Wednesday,* p. 102.

174. "Gaina Sutras," Bk. I, Lecture 2, Chap. 3, *The Sacred Books of the East,* trans. from Prakrit, Vol. XLV, pp. 258-59.

175. "The Upanishads," First Aranyaka, Adhyaya 3, Khanda 2, *The Sacred Books of the East,* trans. by F. Max Müller, Vol. I, p. 177.

176. *Ash Wednesday,* p. 99.

177. See *The Ethical Mysticism of the Buddhist Philosophy,* Chap. II, Sec. VI, pp. 35-36.

178. *Ash Wednesday,* p. 94.

179. *Ibid.,* p. 101.

180. *Ibid.,* p. 103.

181. See the *Traces of Mystification in the Rig-Veda,* Chap. II, Sec. II, pp. 31-32.

182. "Brihadaranyaka-Upanishad," First Adhyaya, Brahmana 4, *The Sacred Books of the East,* trans. by F. Max Müller, Vol. XV, p. 87.

183. *Ash Wednesday,* p. 102.

184. *Ibid.,* p. 97.

185. *Ibid.,* p. 94.

186. See the *Law of Karma,* Chap. II, Sec. III, Footnote No. 13, p. 32.

187. "Akankheyya Sutta," Buddhist Suttas, *The Sacred Books of the East,* trans. by T. W. Rhys Davids, Vol. XI, p. 217.

188. *Ibid.,* pp. 217-18.

189. *Ibid.*

Notes to Chapter Six

1. *L'Oeuvre Poétique de T. S. Eliot* (Montreux, 1940), p. 13.

2. Smith, p. 251.

3. The Logos of Heraclitus "is something which is common to all things, according to which all things happen . . . [It] is a component of each different object, yet has a single collective being: it is the component of order or structure or arrangement, not the whole of an object's structure or shape but that part of it which connects it with everything else."

Heraclitus, *The Cosmic Fragments,* ed. with an Intro. and Commen. by G. S. Kirk, Fr. 50 (Cambridge, 1954), p. 69.

4. Helen Gardner, *The Art of T. S. Eliot* (London, 1949), p. 63.

5. T. S. Eliot, "Burnt Norton," *Four Quartets* (London, 1944—Reprinted 1952), p. 7.

6. See *The Mystical Philosophy of the Advaita Vedanta*, Chap. II, Sec. V, p. 33 ff.

7. Eliot, *Burnt Norton*, p. 7.

8. *Ibid.*

9. *Ibid.*

10. Erich Frank, *Philosophical Understanding and Religious Truth* (New York, 1945), p. 68.

11. *Ibid.*

12. Eliot, *Burnt Norton*, p. 7.

13. *Ibid.*

14. *Ibid.*

15. See *The Mystical Philosophy of St. Augustine*, Chap. II, Sec. IX, pp. 37-38.

16. Eliot, *Burnt Norton*, p. 7.

17. *Ibid.*

18. *Ibid.*

19. *Ibid.*, p. 8.

20. *Ibid.*

21. *Ibid.*

22. *Ibid.*

23. *Ibid.*

24. *Ibid.*

25. *Ibid.*

26. "Perhaps this symbol has its origin in Ancient Egypt. Here it was the symbol of the sun and of life, of immortality and of resurrection . . .

"In Buddhism this flower becomes a symbol denoting the essence of enlightenment of those who have meditated and will meditate on the profound law. The lotus supports the Lord Buddha as the flower supports the world above the chaotic waters of the universe."

William E. Ward, "The Lotus Symbol: its Meaning in Buddhist Art and Philosophy," *The Journal of Aesthetics and Art Criticism*, Vol. XI, No. 2 (December, 1952), p. 135.

27. Melchiori, p. 90.

28. Eliot, *Burnt Norton*, p. 8.

29. *Ibid.*

30. *Ibid.*

31. *Ibid.*

32. *Ibid.*, p. 7.

33. *Ibid.*, p. 8.

34. William Shakespeare, *The Merchant of Venice*, ed. by John Russell Brown, Act II, Sc. VII, ll. 65-69 (London: The Arden Edition, 1955), p. 60.

35. Eliot, *Burnt Norton*, p. 8.

36. *Ibid.*
37. *Ibid.*, p. 9.
38. *Ibid.*
39. *Ibid.*
40. *Ibid.*
41. *Ibid.*
42. *Ibid.*
43. *Ibid.*, p. 10.
44. *Ibid.*
45. *Ibid.*
46. *Ibid.*
47. *Ibid.*
48. *Ibid.*
49. See *the Dark Night of St. John of the Cross,* Chap. I, Sec. III, pp. 28-29 and Chap. II, Sec. XIV, p. 43.
50. Eliot, *Burnt Norton,* p. 10.
51. *Ibid.*
52. *Ibid.*, p. 11.
53. *Ibid.*
54. *Ibid.*
55. *Ibid.*, p. 10.
56. *Ibid.*, p. 11.
57. *Ibid.*
58. ". . . together with the aridity and emptiness which it [the Dark Night] causes in the senses, it gives the soul an inclination and desire to be alone and in quietness."
St. John of the Cross, *The Dark Night of the Soul,* Bk. I, Chap. IX, p. 354.
59. Eliot, *Burnt Norton,* p. 11.
60. *Ibid.*
61. *Ibid.*
62. *Ibid.*, p. 12.
63. William Blissett, "The Argument of T. S. Eliot's 'Four Quartets'," *University of Toronto Quarterly,* Vol. XV, No. 2 (January, 1946), p. 125.
64. Eliot, *Burnt Norton,* p. 12.
65. *Ibid.*
66. *Ibid.*
67. See *The Synthetic Mysticism of St. Thomas Aquinas,* Chap. II, Sec. XI, p. 39.
68. Eliot, *Burnt Norton,* p. 12.
69. *Ibid.*
70. *Ibid.*
71. *Ibid.*
72. ". . . just as men mount by means of ladders and climb up to possessions and treasures and things that are in strong places, even

so also, by means of . . . secret contemplation, without knowing how, the soul ascends and climbs up to a knowledge and possession of the good things and treasures of heaven."

St. John of the Cross, *The Dark Night of the Soul*, Bk. II, Chap. XVIII, p. 432.

73. Eliot, *Burnt Norton*, p. 13.
74. *Ibid.*
75. *Ibid.*
76. *Ibid.*
77. *Ibid.*
78. *Ibid.*
79. *Ibid., East Coker*, p. 15.
80. *Ibid.*
81. In stating that "in my beginning is my end," Eliot gives us an inversion of the motto which was embroidered upon the Chair of State of Mary, Queen of Scots: "En ma fin est mon commencement."

Mr. Sweeney refers to Baring's book on the history of the Scottish Queen and suggests that Eliot might have been interested in this work.

James Johnson Sweeney, "East Coker: A Reading," *T. S. Eliot: A Selected Critique*, ed. by Leonard Unger, p. 399.

In the Preface of this book, we read that "there is no doubt that practically and politically the end of the Queen of Scots was her beginning; for at her death her son, James Stuart, became the heir to the crown of England and Scotland, and he lived to wear both crowns."

Maurice Baring, *In My End Is My Beginning* (London, 1931), p. viii.

82. Eliot, *East Coker*, p. 15.
83. *Ibid.*
84. *Ibid.*, p. 16.
These lines re-echo the following words from "The Boke Named the Gouernour": ". . . as moche as by the association of a man and a woman in daunsinge may be signified matrimonie, I coulde in declarynge the dignitie and commoditie of that sacrament make intiere volumes, if it were nat so communely known to all men, that almoste euery frere lymitour carieth it writen in his bosome."

Sir Thomas Elyot, *The Boke Named the Gouernour*, ed. from the First Edition of 1531 by Henry H. S. Croft, Vol. I, Chap. XXI (London, 1880), pp. 233-34.

85. Eliot, *East Coker*, p. 16.
86. *Ibid.*, p. 17.
87. *Ibid.*
88. *Ibid.*, p. 18.
89. *Ibid.*
90. *Ibid.*

91. See *The Mysticism of the Upanishads,* Chap. II, Sec. III, pp. 31-32.

92. See the "spirit" of humility in *Brahmanic and Hindu Mysticism,* Chap. II, Sec. I, pp. 30-31.

93. See *The Ethical Mysticism of the Buddhist Philosophy,* Chap. II, Sec. VI, pp. 35-36.

94. Smidt, p. 172.

95. See *the Law of Karma,* Chap. II, Sec. III, Footnote No. 13, p. 32.

96. See *the Noble Eightfold Path and the Supreme Enlightenment,* Chap. II, Sec. VI, pp. 35-36.

97. *The Inferno,* Canto I, 11. 1-3, p. 3.

98. Eliot, *East Coker,* p. 18.

99. Sir Arthur Conan Doyle, "The Hound of the Baskervilles," *Sherlock Holmes* (London, 1929), pp. 374-76.

100. Eliot, *East Coker,* p. 18.

101. John Milton, "Samson Agonistes," *The Poetical Works of Milton,* ed. by Helen Darbishire, Vol. II, 11. 80-82 (Oxford, 1955), p. 67.

102. Eliot, *East Coker,* p. 18.

103. *Ibid.,* p. 19.

104. *Ibid.*

105. *Ibid.*

106. *Ibid.*

107. *Ibid.*

108. *Ibid.*

109. *Ibid.*

110. *Ibid.,* p. 20.
In the words of St. John of the Cross:

> In order to arrive at possessing everything,
> Desire to possess nothing.

The Ascent of Mount Carmel, Bk. I, Chap. XIII, p. 59.

111. Eliot, *East Coker,* p. 20.

> In order to arrive at knowing everything,
> Desire to know nothing.

St. John of the Cross, *The Ascent of Mount Carmel,* p. 59.

112. Thomas Merton, *The Ascent to Truth* (London, 1951), pp. 40-41.

113. Eliot, *East Coker,* p. 19.

114. *Ibid., Burnt Norton,* p. 9.

115. "Religio Medici," *The Works of Sir Thomas Browne,* ed. by Geoffrey Keynes, Vol. 1, Pt. 11, Sec. 11 (London, 1928), p. 91.

116. Eliot, *East Coker,* p. 20.

117. *Ibid.*

118. *Ibid.*, p. 21.

119. *Ibid., Burnt Norton,* p. 8.

120. *Ibid., East Coker,* p. 20.

121. *Ibid.*

122. *Ibid.*, p. 21.

123. *Ibid.*

The world of "the ruined millionaire" symbolizes Adam and his descendants.

124. *Ibid.*

The poem was written for the Good Friday of 1940.

125. See *The Mystical Philosophy of St. Augustine,* Chap. II, Sec. IX, pp. 37-38.

126. See *St. Teresa and the Mysticism of the "Interior Castle,"* Chap. II, Sec. XIV, pp. 42-43.

127. See *St. John of the Cross and the Mysticism of the Dark Night,* Chap. II, Sec. XIV, p. 43.

128. Eliot, *East Coker,* p. 20.

129. *Ibid.*, p. 21.

130. *Ibid.*

131. *Ibid.*

132. *Ibid.*, p. 22.

133. Scott, p. 219.

134. Eliot, *East Coker,* p. 22.

135. *Ibid.*

136. *Ibid.*

137. *Ibid.*

138. *Ibid.*

139. *Ibid.*

140. *Ibid.*

141. *Ibid.*, p. 23.

142. *Ibid.*

143. *Ibid.*

144. *Ibid.*

145. "I feel that there is something in having passed one's childhood beside the big river, which is incommunicable to those who have not. Of course my people were Northerners and New Englanders, and of course I have spent many years out of America altogether; but Missouri and the Mississippi have made a deeper impression on me than any other part of the world."

A letter from Eliot to Marquis Childs of *St. Louis Post-Dispatch* from "An Appendix prepared by the Department of English, Washington University," *The Eliot Family and St. Louis.*

The Appendix is attached to *American Literature and the American Language:* An Address delivered at Washington University on June 9, 1953 by T. S. Eliot (St. Louis, 1953), p. 29.

146. Eliot, *The Dry Salvages,* p. 25.

147. *Ibid.*
148. *Ibid.*
149. *Ibid.*
150. *Ibid.*
151. *Ibid.*
152. *Ibid.*, p. 26.
153. *Ibid.*
154. *Ibid.*
155. *Ibid.*
156. *Ibid.*
157. *Ibid.*
158. *Ibid.*
159. *Ibid.*, p. 27.
160. *Ibid.*
161. *Ibid.*
162. *Ibid.*
163. *Ibid.*
164. *Ibid.*
165. *Ibid.*
166. *Ibid.*
167. *Ibid.*, p. 28.
168. Smidt, p. 178.
169. Eliot, *The Dry Salvages*, p. 28.
170. *Ibid.*
171. *Ibid.*
172. *Ibid.*
173. *Ibid.*
174. *Ibid.*
175. *Ibid.*, p. 29.
176. *Ibid.*
177. *Ibid.*
178. *Ibid.*
179. *Ibid.*
180. *Ibid.*
181. *Ibid.*
182. *Ibid.*, p. 28.
183. *Ibid.*
184. *Ibid.*, p. 30.
185. *Ibid.*, p. 26.
186. *Ibid.*, p. 30.
187. *Ibid.*, p. 31.

Eliot expounded the same theme in *The Rock* (1934):

> I say to you: "Make perfect your will."
> I say: take no thought of the harvest,
> But only of proper sowing.

T. S. Eliot, *The Rock*, Pt. I (London, 1934), p. 9.

After his return from a visit to America in 1932-33, Eliot accepted a commission to write a play projected by the Forty-Five Churches' Fund and *The Rock* was completed and performed at Sadler's Wells Theatre: 28 May-9 June, 1934.

188. See *The Mysticism of the Bhagavad-Gita*, Chap. II, Sec. IV, pp. 32-33.

189. See *The Ethical Mysticism of the Buddhist Philosophy*, Chap. II, Sec. VI, pp. 35-36.

190. Eliot, *The Dry Salvages*, p. 31.

191. *Ibid.*

192. (Anon), *The Cloud of Unknowing*, Chap. LVII, Text No. 6, p. 172.

193. St. John of the Cross, *The Dark Night of the Soul*, Bk. II, Chap. XVIII, p. 433.

St. John is referring here to the property of the soul in its communication with God.

194. Eliot, *Epigraph to Four Quartets*, p. 6.

It is taken from Heraclitus' *Cosmic Fragments*, Fr. 60, p. 105.

". . . 'all things are one' in two ways: they are 'one,' first, in that they all have a common component, part of their structure; and secondly, because they all connect up with each other 'because of' this common structure."

Ibid., Fr. 50, p. 70.

195. Eliot, *The Dry Salvages*, p. 31.

196. *Ibid.*

197. *Ibid.*

198. *Ibid.*

199. *Ibid.*, p. 32.

200. *Jonah*, Chap. I, 17; Chap. II, 1, 10.

201. Eliot, *The Dry Salvages*, p. 32.

202. *Ibid.*

203. *Ibid.*, p. 28.

204. *Ibid.*, p. 32.

205. *Ibid.*

206. *Ibid.*

207. *Ibid.*, p. 26.

208. *Ibid.*, p. 32.

209. *Ibid.*, p. 33.

210. *Ibid.*, p. 32.

211. See *The Mysticism of the Upanishads*, Chap. II, Sec. III, pp. 31-32.

212. Eliot, *The Dry Salvages*, p. 33.

213. *Ibid.*

214. *Ibid.*

215. Gardner, p. 177.

216. *Ibid.*

217. Eliot, *The Dry Salvages*, p. 33.

Mr. Nicholson has rightly pointed out that "Eliot is not referring exclusively to the Incarnation of the Son of God in the person of Jesus of Nazareth. He is saying rather that all human apprehension of the timeless has in it something of the quality of the Incarnation."

Norman Nicholson, "T. S. Eliot," *Writers of To-day*, ed. by Denys Val Baker (London, '946), p. 147.

218. Eliot, *The Dry Salvages*, p. 33.

219. *Ibid.*

220. *Ibid.*

221. *Ibid.*

222. "The Quartet takes its title from a village in Huntingdonshire. Here Nicholas Ferrar founded a religious community in 1626. The community was dissolved during the Civil War, and the chapel destroyed by Cromwell's troops. It was restored in the 19th century. Eliot visited it in May 1936. Charles I is reputed to have taken refuge there after his defeat at Naseby in 1646."

C. A. Bodelsen, *T. S. Eliot's 'Four Quartets'* (Copenhagen, 1958), p. 102.

223. Eliot, "Little Gidding," *Four Quartets*, p. 35.

224. *Ibid.*

225. *Ibid.*

226. *Ibid.*

227. *Ibid.*

228. *Ibid.*

229. *Ibid., The Dry Salvages*, p. 32.

230. *Ibid., Little Gidding*, p. 36.

231. *Ibid.*

232. *Ibid.*

233. *Ibid.*

234. *Ibid.*

235. *Ibid.*

236. *Ibid.*

237. *Ibid.*

238. *Ibid.*, p. 37.

239. *Ibid.*

240. *Ibid.*

241. *Ibid.*

242. *Ibid.*

243. *Ibid.*

244. *Ibid.*

245. *Ibid.*

246. *Ibid.*, p. 38.

247. It is reminiscent of the great master Brunetto Latini (1220-94) who was well known for his wisdom and who taught Dante

"how man makes himself eternal." He was among the sinners of Hell because of his blasphemy against God and the Church.

The Inferno, Canto XV, 1. 85, p. 163.

It is also reminiscent of Arnaut Daniel who was to Guido Guinicelli "a better craftsman of the mother tongue."

Ibid., The Purgatorio, Canto XXVI, 1. 117, p. 329.

It is worth noting that Eliot used part of this quotation: "[il] miglior fabbro—the better craftsman" (Ezra Po...nd) in his dedicatory epigraph to The Waste Land.

248. Eliot, Little Gidding, p. 38.

249. Ibid.

250. Ibid.

251. Ibid., East Coker, p. 21.

252. Ibid., Little Gidding, p. 39.

The line is borrowed from Stephane Mallarme's "Donner un sens plus pur aux mots de la tribu."

"Le Tombeau D'Edgar Poe," Vers et Prose (Paris, 1912), p. 74.

253. Eliot, Little Gidding, p. 39.

254. Ibid.

255. Ibid.

256. Ibid.

257. Ibid.

258. Ibid.

259. Ibid., p. 40.

260. Ibid.

261. Ibid.

262. Ibid.

263. Ibid.

264. Ibid.

265. Ibid., p. 41.

266. Frank, p. 69.

267. Ibid., pp. 69-70.

268. Eliot, Little Gidding, p. 41.

269. Ibid.

270. Ibid.

Taking this reference to Milton together with the previous one to "Samson Agonistes" at the beginning of the Third Movement of "East Coker," one may deduce that this poet is regaining his proper place in Eliot's view in conformity with the main trend of Milton's assessment expounded by Sir Maurice Bowra in From Virgil to Milton (1945), Professor Muir in John Milton (1955) and in The Living Milton which is edited by Professor Kermode (a collection of essays by several hands—1960).

271. Eliot, Little Gidding, p. 41.

272. Ibid.

273. Ibid.

274. "Synne is behovabil, but al shal be wel & al shal be wel & al manner of thyng shal be wele."

Dame Julian of Norwich, *The Revelations of Divine Love*, The Thirteenth Revelation, Chap. XXVII, p. 56.

275. Dame Julian tells us that she "saw full surely that all the works that God hath done, or ever shall, were fully known to Him and aforeseen from without beginning. And for Love He made Mankind, and for the same Love would be Man."

Ibid., Chap. LVII, p. 138.

276. Eliot, *Little Gidding*, p. 42.

277. *Ibid.*, p. 38.

278. *Ibid.*

279. *Ibid.*, p. 42.

280. *Ibid.*, p. 40.

281. *Ibid.*, p. 42.

282. Deianira "went into her room and fetched the poisoned ointment which Nessus, the centaur whom Hercules had slain, had left with her. And she took one of Hercules' shirts and ordered one of her women to clean it quickly and to mix the poisoned oil through it." When Hercules "put on the shirt he felt himself filled with many wounds and much sickness, and when the shirt became heated on the skin, it stuck to his body and he became inflamed with the shirt around him."

Gordon Quin (ed. and trans.), *Stair Ercuil Ocus a Bas: The Life and Death of Hercules* (Dublin, 1939), pp. 127, 129.

283. Eliot, *Little Gidding*, p. 42.

284. *Ibid.*, p. 44.

285. *Ibid.*, p. 42.

286. *Ibid.*, p. 43.

287. *Ibid.*, p. 42.

288. *Ibid.*, p. 43.

289. *Ibid.*

290. *Ibid.*, p. 40.

291. *Ibid.*, p. 43.

292. *Ibid.*

293. The original text of "The Cloud of Unknowing" reads:
pe drawзt of pis loue & pe voise of pis cleping.

Phyllis Hodgson (ed.), *The Cloud of Unknowing and the Book of Privy Counselling*, pe secound chapitre, 1. 19 (London, 1944), p. 14.

294. See *The Active Mysticism in the Cloud of Unknowing*, Chap. II, Sec. XIII, pp. 41-42.

295. Eliot, *The Dry Salvages*, p. 32.

296. *Ibid.*, *Little Gidding*, p. 44.

297. *Ibid.*

298. Mr. Preston stresses this theme saying that "it is one measure

of the permanence of 'Four Quartets' that the despair which has been
faced and conquered is not the despair of an age: 'wait without hope
. . .' [the meditation of 'East Coker'] not only directs us to bear
to-day's darkness patiently, but shows us a stage of a man's spiritual
progress in 'any' age."

Raymond Preston, *'Four Quartets' Rehearsed* (London, 1948), p. 63.

299. (Anon), *The Cloud of Unknowing,* Chap. XLVII, Text No. 2,
p. 149.

300. D. S. Savage, *The Personal Principle: Studies in Modern
Poetry* (London, 1944), p. 96.

301. *Ibid.*

302. *Ibid.*

303. *Ibid.,* pp. 96-97.

304. Mr. Edwin Muir has happily considered this point stating
that "the only difference in spirit which I can find between Eliot's
early poetry and his later poetry is that doubt predominates in the
one and faith in the other."

"The Present Age from 1914," *Introductions to English Literature,*
ed. by Bonamy Dobrée, Vol. V (London, 1939), p. 77.

305. See a note on *the objective correlative,* Chap. IV, Sec. I,
Footnote No. 37, p. 67.

306. *Ibid.*

307. Savage, p. 97.

308. *Ibid.*

309. Eliot, "The Dry Salvages," *Four Quartets,* p. 25.

310. *Ibid.,* p. 29.

311. See *Henri Bergson's 'duration,'* Chap. I, Sec. II, p. 24.

312. See *the Theory of Time-sensationalism of Spengler,* Chap. III,
Sec. I, pp. 49-50.

313. Lewis, *Time and Western Man,* p. 283.

314. See F. H. Bradley's concept of "the Absolute" in his *Appearance and Reality,* Chap. III, Sec. I, pp. 47-48.

315. Eliot, *The Dry Salvages,* p. 26.

316. *Ibid.,* p. 29.

317. *Ibid.*

318. *Ibid.*

319. *Ibid.,* p. 28.

320. *Ibid.,* p. 31.

321. *Ibid.,* p. 29.

322. *Ibid., East Coker,* p. 23.

323. *Ibid.*

324. *Ibid.*

325. *Ibid.*

326. *Ibid., Little Gidding,* p. 36.

327. *Ibid.*

328. *Ibid.,* p. 43.

329. *Ibid., East Coker,* p. 22.

330. *Ibid.,* pp. 22-23.

331. *Ibid., Burnt Norton,* p. 8.

332. *Ibid.*

333. *Ibid.,* p. 10.

334. *Ibid., Little Gidding,* p. 40.

335. *Ibid., Burnt Norton,* p. 12.

336. Eliot is drawing here heavily upon St. Augustine's concept of time. After a long meditation on the eternity of the Creator (Chap. XI) and the unreliability of human measurements of time (Chap. XVI), the Bishop of Hippo concludes that "the present time of past things is our memory; the present time of present things is our sight; the present time of future things our expectation" (Chap. XX).

These concepts are re-echoed in the First Movement of Eliot's "Burnt Norton."

St. Augustine, *The Confessions,* Vol. II, Bk. XI, p. 253.

337. Lawrence Durrell, *Key to Modern Poetry* (London, 1952), p. 158.

338. Though Eliot repudiates the influence of Bergson and refers to it as "the epidemic of Bergsonism," he could not fully evade it.

T. S. Eliot, "A Commentary," *The Criterion,* Vol. XII, No. XLVI (October, 1932), p. 74.

In "A Sermon" preached in Magdalene College Chapel, Eliot states: "No one ever attempted to convert 'me'; . . . My only conversion, by the deliberate influence of any individual, was a temporary conversion to Bergsonism."

T. S. Eliot, *A Sermon* (Cambridge, 7 March, 1948), p. 5.

339. Eliot, *The Dry Salvages,* p. 32.

340. *Ibid.*

341. *Ibid.*

342. *Ibid., Little Gidding,* p. 44.

343. See *The Synthetic Mysticism of St. Thomas Aquinas,* Chap. II, Sec. XI, p. 39.

344. Eliot, *Burnt Norton,* p. 8.

345. Unpublished MS. bearing the title *Translation of the Mystical Divinity of Dionysius Areopagita,* kept in the British Museum under Bibliothecae Harleianae (Harley), No. 674 (fol. 15). From the style and expression of ideas, I should locate it in the fifteenth century.

346. " 'Season' Middle English adopted from Old French 'seson, seison' [Modern French 'saison']."

"In the season: at the right and proper time."

The Oxford English Dictionary, a corrected Re-Issue of a New English Dictionary on Historical Principles, Vol. IX (Oxford, 1933), pp. 337-38.

347. Eliot, *East Coker*, p. 16.

348. *Ibid.*

349. *Ibid.*

350. *Ibid., The Dry Salvages*, p. 30.

351. *Ibid.*, p. 26.

352. *Ibid.*

353. *Ibid.*, p. 30.

354. *Ibid., Little Gidding*, p. 43.

355. *Ibid.*

356. "The meaning of history lies in a pattern that transcends the events that compose it: just as at the centre of a turning wheel there is a point which does not move, just as in a dance there is a pattern where the beginning of the movement co-exists with the end."

R. L. Brett, *Reason and Imagination: A Study of Form and Meaning in Four Poems* (London, 1960), p. 131.

357. Mr. Wheelwright scrupulously remarks: "Since the future like the past is an imaginative construction and only the present is actual, an incessantly moving 'now,' rebirth must be an experience of the 'now'—not a future hope but a present embarkation, a resolute 'faring forward.'"

Philip Wheelwright, "Eliot's Philosophical Themes," *T. S. Eliot: A Study of His Writings by Several Hands,* ed. by B. Rajan (London, 1947), p. 105.

358. Eliot, *Little Gidding*, p. 40.

359. *Ibid., The Dry Salvages,* pp. 32-33.

360. *Ibid.*, p. 33.

361. *Ibid., Burnt Norton*, p. 11.

362. *Ibid.*, p. 8.

363. *Ibid., East Coker*, p. 18.

364. *Ibid.*, pp. 17-18.

365. *Ibid., The Dry Salvages*, p. 26.

366. *Ibid.*, p. 28.

367. *Ibid., Burnt Norton*, p. 7.

368. *Ibid.*

369. Mr. Harding is here referring specifically to *Ash Wednesday* (1930) and *Burnt Norton* (1934).

370. D. W. Harding, Review of "T. S. Eliot's Collected Poems, 1909-1935," *Scrutiny*, Vol. V, No. 2 (September, 1936), p. 172.

371. T. S. Eliot, *The Idea of a Christian Society* (London, 1939), p. 13.

372. See the commentary on the definitions of 'Mysticism,' Chap. I, Sec. I, pp. 20-22.

373. *Ibid.*

374. *Ibid.*

375. Eliot, *East Coker*, p. 19.

376. *Ibid., The Dry Salvages*, p. 31.

Notes to the Conclusion

1. T. S. Eliot, "The Perfect Critic," *The Sacred Wood: Essays on Poetry and Criticism* (London: Second Edition, 1928), p. 15.
2. Eliot, "The Love Song of J. Alfred Prufrock," *Collected Poems,* p. 12.
3. *Ibid.,* "Portrait of a Lady," p. 19.
4. *Ibid.,* "Rhapsody on a Windy Night," p. 24.
5. The quotation is taken from St. John of the Cross:
 . . . since no creature whatsoever, and none of its actions or abilities, can conform or can attain to that which is God, therefore must the soul be stripped of all things created . . . so that, when all that is unlike God and unconformed to Him is cast out, the soul may receive the likeness of God.
The Ascent of Mount Carmel, Bk. II, Chap. V, p. 76.
It is cited by Eliot as an Epigraph to his Aristophanic Melodrama *Sweeney Agonistes.*
Eliot, *Collected Poems,* p. 117.
6. *Ibid.,* "East Coker," *Four Quartets,* p. 19.
7. *Ibid., Burnt Norton,* p. 11.
8. *Ibid.*
9. *Ibid., East Coker,* p. 20.
10. *Ibid., Burnt Norton,* p. 9.
11. *Ibid., East Coker,* p. 20.
12. *Ibid.*
13. *Ibid.,* p. 19.
14. *Ibid.,* "Portrait of a Lady," p. 16.
15. *Ibid.,* "Preludes," p. 21.
16. *Ibid.,* "A Game of Chess," p. 64.
17. *Ibid.,* "The Fire Sermon," p. 68.
18. *Ibid.,* pp. 69-70.
19. *Ibid.,* "Mr. Eliot's Sunday Morning Service," p. 55.
20. *Ibid.,* p. 56.
21. *Ibid.,* "What the Thunder said," p. 74.
22. *Ibid., Little Gidding,* p. 42.
23. *Ibid.*
24. *Ibid.*
25. *Ibid.,* p. 44.
26. *Ibid., Ash Wednesday,* p. 97.
27. *Ibid.,* "Marina," p. 113.
28. *Ibid., Little Gidding,* p. 42.
29. *Ibid.,* p. 36.
30. *Ibid.,* p. 38.
31. *Ibid.*
32. *Ibid.*
33. *Ibid., East Coker,* p. 22.
34. *Ibid.,* p. 21.

35. *Ibid.*, p. 22.
36. *Ibid.*
37. *Ibid.*
38. *Ibid.*, *Little Gidding*, p. 43.
39. *Ibid.*, "Whispers of Immortality," *Collected Poems*, p. 53.
40. *Ibid.*
41. *Ibid.*, *The Waste Land*, 1. 403.
42. *Ibid.*, 11. 418-19.
43. *Ibid.*, 1. 422.
44. *Ibid.*, "The Hollow Men," p. 87.
45. *Ibid.*
46. *Ibid.*, "Journey of the Magi," p. 108.
47. *Ibid.*, "A Song for Simeon," p. 110.
48. *Ibid.*
49. *Ibid.*
50. *Ibid.*, "The Burial of the Dead," *The Waste Land*, 1. 60.
51. *Ibid.*, "Animula," *Collected Poems*, p. 111.
52. *Ibid.*
53. *Ibid.*, *The Cultivation of Christmas Trees*, An Ariel Poem illustrated by David Jones (London, 1954), p. (2).
54. *Ibid.*, *Burnt Norton*, p. 8.
55. *Ibid.*, *The Waste Land*, 11. 40-41.
56. *Ibid.*, 11. 320-21.
57. *Ibid.*, "The Hollow Men," p. 89.
58. *Ibid.*, *Ash Wednesday*, p. 100.
59. *Ibid.*, *Burnt Norton*, p. 9.
60. *Ibid.*
61. *Ibid.*
62. *Ibid.*, "Marina," p. 114.
63. *Ibid.*, *Ash Wednesday*, p. 102.
64. *Ibid.*, *East Coker*, p. 20.
65. *Ibid.*, *The Dry Salvages*, p. 33.
66. *Ibid.*, *Burnt Norton*, p. 10.
67. *Ibid.*, p. 13.
68. *Ibid.*
69. *Ibid.*, p. 12.
70. *Ibid.*, *Little Gidding*, p. 43.
71. *Ibid.*, *The Dry Salvages*, p. 31.
72. *Ibid.*, p. 32.
73. Richard Lea, "Forum: T. S. Eliot's 'Four Quartets,'" *The Adelphi*, Vol. XXI, No. 4 (July-September, 1945), p. 186.
74. In the same interview with the poet, I raised this matter by asking him, "Do you think the religious image in poetry and the mystic vision meet somewhere?" To which he answered, "Yes. But I don't claim to have had more of any mystical experience than any other religious poet. I have never had but gleams."

My personal interview with T. S. Eliot on October 19, 1961.

75. See *The Components of the Mystic Way*, Chap. I, Sec. III, pp. 26-29.

76. Eliot, *Burnt Norton*, p. 12.

77. See *the State of Absorption*, Chap. II, Sec. V, Footnote No. 26, p. 34.

78. "In the morning I shall stand in thy presence and shall see the health of my countenance, even my God, who shall quicken our mortal bodies, by the Spirit that dwelleth in us: because he hath in mercy moved upon our inner darksome and unquiet deep: from whom in this our pilgrimage we have received such a pledge, as that even now we are light: whilst hitherto we are saved by hope, made the children of light, and the children of the day."

St. Augustine, *The Confessions*, Vol. II, Bk. XIII, Chap. XIV, p. 403.

79. George Herbert, "The Collar," *Metaphysical Lyrics and Poems of the Seventeenth Century*, ed. by H. J. C. Grierson, p. 112.

80. *My Personal Interview with T. S. Eliot.*

81. Eliot, *The Use of Poetry and the Use of Criticism*, p. 154.

82. G. Rostrevor Hamilton, *The Tell-Tale Article: A Critical Approach to Modern Poetry* (London, 1950), p. 59.

83. T. S. Eliot, "Books of the Quarter Reviewed," *The Criterion* (January, 1930), p. 334.

84. Stephen Spender, *The Destructive Element* (London, 1935), p. 135.

85. T. S. Eliot, *The Adelphi* (July-September, 1945), p. 154.

86. *Ibid.*

87. Albert Schweitzer, *Out of my Life and Thought*, trans. by C. T. Campion (New York, 1949), p. 53.

88. George Seaver, *Albert Schweitzer: Christian Revolutionary* (London, 1944—Reprinted and Revised, 1955), pp. 29-30.

89. Albert Schweitzer, *The Mysticism of Paul the Apostle*, trans. by William Montgomery from the German *Die Mystik des Apostels Paulus* (London, 1931), p. 297.

90. *Ibid.*, "The Decay and the Restoration of Civilization," *The Philosophy of Civilization*, Pt. I, trans. by C. T. Campion (London, 1923), p. 64.

91. T. S. Eliot, "A Commentary," *The Criterion*, Vol. XII, No. XLVI (October, 1932), p. 78.

92. Eliot "n'a pas seulement modifié le langage de la poésie en forgeant un nouvel idiome et en posant une norme d'exigence critique, il a fait école."

Georges Cattaui, *T. S. Eliot* (Paris, 1957), p. 36.

93. Eliot, "Little Gidding," *Four Quartets*, p. 39.

94. See the *Appendix* on *Rilke and Eliot's 'Four Quartets,'* *infra*, p. 156 ff.

95. Professor Matthiessen holds a contrary view by asserting that

there is harmony "between his [Eliot's] 'revolutionary' creative work and his 'traditionalist' criticism."

F. O. Matthiessen, "Eliot's Quartets," *The Kenyon Review*, Vol. V (Spring, 1943), p. 162.

It is also the same case with Mr. Partridge who maintains that "there is no real divergence between his theory and practice, no matter how lucid he may contrive to make his criticism, or how obscure his poetry."

A. C. Partridge, "T. S. Eliot," *Arts and Social Sciences*, Series III, No. 4 (Pretoria, 1937), p. 3.

96. T. S. Eliot, *After Strange Gods: A Primer of Modern Heresy* (London, 1934), p. 28.

Notes to Appendix

1. Elsie Weigand, "Rilke and Eliot: The Articulation of the Experience," *The German Review*, Vol. XXX, No. 3 (October, 1955), p. 199.

2. Rainer Maria Rilke, "The Fifth Elegy," *Duino Elegies*, trans. by J. B. Leishman and Stephen Spender (London, 1939—Reprinted 1948), p. 55.

3. Eliot, *Burnt Norton*, p. 8.

4. Rilke, *The Fifth Elegy*, p. 55.

5. *Ibid.*

6. *Ibid., The Ninth Elegy*, p. 83.

7. *Ibid.*, "Requiem," *Requiem and Other Poems*, trans. by J. B. Leishman (London, 1949), p. 133.

8. *Ibid., Tombs of the Hetaerae*, p. 100.

9. *Ibid., Requiem*, p. 133.

10. *Ibid.*, p. 136.

11. *Ibid., Bowl of Roses*, p. 109.

12. John Donne, "A Hymn to God the Father," *Metaphysical Lyrics and Poems of the Seventeenth Century*, ed. by Herbert J. C. Grierson, p. 93.

13. Herbert, *Affliction*, p. 105.

14. *Ibid.*

15. *Ibid.*, "The Collar," p. 112.

16. In the case of Rilke, his biographer tells us that "all his [Rilke's] life had been tormented by the gulf that yawned between him and his fellow-humans, by the haunting horror of loneliness and death, by an unappeasable nostalgia for reality and by his own incapacity to create the work of art which would release him."

Nora Wydenbruck, *Rilke: Man and Poet* (London, 1949), p. 334.

17. Rilke, "The First Elegy," *Duino Elegies*, pp. 29, 31.

18. *Ibid., The Sixth Elegy*, p. 67.

19. *Ibid.*, "The Spectator," *Requiem and Other Poems*, p. 77.

20. *Ibid.*, "The Third Elegy," *Duino Elegies*, p. 41.

21. Eliot, *Burnt Norton*, p. 8.

22. Marvell, *Metaphysical Lyrics and Poems of the Seventeenth Century*, p. 163.

23. Rilke's first visit to Russia, "too short and bewildering to allow painful impressions to intrude, brought forth an immediate poetical harvest: 'The Book of Monkish Life' in verse and 'Tales about God' in prose, written in the autumn and winter of 1899. Partly inspired by Russia, both works originated in Italy, and derive from the Tuscan diary, the cyclic poem in particular being a beautifully ambiguous and highly mysterious expression of Rilke's overweening ideas about art."

During his second visit in the winter of 1899-1900, he met Nikolai Tolstoy who was to Rilke "the eternal Russian."

E. M. Butler, *Rainer Maria Rilke* (Cambridge, 1941), pp. 51, 67.

24. Rainer M. Rilke, "The Book of the Monastic Life," *Selected Works*, trans. by J. B. Leishman, Vol. II (London, 1960), p. 40.

25. It is worth remarking that Rilke's concept of God, from the purely mystical point of view, is that He is immanent rather than transcendent, *i.e.*, He is indwelling all phenomena and everyday life. In this sense, Rilke follows the Spinozaic theory of immanental causation which has exercised remarkable influence on the pantheistic mysticism of the Romantic Movement.

26. Rilke, "The Book of Pilgrimage," *Selected Works*, Vol. II, p. 79.

27. *Ibid.*, "The Book of Poverty and Death," p. 92.

28. In a letter to his wife Clara from 11 Rue Toullier, Paris, dated 27th September, 1902, Rilke tells her that "from everywhere people pop out . . . grave, sad, quiet and lonely people . . . Such as have sat many hours on a remote bench as though waiting for something . . . and then others who live on the benches during the daytime, eat, sleep and read a newspaper. It is rather like a Last Judgment . . . And Paris becomes narrow, garish and rowdy and begins one of its hectic nights again, stimulated by spices, wine [and] music."

R. F. C. Hull (trans.), *Selected Letters of Rainer Maria Rilke: 1902-1926* (London, 1946), p. 13.

29. Rilke, "The Boy," "The Book of Images," *Selected Works*, Vol. II, p. 112.

30. *Ibid.*, "The Spectator," p. 137.

31. F. W. Van Heerikhuizen, *Rainer Maria Rilke: His Life and Work*, trans. by Fernand G. Renier and Anne Cliff (London, 1951), p. 269.

32. *Ibid.*

33. Stephen Spender, *The Creative Element* (London, 1953), p. 73.

34. J. F. Angelloz, *Rainer Maria Rilke: L'Evolution Spirituelle du Poete* (Paris, 1936), p. 146.

35. Eliot, "Burnt Norton," *Four Quartets*, p. 12.

36. C. M. Bowra, "The Neue Gedichte," *Rainer Maria Rilke: Aspects of his Mind and Poetry*, ed. by William Rose and G. Craig Houston (London, 1938), p. 89.

37. Rilke, "The Second Elegy," *Duino Elegies*, p. 33.

38. *Ibid.*, "The Ninth Elegy," p. 83.

39. Eliot, "Conversation Galante," *Collected Poems*, p. 33.

40. Rilke, "The Ninth Elegy," *Duino Elegies*, p. 71.

Selected Bibliography

I

Unpublished MSS.

A ladder to heaven of twelve staves (London: The British Museum, Royal 17.c.XIII). The MS. is dated at the beginning of the 17th century.

Thomas Aquinas of the Angelical Salutation, trans. by Henry P. Kt. Lord Morley (London: The British Museum, Royal 17.c.XVI). The MS. is dated between A.D. 1528 and 1547.

Translation of the Mystical Divinity of Dionysius Areopagita (London: The British Museum, Bibliothecae Harleianae No. 674). The MS. is dated in the 15th century.

II

Mysticism
Eastern and Western

APPLETON, GEORGE. *The Christian Approach to the Buddhist*. London: Edinburgh House Press, 1958.

BERGSON, HENRI. *Durée et Simultanéité: A Propos de la Théorie d'Einstein*. Paris: Librairie Felix Alcan, 1922.

BUCKE, R. MAURICE (ed.). *Cosmic Consciousness: A Study in the Evolution of the Human Mind*. Philadelphia: Innes & Sons, 1905.

BUTLER, DOM CUTHBERT. *Western Mysticism: Neglected Chapters in the History of Religion*. London: Constable & Co. Ltd., 1922.

ELIADE, MIRCEA. *Patterns in Comparative Religion*. Trans. by Rosemary Sheed. London: Sheed & Ward, 1958.

GELL, C. W. "Schweitzer and Radhakrishnan: A Comparison," *The Hibbert Journal* (October, 1952-July, 1953), Vol. LI.

INGE, DEAN W. RALPH. *Christian Mysticism*. The Bampton Lectures. London: Methuen & Co., 1899.

JONES, RUFUS. *The Flowering of Mysticism*. New York: The Macmillan Company, 1939.

MARITAIN, JACQUES. *The Degrees of Knowledge*. Trans. under the supervision of Gerald B. Phelan. London: Geoffrey Bles, 1959.

MASUTANI, FUMIO. *A Comparative Study of Buddhism and Christianity*. Tokyo: The Young East Association, 1957.

MÜLLER, F. MAX. *The Sacred Books of the East*. Trans. by various

Oriental Scholars. Oxford: The Clarendon Press, 1879-1910, 50 Vols.

OSBORNE, ARTHUR. *Buddhism and Christianity in the Light of Hinduism*. London: Rider & Co., 1959.

OTTO, RUDOLF. *Mysticism: East and West*. A Comparative Analysis of the Nature of Mysticism. Trans. by B. L. Bracey and R. C. Payne. London: Macmillan & Co., 1932.

RADHAKRISHNA, SIR S. *East and West in Religion*. London: George Allen and Unwin Ltd., 1933.

SANTAYANA, G. *The Life of Reason*. London: Constable & Co., 1954.

SCHWEITZER, ALBERT. *Christianity and the Religions of the World*. Trans. by J. Powers. London: G. Allen & Unwin, 1923.

UNDERHILL, EVELYN. *Mysticism: A Study in the Nature and Development of Man's Spiritual Consciousness*. London: Methuen & Co., 1911—Reprinted 1930.

WINSLOW, JACK C. *The Christian Approach to the Hindu*. London: Edinburgh House Press, 1958.

III

References on T. S. Eliot

BERGSTEN, STAFFAN. *Time and Eternity: A Study in the Structure and Symbolism of T. S. Eliot's "Four Quartets."* Stockholm: Svenska Bokforlaget, 1960.

BLISSETT, WILLIAM. "The Argument of T. S. Eliot's 'Four Quartets,'" *University of Toronto Quarterly* (January, 1946), Vol. XV, No. 2.

BODELSEN, C. A. *T. S. Eliot's "Four Quartets."* Copenhagen: Rosenkilde & Bagger, 1958.

BOWRA, C. M. "The Waste Land," *The Creative Experiment*. London: Macmillan, 1949.

BRADBROOK, M. C. "The Lyric and the Dramatic in the Latest Verse of T. S. Eliot," *Theology* (February, 1942), Vol. XLIV, No. 260.

BROOKS, CLEANTH. "The Waste Land: Critique of the Myth," *Modern Poetry and the Tradition*. London: Cole & Co., 1948.

COATS, R. H. "An Anchor for the Soul: A Study of Mr. T. S. Eliot's Later Verse," *The Hibbert Journal* (October, 1945-July, 1946), Vol. XLIV.

DOBRÉE, BONAMY. *The Lamp and the Lute: Studies in Six Modern Authors*. Oxford: The Clarendon Press, 1929.

DREW, ELIZABETH. *T. S. Eliot: The Design of his Poetry*. London: Eyre and Spottiswoode, 1950.

FOSTER, GENEVIEVE. "The Archetypal Imagery of T. S. Eliot," *Publications of the Modern Language Association of America*. June 1945, Vol. LX.

FRY, EDITH. "The Poetic Work of T. S. Eliot," *The British Annual of Literature.* London: The British Authors' Press, 1948, Vol. V.

GAMBERINI, SPARTACO. *La Poesia di T. S. Eliot.* Genoua: Pubblicazioni Dell'Instituto Universitario di Magistero, 1954.

GARDNER, HELEN. *The Art of T. S. Eliot.* London: The Cresset Press, 1949.

GREENE, EDWARD. *T. S. Eliot et la France.* Paris: Boivin et Cie, 1951.

HÄUSERMANN, HANS W. *L'Oeuvre Poétique de T. S. Eliot.* Montreux: Editions du Mois Suisse, 1940.

KERMODE, FRANK. "Dissociation of Sensibility," *The Kenyon Review* (Spring, 1957), Vol. XIX, No. 2.

LEAVIS, F. R. *New Bearings in English Poetry.* London: Chatto & Windus, 1932.

LUCAS, F. L. "Review of the Waste Land," *The New Statesman* (3 Nov., 1923), Vol. XXII, No. 551.

MARTIN, PHILIP. *Mastery and Mercy: A Study of two Religious Poems, 'The Wreck of the Deutschland' by G. M. Hopkins and 'Ash Wednesday' by T. S. Eliot.* London: Oxford University Press, 1957.

MARTIN, P. W. *Experiment in Depth: A Study of the Work of Jung, Eliot and Toynbee.* London: Routledge and Kegan Paul, 1955.

MARTZ, L. L. "The Wheel and the Point: Aspects of Imagery and Theme in Eliot's Later Poetry," *Sewanee Review* (January, 1947), Vol. LV.

MATTHIESSEN, F. O. *The Achievement of T. S. Eliot.* New York: Oxford University Press, 1935—Reprinted 1958.

————. "Eliot's Quartets," *The Kenyon Review* (Spring, 1943), Vol. V.

MAXWELL, D. E. S. *The Poetry of T. S. Eliot.* London: Routledge and Kegan Paul, 1952.

MOORMAN, CHARLES. "Myth and Organic Unity in 'the Waste Land,'" *The South Atlantic Quarterly* (Spring, 1958), Vol. LVII.

MORRISON, THEODORE. "Ash Wednesday: A Religious History," *New England Quarterly* (June, 1938), Vol. XI.

MUSGROVE, S. *T. S. Eliot and Walt Whitman.* Wellington, New Zealand: The University Press, 1952.

MUSURILLO, H. "Note on 'the Waste Land,'" *Classical Philology* (July, 1956), Vol. LI.

PAIGE, D. D. (ed.). "Letters of Ezra Pound to T. S. Eliot concerning 'the Waste Land,'" *The Hudson Review* (Spring, 1950), Vol. III, No. I.

PASSMORE, J. A. *T. S. Eliot.* Sydney: The University Literary Society, 1934.

PETER, JOHN. "A New Interpretation of 'the Waste Land,'" *Essays in Criticism* (July, 1952), Vol. II, No. 3.

POWELL, DILYS. "The Poetry of T. S. Eliot," *Life and Letters,* ed. by D. MacCarthy (London: Kingsway, July-December, 1931), Vol. VII, pp. 386-419.

RAJAN, B. (ed.). *T. S. Eliot: A Study of his Writings by Several Hands*. London: Dennis Dobson Ltd., 1947.

REINSBERG, M. "Footnote to 'Four Quartets,'" *American Literature* (November, 1949), Vol. XXI.

SCHWARTZ, DELMORE. "The Literary Dictatorship of T. S. Eliot," *Partisan Review* (February, 1949), Vol. XVI, No. 2.

SMITH, GROVER. *T. S. Eliot's Poetry and Plays: A Study in Sources and Meaning*. Chicago: The University Press, 1956.

SPENDER, STEPHEN. *The Creative Element*. London: Hamish Hamilton, 1953.

————. *The Destructive Element*. London: Jonathan Cape, 1938.

STROTHMANN, F. W. "Hope for T. S. Eliot's Empty Men," *Publications of the Modern Language Association* (September, 1958), Vol. LXXIII.

TATE, ALLEN. *Reactionary Essays on Poetry and Ideas*. New York: Charles Scribner's Sons, 1936.

TRAVERSI, DEREK. "The Waste Land Revisited," *The Dublin Review* (Second Quarter, 1948), No. 443.

UNGER, LEONARD (ed.). *T. S. Eliot: A Selected Critique*. New York: Rinehart & Co., 1948.

WAGNER, R. D. "Meaning of Eliot's Rose-garden," *Publications of the Modern Language Association* (March, 1954), Vol. LXIX.

WEITZ, M. "T. S. Eliot: Time as a Mode of Salvation," *Sewanee Review* (January, 1952), Vol. LX.

WORTHINGTON, JANE. "The Epigraphs to the Poetry of T. S. Eliot," *American Literature* (March, 1949), Vol. XXI, No. 1.

Index

Advaita Vedanta, 33-34, 108
After Strange Gods: A Primer of Modern Heresy (T. S. Eliot), 155
"Animula," 97-98, 141
Ara Vos Prec, 143
Aristotelianism, 37-39, 111
Ash Wednesday, 48, 52, 87 ff., 91-94, 97-101, 103-5, 136, 139, 142-43, 145
Atman, 30, 36
Auden, W. H., 50
Augustinianism, 22, 37-39, 52-53, 77
Averroes (Ibn Rushd), 39
Avicenna (Ibn Sina), 39

Baudelaire, Charles, 66, 139, 154
Berdyaev, Nicolas, 14, 18, 20
Bergson, Henri, 24, 48, 130, 209
Bhagavad-Gita, 32-33, 119-20, 129
Bowra, C. M., 79, 85, 125, 206
Bradley, F. H., 47, 130, 208
Brahmanism, 30, 32, 72, 113
Bremond, Henri, 14
Brooks, Cleanth, 66, 85
Buddhism, 30, 35, 54, 69-71, 77, 79, 82, 103-5, 113, 120, 132, 147
Bullough, Geoffrey, 66, 80, 85, 95
"Burbank with a Baedeker: Bleistein with a Cigar," 58, 62
Burnt Norton, 51, 108-12, 115-16, 129, 131, 133-34, 137-39, 142-45, 156, 158, 160
Butler, Dom Cuthbert, 14, 17

The Cambridge Platonists, 44
Cattaui, Georges, p. 80
Cavalcanti, Guido, 87, 190
Civitate Dei, De, 38
Clement of Alexandria, 26
The Cloud of Unknowing, 41-42, 88, 120, 128, 207
The Confessions (St. Augustine), 70, 108, 116, 131, 145, 209, 213

"Conversation Galante" (T. S. Eliot), 161
"A Cooking Egg," p. 57
Corpus Hermeticum, 68
Cosmic positivism, 25
Croce, Benedetto, 45
The Cultivation of Christmas Trees (T. S. Eliot), 142

Daiches, David, 85
Dame Julian of Norwich, 22, 43, 126, 130, 207
"Dans le Restaurant," 58, 69
Dante Alighieri, 27, 40-41, 83-84, 87, 93, 102, 113, 135
"Dante," *Selected Essays* (T. S. Eliot), 83-84, 87, 95, 129, 189
The Dark Night of the Soul, 28, 43, 87-88, 90, 99, 110-12, 114, 116, 120, 133, 152, 204
Descartes, René, 23
Desdichado, El (Gérard de Nerval), 74, 183-84
Dionysius the Areopagite, 37, 89, 191, 209
"Dissociation of sensibility," 52-53
Dobrée, Bonamy, 77, 129
Donne, John, 158
Drew, Elizabeth, 85
The Dry Salvages, 117 ff., 123, 129-31, 133-35, 144

East Coker, 112-17, 129-30, 133, 135, 137-39, 143, 206
Eckhart, Meister, 13
Einstein, Albert, 23, 25
Emanation, 18, 162
Empiricism, 23, 25
Eyes that last I saw in tears, 76

Ferrar, Nicholas, 125, 133
Fisher King, 79, 187
Four Quartets, 24, 50, 107 ff.

From Ritual to Romance (Jessie L. Weston), 65, 68, 73-74, 79, 180

Gamberini, Spartaco, 81
Gardner, Helen, 78, 89, 108, 122
"Gerontion," 55-56, 63, 72, 84, 96, 100, 141
Godhead, 14, 42
The Golden Bough (Sir James Frazer), 66, 69, 82
Goldsmith, Oliver, 67
Greene, Edward J. H., 78, 81

"Hamlet," *Selected Essays* (T. S. Eliot), 52
Häusermann, Hans W., 80, 107
Heart of Darkness (Joseph Conrad), 75
Heidegger, Martin, 45, 49-50
Heraclitean philosophy, 34, 107-8, 117, 120, 123, 130, 197, 204
Herbert, George, 15, 146, 158
Hercules Furens (Seneca), 100, 196
Hinduism, 30 ff., 103-6, 121, 132, 147
"The Hippopotamus," 54, 61, 63
"The Hollow Men," 75-77, 83, 137, 141, 143, 145, 148-49
Hume, David, 23
"Humouresque," 60
Huxley, Aldous, 14

The Idea of a Christian Society (T. S. Eliot), 134
Immanence, 17, 19, 26, 32, 34, 36, 133, 162
Inferno (Dante), 40, 52, 67, 71, 75, 113, 124, 205-6
Inge, Dean W. Ralph, 13, 25
Intuitionism, 23-25, 27, 37, 39
Islam, 14, 32

"Journey of the Magi," 96, 98, 141

Kermode, Frank, 125, 206
Kierkegaard, Sören, 45
Knight, G. Wilson, 77, 185-86

"La Figlia Che Piange," 57
Leavis, F. R., 78-79
Leibniz, Gottfried W., 23
Lewis, Cecil D., 51

Lewis, Wyndham, 45, 49-50, 130
Little Gidding, 123 ff., 130-31, 133, 138-39, 144, 154
Locke, John, 23
"The Love Song of J. Alfred Prufrock," 53, 57-59, 61-62, 90, 137-38

MacNeice, Louis, 51
"Marina," 98, 101, 139, 143, 196
Maritain, Jacques, 45, 48
Marvell, Andrew, 158
Matthiessen, F. O., 66, 75, 89, 155
Melchiori, Giorgio, 85, 109
Metapsychosis, 15
Middleton, Thomas, 67
Monasticism, 20
Monotheism, 31
"Mr. Eliot's Sunday Morning Service," 54, 63, 138
Muir, Kenneth, 125, 206
Mystical experience, 18, 20-21, 25-26, 44, 46, 78, 145
Mystical philosophy, 16, 18, 48, 50-51, 71, 105, 132-33, 146, 152
Mysticism, Comparative, 13-14, 22, 30; Components of the Mystic Way, 26 ff., 71, 133, 145; Definition of, 17 ff.; European, 36 ff., 98, 135, 139, 145-47, 154; Indian, 30 ff., 103-6, 119-20, 129, 132, 147-48, 155; Sociological, 21, 51, 135, 150, 152

Naturalism, 25
Neo-Platonism, 36-38, 44, 52, 88, 132
Neo-Thomism, 45, 48
Nirvana, 35
The Noble Eightfold Path (Buddha), 35, 104, 113, 201

"Objective correlative," 67, 129, 179, 208
Occultism, 17, 46
"On a Portrait," 60
Origen (Origenes Adamantius), 26

Pantheism, 17, 162
Paradiso (Dante), 40, 52, 76, 93, 102, 191
Pervigilium Veneris, 74, 184

Philo (Judaeus), 36-37
Platonism, 36, 101, 132, 138
"Portrait of a Lady," 53, 57, 59, 137-38, 141
"Preludes," 59, 138
Purgatorio (Dante), 26, 40, 52, 74, 78, 89, 97, 102, 124, 145, 152, 192, 205-6

Radhakrishnan, Sir Sarvepalli, 13
Rationalism, 22, 25, 44, 46, 50
"Rhapsody on a Windy Night," 137
Richards, I. A., 81
Rig-Veda, 31, 105
Rilke, Rainer Maria, 154, 156 ff.
The Rock (T. S. Eliot), 120, 203-4
Rosa Mystica, 139
Russell, Bertrand, 23-24, 49

The Sacred Books of the East, 70, 103-5
The Sacred Wood: Essays on Poetry and Criticism (T. S. Eliot), 137
Samson Agonistes (Milton), 114
Sankara, Acharya, 13, 33
Santayana, George, 24
Satyricon (Petronius), 67, 179
Schopenhauer, Arthur, 24, 31, 44
Schweitzer, Albert, 14, 150-51
Seneca, Lucius A., 100
Shakespeare, William, writings of: *The Merchant of Venice*, 109; *Pericles*, 98, 195; *The Sonnets*, 99, 195; *The Tempest*, 68, 180
Simultaneity of Being, 34, 124, 131-33
Smidt, Kristian, 83, 113
Smith, Grover, 78, 80
"A Song for Simeon," 97, 141
The Spanish Tragedy (Thomas Kyd), 74
Spender, Stephen, 51, 81, 84, 149, 160
Spengler, Oswald, 49, 130
Spinoza, Benedictus de, 23-24
"Spleen," 60
St. Athanasius of Alexandria, 20
St. Bonaventura, 19-20
St. Catherine of Genoa, 26
St. Catherine of Siena, 28
St. John of the Cross, 15, 43, 100, 112, 115-16, 129, 137, 211

St. Teresa of Avila, 22, 42-43, 116, 190
Sweeney Agonistes, 137, 211
"Sweeney Among the Nightingales," 53, 101

Taoism, 14, 31
Tate, Allen, 94-95
Thomism, 39, 44, 52-53, 93, 111, 132, 194
"Thoughts After Lambeth," *Selected Essays* (T. S. Eliot), 81, 91, 192
Tradition and the Individual Talent (T. S. Eliot), 84, 85, 189
Traherne, Thomas, 15
Trans-animation, 15
Transcendence, 17, 21, 25, 28-29, 32, 36-37, 48, 50, 133, 144, 151, 162
Tristan und Isolde (Richard Wagner), 78, 186
"Triumphal March," 138

Underhill, Evelyn, 13, 19-20, 28
Unger, Leonard, 100, 196
Universal Spirit, 18
Upanishadic philosophy, 31-32, 72, 74-75, 78, 86, 105, 113, 121, 148
The Use of Poetry and the Use of Criticism (T. S. Eliot), 61, 82, 148

Vaughan, Henry, 15
Via Affirmativa, 150
Via Contemplativa, 88
Via Mystica, 50-51, 78
Via Negativa, 43, 88, 111, 135, 148, 150

The Waste Land, 65 ff.; "The Burial of the Dead," 65-68, 73, 78-80, 84-85, 141-42; "Death by Water," 68-70, 73, 142-43; Epigraph, 124, 206; "The Fire Sermon," 67, 71-72, 86, 138; "A Game of Chess," 66, 72, 86, 138; "What the Thunder Said," 73-75, 78-80, 84, 86, 95, 138
Webster, John, 66, 140
"Whispers of Immortality," 63, 140